Calf Fries to Caviar

by Janel Franklin & Sue Vaughn

★ TRUE CONFESSIONS OF TWO TEXAS COOKS ★

by
Janel Franklin
Sue Vaughn
Jan-Su Publications

A collection of recipes from West Texas

Library of Congress No. 83-090235
ISBN 0-9610956-0-1

Additional copies may be obtained at the cost of 11.95
per book, plus 2.00 postage and handling.
Texas residents add .63 sales tax. Send to:
JAN-SU PUBLICATIONS
1012 North 9th
Lamesa, Texas 79331
806-872-8667
806-998-5010

First Printing August, 1983   5,000 copies
Second Printing February, 1984   20,000 copies
Third Printing February, 1986   20,000 copies

Printed in the United States of America
by
Wimmer Brothers
4210 B.F. Goodrich Blvd.
Memphis, Tenn. 38118

Foreword

Characteristic of West Texas living, **Calf Fries to Caviar** is a collection of recipes ranging from "down-home" to "elegant gourmet" cooking.

Having raised six children between us, plus our husbands, we have had the opportunity and need for a wide range of cooking and entertaining. The fabulous part about our life style is the variety it offers.

In this book, we have compiled recipes for any occasion—elegant dinner parties to backyard cook-outs. In writing the recipes, we have tried to keep in mind our busy life styles. We have included many make-ahead, microwave, quick and easy recipes, and Hints for short-cut cooking. The Comments are to remind you that cooking is fun, relaxing and rewarding, if you let it be.

We intend for this book to reflect the years we have spent cooking for our families and friends. Many good memories are made while preparing food and eating together. Most of our recipes have been given to us through the years by these same family members and good friends, and to them we say, "Thank you for sharing!" The majority of the recipes have been scribbled on the backs of checks, on paper napkins, envelopes and paid bills, and buried in the bottom of cabinet drawers, where they were searched for frantically and retrieved with relief countless times over the years. At last, we've had to get organized!

The style of the recipes provides even the beginning cook with easy, step-by-step instructions (on the left) and all necessary ingredients in *capital letters* (on the right). We also capitalized any *new* ingredient not listed previously that appears in the method below. So, at a glance you may check the items you have on hand and know immediately what you will need to buy at the market.

Since cooking is an art, regard the recipes as guidelines for your own creativity. Do not hesitate to vary, add or delete to suit your own personal taste, as we have.

We say a SPECIAL "Thank You" to our husbands, Don Vaughn and H. G. Franklin, for being so supportive and encouraging. And especially for being our best tasters and critics.

We are grateful to Bill Price for the loan of his saddle, and to Joe Belt for his artistic talent in turning it into our cover design. Thanks also to Nan Mulvaney and Sheryn R. Jones who helped coordinate our book; to Sheri Holmes for her extra special "touch" with the typewriter, and last, but not least, to I.G. Holmes for the title, our utmost gratitude.

We dedicate to you, our readers, **Calf Fries to Caviar,** for your own personal enjoyment. It is our conclusion that perhaps "tasteful" simplicity is one of life's ultimate pleasures.

Sue and Janel

CALF FRIES

CALF FRIES or "Mountain Oysters" are the delicacies eaten on the working ranches of Texas. They are the part of the bull removed to make the animal a steer. They are fried in batter or crumb or cornmeal coatings. AND THEY ARE DELICIOUS.

CAVIAR

CAVIAR is roe of the sturgeon treated by heating, straining, and salting. The best caviar is made only in winter, and one of the causes of its high price is the great difficulty in preserving it. It should be spread on toast and flavored with a few drops of lemon squeezed over it, and is usually eaten as hors d'oeuvres.

Table of Contents

Party Food/Beverages

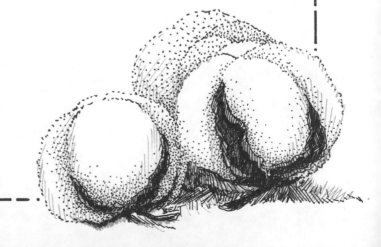

TEXAS CALF FRIES
Usually eaten as an hors d'oeuvre but may be an entree.

Dip frozen **CALF FRIES** in hot, but not boiling, **WATER.** Leave 3 to 4 minutes. Drain and peel off outer membrane. Cut into bite-size chunks. Pat dry with paper towels. Sprinkle with **SALT** and **PEPPER.** Dredge in **CORNMEAL,** pressing the meal on with your finger tips so that it adheres. Shake off any excess. Let stand a few minutes so the coating will have a chance to set. Heat about ½-inch **SHORTENING** in a large heavy skillet. Fry the calf fries a few at a time until crisp and brown on all sides. Drain on paper towels. Serve warm. Delicious with **SCRAMBLED EGGS** or with dips.

MOUNTAIN OYSTERS
Definition: Same as Calf Fries—ask any COWBOY

Prepare same as Calf Fry recipe. Beat together 1 **EGG** and 1 cup **MILK.** Dip fries in liquid, then in mixture of equal parts **FLOUR** and **CORNMEAL** that has been seasoned with **SALT** and **PEPPER.** Fry in deep hot **SHORTEN-ING.** (They are done when they float to the top.) Drain on paper towels and serve warm with your favorite dip.

FRIED WILD TURKEY
Brad uses only the breast

Slice **TURKEY BREAST** across grain into very thin strips. Season with **SALT** and **PEPPER.** Dip in flour, then **MILK.** Repeat flour, then milk. Drop in deep hot melted **SHORTENING.** Cook until golden brown.

CALF FRIES KANSAS LEGION STYLE

Dip **CALF FRIES** in
    mixture of . . . .   1 dozen **EGGS**
                                       1 quart **BUTTERMILK**
Then dip in . . . .   3 cups **CRACKER MEAL**
                                       1 cup **FLOUR** seasoned w/black
                                            pepper

Deep fry in hot shortening until crisp and brown. Drain on paper towels and serve with Kansas Treat.

KANSAS TREAT: Combine 1 quart **CATSUP,** ½ jar **HORSERADISH,** 3 tablespoons **WORCESTERSHIRE SAUCE** and **HOT PEPPERS** to taste. (More horseradish, if you prefer, and the peppers are optional.)

COTTON PICKIN' DIP: Combine 1 cup **MAYONNAISE,** ½ cup (wet) **HORSERADISH,** ½ teaspoon **ACCENT,** 2 tablespoons **LEMON JUICE,** and ½ teaspoon **SALT.** Serve either hot or cold. (Adjust horseradish to your taste, but the sauce should speak with authority!)

MEXICAN QUESO: Heat until melted, 1 can **RO-TEL,** 1 pound **VELVEETA CHEESE,** and 2 **TOMATOES,** chopped. Serve warm.

CREAM CHEESE AND CAVIAR

Soften to room temperature . . . .   1 pkg. (8 oz.) **CREAM CHEESE**
Add and blend well . . . .   **MAYONNAISE**
                                       WORCESTERSHIRE SAUCE
                                       TABASCO
                                       LAWRY'S SEASONED SALT
                                  1 pkg. dried **ONION SALAD**
                                         SEASONING
                                  1 small jar **BLACK CAVIAR**

Make consistency desired by thinning with milk. (For canapes, thick; dips, thinner.)

CAVIAR N' PUMPERNICKEL
Served at Becky Taylor's Monte Carlo party.

Blend together . . . .   1 pkg. **CREAM CHEESE**
    2 cartons **SOUR CREAM**
    1 bunch **FRESH ONIONS**, chopped
       fine (tops, also)
    dash **PEPPER**
Have on hand . . . .   1 round **PUMPERNICKEL** loaf

Cut top out of pumpernickel. Pull bread from the middle of loaf to make indention to hold cream cheese mixture. (Reserve bread for dipping.) Sprinkle 1 jar **BLACK CAVIAR** over mixture inside bread. Serve with chunks of **PUMPERNICKEL** and **CRACKERS**.

BAIER CHEESE SNACK

Place on serving plate . . . .   1 pkg. (8 oz.) **CREAM CHEESE**
       (whole block)
Cover generously with . . . .   1 bottle **PICKAPEPPER SAUCE**

Serve with **CRACKERS**.

DEVILED CHEESE BALL

Combine . . . .   1 small can **DEVILED HAM**
    1 pkg. (8 oz.) **CREAM CHEESE**

Mix well. Roll in crushed **PECANS**. Chill.

READY CHEESE: Grate a large quantity of cheese at a time in food processor. Seal in tight containers and freeze. Cheddar and Swiss freeze well. Use as needed.

DOUBLE-NUT CHEESE BALL

Combine . . . . 2 cups shredded **CHEDDAR CHEESE**
　　　　　　　　　　　　　　　1 pkg. (8 oz.) **CREAM CHEESE,** room temperature
　　　　　　　　　　　　　　　6 Tbsp. **COCONUT RUM LIQUEUR**
　　　　　　　　　　　　　　　½ cup **RAISINS**
　　　　　　　　　　　　　　　¼ cup finely chopped toasted **ALMONDS**

Mix well. Place on waxed paper; shape into a ball. Chill 2 to 3 hours. Roll in sliced **ALMONDS.**

YIELD: 1 BALL, ABOUT 4 INCHES IN DIAMETER

"FOUR-CHEESE" CHEESE BALL

Grind and mix well . . . . 1 pkg. (8 oz.) **CREAM CHEESE**
　　　　　　　　　　　　　　　½ pound **AMERICAN CHEESE**
　　　　　　　　　　　　　　　½ pound **SHARP CHEDDAR CHEESE**
　　　　　　　　　　　　　　　½ pound **VELVEETA CHEESE**
Add, to taste . . . . **GARLIC POWDER**
　　　　　　　　　　　　　　　WORCESTERSHIRE SAUCE

Make into a roll or ball and roll in 1 cup finely chopped **PECANS.** Sprinkle with **PAPRIKA.** (Optional: add **TABASCO** to taste.) Serve with **CRACKERS.**

"THREE-CHEESE" CHEESE BALL

Mix together . . . . ¼ pkg. **BLUE CHEESE**
　　　　　　　　　　　　　　　1 pkg. (10 oz.) **CREAM CHEESE**
　　　　　　　　　　　　　　　1 pkg. (10 oz.) **SHARP CHEDDAR CHEESE**
　　　　　　　　　　　　　　　½ tsp. **WORCESTERSHIRE SAUCE**
　　　　　　　　　　　　　　　dash **ONION SALT**
　　　　　　　　　　　　　　　dash **GARLIC SALT**
　　　　　　　　　　　　　　　2 Tbsp. **MAYONNAISE**

Roll in crushed **NUTS.** Place ball in foil and refrigerate. Chill.

BAKED BRIE AND APPLES

Place in an oven-proof serving
    dish .... 1 wheel (8 oz.) **BRIE**
Spread with .... ¼ stick softened **BUTTER**
Arrange over top .... ¼ cup sliced **ALMONDS**

Bake in preheated 350 degree oven until softened and heated through, about 12 to 15 minutes. Serve warm with **FRENCH BREAD** and slices of **APPLES**.

BRIE APPETIZER ROUND

Purchase .... 1 round (2½ lb.) **RIPENED BRIE**
Remove rind, cutting to within ¼-inch of outside edges. Place on ungreased
    cookie sheet.
Arrange over top .... ⅔ cup coarsely chopped **PECANS**
Sprinkle with .... 2 to 3 Tbsp. **BROWN SUGAR**

Broil 8 inches from heat for 3 to 5 minutes, or until sugar and cheese are bubbly. Serve with **CRACKERS**.

CAVIAR

Serve Caviar (3 to 4 ounces) chilled and nestled in a bowl of crushed **ICE**.
Surround with tiny bowls of.... 2 **EGGS,** hard boiled and shredded
                               1 **ONION,** minced
                                  SOUR CREAM or **YOGURT**
                                  LEMON WEDGES, seeded

Serve with thin-sliced **WHITE** or **BROWN PARTY BREAD, UNSALTED CRACKERS** and **COCKTAILS**.

CHEESE: Freeze for 15 minutes before grating.

CHEEZIEST JALAPENO CHEESE SQUARES

Combine .... | 4 **EGGS,** well beaten
1 tsp. minced **ONION**
4 **JALAPENO PEPPERS,** seeded and chopped, or, 1 can (4 oz.) chopped **GREEN CHILIES**
4 cups shredded **CHEDDAR CHEESE** (16 oz.)

Mix well. Spread into an ungreased 8-inch square pan. Bake in a preheated oven at 350 degrees for 30 minutes.

YIELD: 6 SERVINGS

BAC-OOOOS

Buy .... | 1 box **SARATOGA CRACKERS** (long, perforated lengthwise)

Have butcher slice *very* thin .... | 1 pound **BACON**

Break the crackers along perforation. Wrap ½ piece bacon around cracker. Place on cookie sheet. Sprinkle heavily with **PAPRIKA.** Bake in slow oven (200 degrees) for 45 minutes, or until bacon is cooked. Let set a few minutes so bacon can crisp. Serve warm. (To freeze, wrap baked, cooled bacon in foil. To serve, place frozen Bac-Os in slow oven and heat. Open foil and let stand to crisp.

BACON TID-BITS
Scrumptious.

Place in single layers on a microwave roasting rack or in a glass baking dish .... | 2 pounds **BACON,** *thick* sliced
Combine and sprinkle over..... 1½ cups **BROWN SUGAR,** packed
1½ tsp. **DRY MUSTARD**

Cook in microwave for 1 minute per slice, or until crisp. Drain on paper towel and break into bite-sized pieces. (I have never tried this recipe in a conventional oven, but I'm sure it can be done. Just as long as the sugar caramelizes and the bacon is done.)

BACON WRAPPED WATER CHESTNUTS

Drain well . . . .   2 cans (5 oz. each) **WATER CHESTNUTS**

Marinate 2 to 3 hours in . . . .   2 to 3 Tbsp. **SOY SAUCE**
½ tsp. **PEPPER**
2 Tbsp. **BROWN SUGAR**

Drain well. Wrap ⅓ slice **BACON** around each chestnut and secure with a toothpick. Bake on a cookie sheet in a 350-degree oven until brown and bacon is crisp.

YIELD: 16 TO 18 HORS D'OEUVRES

COCKTAIL WIENERS

Heat . . . .   1 small jar **JELLY,** any kind (my-favorite—**JALAPENO JELLY**)
Equal amount **CATSUP**

Cut into one-fourths . . . .   1 pound **WIENERS**

Cook for about 20 minutes on simmer. Serve in a chafing dish. Use toothpicks to spear wiener chunks.

HAM LOG

Combine in a medium bowl . . . . .   1 cup **GROUND COOKED HAM**
8 ounces **CREAM CHEESE,** softened
3 Tbsp. finely chopped **GREEN PEPPER**
2 Tbsp. finely chopped **ONION**
2 Tbsp. finely chopped **PIMIENTO**
1 Tbsp. **PREPARED HORSERADISH**
1 tsp. **WORCESTERSHIRE SAUCE**
⅛ tsp. ground **FRESH PEPPER**

Mix well to blend. Divide mixture in half. Spoon onto waxed paper. Roll into logs 3 to 4 inches long, and wrap and chill several hours or overnight. To serve, combine ½ cup finely chopped **CHIVES** and 3 Tbsp. **SALAD SEASONING** on a piece of waxed paper. Roll chilled logs in mixture, coating generously. Place on serving plate and garnish with **CRACKERS**.

PICNIC BEEF BOLOGNA
W. J. McLaurin's gift to neighbors at Christmas.

In a large bowl, mix
thoroughly . . . .   2 pounds **HAMBURGER MEAT,**
extra lean
2 Tbsp. **MORTON'S TENDER-
QUICK** curing salt
½ Tbsp. **LIQUID SMOKE**
⅛ tsp. **GARLIC POWDER**
¼ tsp. ground **BLACK PEPPER**
1 cup **RED WINE** (or **WATER**)

Chill two hours. Form into rolls, 6 inches long, and about 2 inches in diameter. Wrap in plastic wrap. Refrigerate for 24 hours.

Unwrap, place on a broiler pan rack. Bake in a 225 degree oven for 3 hours. Remove from oven. Pat with paper towels to remove excess fat. Cool slightly and wrap in foil. Refrigerate or freeze.

May be cooked in a smoker.

SAUSAGE PINWHEELS
Dot Roberts's recipe. Much easier than the sausage balls.

Set sausage out of refrigerator for 30 minutes, for easier mixing.
Make dough of . . . .   4 cups **BISQUICK**
1 stick **MARGARINE,** melted
1 cup **MILK**
Refrigerate 30 minutes.
Mix together . . . .   1 pound **HOT PORK SAUSAGE**
1 pound **REGULAR PORK
SAUSAGE**

Divide dough into 3 batches. Put a batch on a floured board or waxed paper. Roll into a rectangle. Spread with ⅓ of the raw sausage mixture. Roll as for a jelly roll. Do the same with the remaining dough and sausage. Wrap each roll in waxed paper or foil. Put in the freezer or refrigerator. Bake all at one time, or just as many as you need. May also bake, and then freeze. Reheat in a warm oven or microwave.

To bake, slice ¼-inch thick, place on an ungreased cookie sheet and bake in a preheated 350-degree oven for 15 minutes.

YIELD: 4 OR 5 DOZEN

VARIATION: Omit 1 cup of **SAUSAGE** and add 1 cup grated **SHARP CHEDDAR CHEESE.**

SCRUMPTIOUS PARTY PORK
Different! Your guests will want the recipe.

Have butcher to cut a . . . .   3 pound **PORK TENDER**
Rub with "a lot" of . . . .   **SALT, PEPPER, COMINO**

Wrap with foil and bake 6 hours at 250 degrees. Slice and mix with **SWEET AND SOUR MIXTURE.** (The meat will probably crumble and resemble tuna.)

SWEET AND SOUR MIXTURE
Mix well . . . .   1 jar **SWEET AND SOUR SAUCE**
   1 small jar **RED PEPPER JELLY**
   (found in the Deli)

Stir mixture into the **PORK TENDER.** Serve with tiny **ROLLS.** (Baker will make these for you special, or try the Featherweight Rolls.) Serve with **DIJON MUSTARD, CHIPS, PICKLES, OLIVES,** etc.

FRIED OYSTERS

Wash, clean and pat **OYSTERS** dry with paper towels. Dip in **MILK** or **BUTTERMILK.** Shake excess off oysters and dip in **CORNMEAL** with **SALT** and **PEPPER.** Fry in very hot **OIL.** Dip in **COCKTAIL SAUCE** or our favorite, "SALSA PARA OSTIONES".

SALSA PARA OSTIONES

Saute until golden brown . . . . . .   2 **GREEN ONIONS** slivered with
   part of their tops
   2 cloves **GARLIC,** crushed
   3 Tbsp. **OLIVE OIL**
Add and cook gently 3
  minutes . . . .   ½ cup chopped, peeled, seeded
   TOMATO
Stir in . . . .   ⅓ cup minced fresh **PARSLEY**
   SALT and **PEPPER** to taste.

Remove from heat. Serve warm with **FRIED OYSTERS.**

LEMONY BARBEQUED SHRIMP
Straight from the Texas coast.

Melt . . . .   ½ cup **BUTTER**
Add . . . .   2 Tbsp. **WORCESTERSHIRE SAUCE**
  2 Tbsp. **LEMON JUICE**
Remove from heat and add . . . . .   2 pounds **SHRIMP,** peeled and deveined

Marinate for 2 hours. Do not refrigerate. Cook 2 to 5 minutes on barbeque grill. Baste while cooking.

PEEL-YOUR-OWN PEPPERED SHRIMP
Recipe from our Cajun friend, Drew Mouton.

Cut up in a skillet and melt . . . . .   1 stick **BUTTER**
Add . . . .   36 to 40 **SHRIMP**
  lots of **CRACKED PEPPER**
  1 **LEMON** (rind and all, cut up very fine)
  SALT
  ½ to ¾ cup **WHITE WINE**

Cover with lid and steam for 15 to 20 minutes. Serve shrimp warm in the shells.

SHRIMP SAUCE

Mix all together . . . .   2 cups **CATSUP**
  2 cups **CHILI SAUCE**
  ¼ cup **CIDER VINEGAR**
  6 drops **TABASCO SAUCE**
  ¼ cup **HORSERADISH**
  ¼ cup finely minced **CELERY**
  ¼ cup finely minced **ONION**
  2 tsp. **WORCESTERSHIRE SAUCE**

Blend well. Store in the refrigerator in an air-tight container. Serve with **SHRIMP,** boiled in **BEER.**

MINI MEATBALLS

Combine .... 1 pound **HOT BULK PORK SAUSAGE**
1 pound **MILD BULK PORK SAUSAGE**

Shape into 1-inch meatballs. Cook in a large skillet over medium heat until browned. Drain off drippings.
Combine and pour over
meatballs .... 1¼ cups **CATSUP**
¼ cup **WATER**
¼ cup **BROWN SUGAR,** packed
1 Tbsp. **SOY SAUCE**
1 Tbsp. **LEMON JUICE**

Simmer 10 minutes, stirring occasionally. Add 1 can (15½ oz.) **PINEAPPLE CHUNKS,** drained. Simmer an additional 10 minutes, stirring often.

YIELD: 3½ DOZEN

PARTY TARTS
The right start for holiday parties.

MINI PATTY SHELLS:
Combine .... 1 pkg. (3 oz.) **CREAM CHEESE,** softened
½ cup **BUTTER** or **MARGARINE,** softened
1½ cups **FLOUR**

Cream until smooth. Shape into 30 (1-inch) balls. Place in ungreased muffin pans. Shape each ball into a shell.

FILLING:
Place on paper towels and
squeeze until almost dry ..... 1 pkg (10 oz.) frozen **CHOPPED SPINACH,** thawed and drained
Combine with .... 1 **EGG,** well beaten
¼ tsp. **SALT**
⅛ tsp. **PEPPER**
2 Tbsp. chopped **ONION**
1 cup grated **ROMANO CHEESE**
¼ cup **BUTTER** or **MARGARINE,** melted

Fill each shell with 1 heaping teaspoonful of the mixture. Sprinkle with more **ROMANO CHEESE.** Bake at 350 degrees for 30 to 35 minutes.

YIELD: 2½ DOZEN

WON TON STRIPS AND SAUCE
Prepare the morning of the party.

Fry and store in an air-tight
 container.................. 16 **WON TON SKINS** (3-inch
 square) or 4 **EGG ROLL SKINS**

(Quarter egg roll skins. Cut won ton skins or quartered egg roll skins in ½-inch wide strips.) Drain on paper towel.

Blend .... ¼ cup **SOY SAUCE**
 2 Tbsp. **LEMON JUICE**
 2 tsp. **BROWN SUGAR**
 2 Tbsp. **RED BEAN PASTE**
 (optional)

Refrigerate until ready to serve. Arrange won ton strips around bowl of sauce.

YIELD: THIS MAKES ONLY ½ CUP SAUCE. MAY NEED TO DOUBLE OR TRIPLE ENTIRE RECIPE FOR PARTY.

TEXAS JALAPENO JELLY
Try this on top of crackers spread with cream cheese,
for a snappy appetizer.

Combine in blender .... 3 medium **GREEN PEPPERS,**
 seeded and chopped
 2 **JALAPENO PEPPERS,** seeded
 and chopped
 1 cup **WHITE VINEGAR**

Blend until pureed. Pour into a
 large deep saucepan,
 and add .... 6½ cups **SUGAR**
 ½ cup **WHITE VINEGAR**
 1 tsp. **CAYENNE PEPPER**

Bring to a rolling boil, stirring
 frequently. Stir in .... 6 ounces **CERTO** liquid fruit pectin

Boil 1 minute longer, stirring constantly. Remove from heat and skim off foam. Pour into sterilized jars and seal.

YIELD: 6 TO 7 HALF-PINT JARS

MARINATED MUSHROOMS

Wash, dry and set aside	1 pound small **MUSHROOMS**
Mix together	¾ cup **SALAD OIL**
	¾ cup **RED WINE VINEGAR**
	¼ cup grated **ONION**
	¼ cup diced **GREEN PEPPER**
	¼ cup chopped **PARSLEY**
	2 cloves **GARLIC,** crushed
	1 tsp. **SALT**
	1 tsp. **SUGAR**

Add marinade to mushrooms at least 1½ hours before serving. (Overnight, if possible.) To serve, lift out with a slotted spoon onto a bowl of crushed ice.

ARTICHOKE JUSTIN'

Wash and remove stems from . .	3 large **ARTICHOKES**
Cut spikes off leaves.	
Mix together	1 large can **PARMESAN CHEESE**
	3 pieces crushed **DRY TOAST**
	2 tsp. **LEMON JUICE**
	GARLIC SALT to taste
Add	1 **BOUILLON CUBE** mixed with less than ¼ cup **WATER**

Mixture has a paste-like texture. Make cavity in center of artichoke. Place stuffing in cavity and on each leaf. (Be careful not to spread the artichoke apart.) Place artichokes in a large pan with 1 inch of **WATER** in the bottom. Add 2 cloves **GARLIC** to liquid. Steam for 1 hour. Remove and drain. Serve warm or cold.

POTATO SKINS

A favorite appetizer in West Texas.

Bake at 350 degrees for 1 hour .	4 **POTATOES,** do not peel
Cut in half and scoop out, leaving only the shell. Fill shells with a mixture of	½ cup shredded **CHEDDAR CHEESE**
	8 slices **BACON,** cooked and diced
	2 **GREEN CHILI PEPPERS** cut in thin strips

The filling will be very thin in the shells. Place under broiler for 5 minutes. Serve with **QUICK VEGGIE DIP.** (See index.)

FRITTER BATTER
For squash, onion, etc.

Mix and stir until smooth . . . . . .   1 cup **FLOUR**
                                    3 tsp. **BAKING POWDER**
                                    ½ tsp. **SALT**
                                    ¼ tsp. **SUGAR**
                                    1 Tbsp. **OIL**
                                    2 **EGGS,** beaten
                                    ⅓ cup **MILK**
More liquid may be added if needed.

Wash any kind of **VEGETABLE,** slice, or cut up the way you prefer. Dry *very well* on paper towels. Dip in batter. Fry in hot **FAT**. Drain well.

Vegetables that are excellent are:
SQUASH   **MUSHROOMS**   **CAULIFLOWER**   **EGGPLANT**
ZUCCHINI   **ONIONS**   **FRESH GREEN ONIONS** (leave whole)

Also try **CUBED CHEESE.** (Have very cold.)

DEEP FRIED ZUCCHINI
Babette's specialty.

Mix together . . . .   1 cup **CORN MEAL**
                                    ½ cup **FLOUR**
                                    ½ tsp. **SALT**
Add to make a thick batter . . . . .   **BUTTERMILK**
Dip into batter . . . .   **ZUCCHINI,** slices or spears

Fry in hot **VEGETABLE OIL** until golden brown. Drain on paper towels. Serve with **RANCH STYLE DRESSING.** This can be served as a side dish or appetizer.

YIELD: 4 SERVINGS

VARIATION: An **EGG** can be added to the batter for a thicker crust.

APPETIZERS: Whet the appetite, don't satisfy it. Plan them to complement the menu.

MRS. SUTTON'S SPINACH BALLS

Cook according to directions . . . . 2 pkgs. (10 oz. each) **CHOPPED FROZEN SPINACH**

Drain well and add . . . . 1 **ONION,** chopped
¾ cup **MARGARINE,** melted
6 **EGGS,** beaten
½ cup grated **PARMESAN CHEESE**
3 cups **HERB STUFFING MIX**
1 Tbsp. **PEPPER**
1½ tsp. **GARLIC SALT**
1½ tsp. **THYME**

Mix all together and shape into ¾-inch balls. Place on a lightly greased cookie sheet. Bake in a preheated 325-degree oven for 25 minutes. Can be frozen before baking. (If frozen, allow 10 minutes more baking time.)

DIPPERS

MILDRED LeMOND'S BROCCOLI DIP
Expected at every Bridge party.

Cook according to directions . . . . 1 pkg. chopped **FROZEN BROCCOLI**

Drain *well.* Set aside.
Saute . . . . 1 small **ONION,** chopped
2 Tbsp. **MARGARINE**
Add . . . . 1 can **MUSHROOM SOUP,** undiluted
1 roll (6 oz.) **GARLIC CHEESE**
1 tsp. **ACCENT**
½ tsp. **SALT**
½ tsp. **PEPPER**
1 tsp. **WORCESTERSHIRE SAUCE**
½ tsp. **TABASCO**

Heat until cheese is melted.
Add and cook 1 minute . broccoli
Remove from heat and add . . . . . 4 ounces chopped canned **MUSHROOMS**
¾ cup slivered **ALMONDS**

Put mixture in chafing dish. Serve hot with **CORN CHIPS.**

ARTICHOKE DIP

Combine . . . . 1 can (13½ oz.) **ARTICHOKE HEARTS,** drained and chopped
1 cup **MAYONNAISE** (do not use salad dressing)
1 cup grated **PARMESAN CHEESE**
GARLIC POWDER and **SALT** to taste

Bake at 225 degrees 20 minutes. Serve warm.

VEGETABLE DIP

Mix together and chill . . . . ½ cup **SOUR CREAM**
½ cup **MAYONNAISE**
1 Tbsp. **DRIED ONION**
1 Tbsp. **DRIED PARSLEY**
1 tsp. **DILL**
1 tsp. **BEAU MONDE SEASONING**

MEXICAN DIP

In a medium skillet brown . . . . . . 1 pound **GROUND ROUND**
1 small **ONION,** chopped
Add . . . . 1 pound **VELVEETA CHEESE**
Stir until melted.
Add . . . . 1 can **RO-TEL**
Remove from heat and add . . . . . 2 **TOMATOES,** chopped

Serve with **CORN CHIPS.** *Keep warm.*

JALAPENO BEAN DIP

Heat together . . . . 1 pound **VELVEETA JALAPENO CHEESE**
1 can (No. 2) **REFRIED BEANS**
1 cup **MILK**

Serve warm.

QUICK VEGGIE DIP

Mix and chill . . . .
    1 pint **MAYONNAISE**
    1 carton **SOUR CREAM**
    2 packages **RANCH DRESSING MIX**

SHRIMP DIP

Mix and chill . . . .
    1 pkg. **DRY ONION SOUP**
    2 cups **SOUR CREAM**
    1 cup **MAYONNAISE**
    ⅓ cup **CATSUP**
    1 pound **COCKTAIL SHRIMP,** cooked and chopped

TAMALE-CHILI DIP

Heat until cheese is melted . . . . .
    1 large can **TAMALES,** mashed
    1 pound **VELVEETA CHEESE**

Add . . . .
    1 can **RO-TEL**
    2 cans (15 oz.) **CHILI**

Serve warm.

CHILI CON QUESO

Cook in heavy skillet . . . .
    3 Tbsp. **BUTTER**
    3 **ONIONS,** chopped

Add . . . .
    4 cans (3 oz. each) **CHOPPED CHILIES**

Add and stir constantly . . . . 3½ pounds **AMERICAN CHEESE,** grated

Stir in . . . .
    5 Tbsp. **WORCESTERSHIRE SAUCE**
    SALT and **PEPPER**
    TABASCO to taste

Serve immediately on toasted **CRACKERS** or with crisp fried **TORTILLAS.** (If cheese becomes to thick, thin with **MILK.**)

YIELD: 20 TO 25 SERVINGS

AVOCADO DIP

Mix and chill ....
- 2 **AVOCADOS**, mashed
- 2 tsp. grated **ONION**
- **JUICE** of 1 **LEMON**
- **SALT**
- 1 **ORTEGA CHILI**, diced
- 1 Tbsp. **MAYONNAISE**, heaping

SUZIE'S LAYERED DIP

In a large, round, flat dish, layer
the following in the order
given ....
- 2 cans (10½ oz. each) **BEAN DIP**
- 3 large **AVOCADOS**, chopped and sprinkled with 2 Tbsp. **LEMON JUICE**
- 1 cup **SOUR CREAM**, mixed with ½ cup **MAYONNAISE** and 1 pkg. dry **TACO SEASONING**
- 1 bunch **GREEN ONIONS**, chopped (tops, also)
- 3 **TOMATOES**, chopped
- 2 cans (3½ oz. each) chopped **RIPE OLIVES**
- 2 cups grated **MONTEREY JACK CHEESE**

Refrigerate until ready to serve. (Seal with plastic wrap.) Serve with
DORITOS OR **CORN CHIPS**.

SEAFOOD CHILI DIP

Mix in a blender until smooth...
- 1 bottle **HEINZ CHILI SAUCE**
- 1 bunch **GREEN ONIONS**, chopped (tops, also)
- 3 stalks **CELERY**, chopped
- 1 **GREEN PEPPER**, chopped
- 3 Tbsp. **PICANTE SAUCE**
- 1 Tbsp. **WORCESTERSHIRE SAUCE**

Refrigerate 24 hours.
Spread on a large flat plate ....
- 2 pkgs. (8 oz. each) **CREAM CHEESE**, softened

Layer on top of the cheese .....
- ½ pound **POPCORN SHRIMP** or **CRAB MEAT**

Spread sauce over the seafood. Chill. Serve with **CRACKERS** or **CHIPS**.

WINTER TIME DIP

Brown and drain	1	cup **PECAN PIECES**
	2	Tbsp. **BUTTER**
Set aside.		
Heat	16	ounces **CREAM CHEESE**
	¼	cup **MILK**
	2	cans (4 oz. size) **CHIPPED BEEF**
	½	tsp. **GARLIC SALT**
	4	tsp. minced **ONION**
	1	cup **SOUR CREAM**
	1	can **CHOPPED CHILIES**

Mix well. Sprinkle with the pecans. Bake in a preheated 350-degree oven for about 20 minutes, or until heated through. Serve warm with **CRACKERS**.

TEASERS

Remove crusts from	1	loaf (1 pound) **SANDWICH BREAD**
Cut slices into 4 triangles and toast on both sides.		
Spread with mixture of	2	bunches **GREEN ONIONS,** chopped (tops, also)
	1	pound **BACON,** cooked and crumbled
	¾	cup **MAYONNAISE**
		Dash of **PEPPER**

Use about 1 teaspoon mixture on each triangle.

YIELD: 5 DOZEN

CHIPPED BEEF DIP

Soften	2	pkgs. (8 oz. each) **CREAM CHEESE**
Add	2	bunches **GREEN ONIONS,** chopped very fine (tops, also)
	1	jar dried **CHIPPED BEEF**

Chill.

PARTY SANDWICHES

Make ahead and refrigerate or freeze.

Make out of **WHOLE WHEAT BREAD,** for one side, and **WHITE BREAD** for the other side.

Ask baker to make **COLORED BREAD** for special holidays—*Red* for Christmas parties, *Orange* for Halloween or Thanksgiving, etc.

Party sandwiches are a little more attractive if the crusts are removed, but it is not necessary.

Cut whole loaves of **BREAD** diagonally into 3 or 4 slices. Spread on **FILLING** and stack like a layered cake. Slice.

Cut into shapes with cookie cutters for different occasions.

FILLINGS

PINEAPPLE: Drain well 1 can (14 oz.) **CRUSHED PINEAPPLE.** Mix with 16 ounces **CREAM CHEESE,** chopped **PECANS,** and enough **MAYONNAISE** to spread easily. (Optional: dry **PARSLEY**)

ONION: Combine 16 ounces **CREAM CHEESE,** 1 cup chopped **PECANS,** 1 Tbsp. minced **ONION,** 2 Tbsp. **LEMON JUICE,** enough **MAYONNAISE** to spread easily. (Optional: chopped **CHIVES**)

CREAM CHEESE-EGG: Combine 8 ounces **CREAM CHEESE,** ¼ cup chopped **RIPE OLIVES,** ¼ cup minced **ONION,** 3 hard boiled **EGGS** (mashed,) 1 Tbsp. **CATSUP,** 1 or 2 chopped **PIMIENTOS,** ½ cup chopped **NUTS, SALT** and **PEPPER.**

DIP FOR STRAWBERRIES

In a small mixing bowl
add...................... **POWDERED SUGAR** to taste
to .... 2 cups **SOUR CREAM**
dash of **CINNAMON**
2 Tbsp. **POPPY SEED**

Wash **STRAWBERRIES.** Leave stems on to hold for dipping. Serve chilled.

FRUIT DIP

Mix until smooth . . . . 1 pkg. (8 oz.) **CREAM CHEESE**
½ carton **SOUR CREAM**
3 Tbsp. **APRICOT PRESERVES**
½ can **ANGEL FLAKE COCONUT**
½ cup **PECANS,** chopped very fine

If too thick, add more **PRESERVES.** Chill and serve with **PINEAPPLE SPEARS** or whole **STRAWBERRIES.**

FRIED FRUIT

Be sure and fry enough so there will be plenty for seconds (and thirds).

Beat until they form stiff
  peaks . . . . 5 **EGG WHITES**
Set aside.
Use a mixer or whisk and beat
  until very creamy . . . . 2 cups **FLOUR**
1 can **BEER**
½ tsp. **SUGAR**
Fold in egg whites.

Wash any kind of fruit very well. *Dry completely* with paper towels. Be sure all moisture is removed. Dip each piece of fruit in the batter. Deep fry until golden brown. Drain on paper towels. Roll fruit in a **CINNAMON-SUGAR** mixture. Serve with **SOUR CREAM-POWDERED SUGAR** mixture. (Stir powdered sugar into 1 carton of sour cream until a creamy consistency. Add a dash of **CINNAMON** and 2 Tbsp. **POPPY SEED.**)

MALLOW FRUIT DIP

Blend together gradually . . . . 1 jar (7 oz.) **MARSHMALLOW CREAM**
1 pkg. (8 oz.) **PHILADELPHIA CREAM CHEESE**
Add and whip until fluffy . . . . . . 1 Tbsp. **ORANGE RIND**
dash of **GINGER**

Refrigerate until ready to serve. Arrange fresh **FRUIT** on plate and serve with dip.

CHERRIES RENAISSANCE
So pretty on a party table and so GOOD!

Wash approximately 8 medium-size **DARK SWEET CHERRIES,** per person. Set aside to drain. If long stems not available, use frilly toothpicks to spear. Chop into small pieces and put
in double boiler . . . . 1 pound **SEMI-SWEET DARK**
                                      BAKER'S CHOCOLATE
Stir constantly until chocolate reaches 95 degrees.
Use same procedure with . . . . . . 1 pound **WHITE CHOCOLATE**

Dip half of the cherries in white chocolate and half in dark chocolate. Place waxed paper on a cookie sheet. Place dipped cherries on waxed paper and refrigerate.

YIELD: ABOUT 64 CHERRIES

VARIATION: For a conversation stopper—dip ½ of *each cherry* in the white chocolate and the other ½ in the dark chocolate.

(Follow the directions in microwave manual to melt the chocolate, if you wish.)

JAN-SU JUNQUE

Combine equal parts; **BEER NUTS, SHOE-STRING POTATOES, CHEESY-POPCORN** and extra thin **PRETZELS.** Serve with drinks.

TEXAS TRASH

Mix and stir constantly until it
boils. . . . . 1 cup **BUTTER**
                                         2 Tbsp. **LAWRY'S SEASON SALT**
                                         2 Tbsp. **GARLIC**
                                         2 Tbsp. **TABASCO SAUCE**
                                         2 Tbsp. **WORCESTERSHIRE**
                                               SAUCE
Set aside and mix in large
mixing bowl . . . . 1 box **WHEAT CHEX**
                                        1 box **CHEERIOS**
                                        2 pounds **NUTS**
                                        1 box **RICE CHEX**

Stir all together until cereal is moist. Bake in long pan, stirring occasionally at 250 degrees, for 1 hour.

NUTS!

TERIYAKI ALMONDS

Spread on an ungreased cookie
    sheet and toast for 20 minutes
    at 300 degrees . . . .   2 cups blanched **ALMONDS**
Melt . . . .   ¼ cup **BUTTER**
Add . . . .   2 Tbsp. **SOY SAUCE**
                             2 Tbsp. **DRY SHERRY**
                             ¼ tsp. **GINGER**

Pour over almonds. Bake 10 to 20 more minutes. Stir occasionally to coat evenly. Sprinkle with **GARLIC SALT** to taste. Cool on paper towels. Refrigerate.

CRYSTALLIZED ORANGE PECANS

Combine and microwave on
    Roast (70% power) for 6
    minutes . . . .   ¼ cup **ORANGE JUICE**
                             1 cup **SUGAR**
                             2 to 3 cups **PECAN HALVES**
                             ¼ tsp. **CINNAMON**

Stir and continue cooking on Roast until crystallized (8 to 10 more minutes.) Stir occasionally. Spread on waxed paper, separating pecans.

CRYSTALLIZED PEANUTS

Combine in a heavy
    saucepan . . . .   2 cups **RAW PEANUTS**
                             1 cup **SUGAR**
                             ½ cup **WATER**

Cook over medium heat until mixture crystallizes and coats peanuts (about 10 minutes). Stir constantly. Spread peanuts in a buttered jelly roll pan. Sprinkle with **SALT**. Bake for 15 minutes at 300 degrees. Lift and turn peanuts with a spatula and continue to cook 15 minutes more. Cool.

CANDIED NUTS

Beat until frothy . . . . 1 tsp. **WATER**
 1 **EGG WHITE**
Mix well with . . . . 1 pound **PECAN** or **WALNUT**
 HALVES
Combine and mix
  with nuts . . . . 1 cup **SUGAR**
 1 tsp. **CINNAMON**
 1 tsp. **SALT**

Spread on a cookie sheet. Bake at 225 degrees for 1 hour. Stir occasionally.

VIVIAN'S SUGARED PECANS

Beat until stiff . . . . 1 **EGG WHITE**
 ¼ tsp. **CINNAMON**
Add and continue beating until
  very stiff . . . . 1 cup **BROWN SUGAR**
 pinch of **SALT**
Fold in . . . . 1½ cups **PECAN HALVES**

Drop pecan halves, one at a time, onto a buttered cookie sheet. Bake at 225 degrees for 1 hour and 15 minutes.

CHOCOLATE MEJICANO

Heat, but do not boil . . . . 1 quart **MILK**
Add . . . . 4 tsp. **INSTANT COFFEE** (heaping)
 ½ cup **CHOCOLATE SYRUP**
 ½ tsp. **VANILLA**
 ⅛ tsp. **SALT**

Mix well and pour into mugs. Top with **WHIPPED CREAM**. Sprinkle with ground **CINNAMON**.

YIELD: 4 SERVINGS

VARIATION: Put a jigger of **KAHLUA** in mug before adding Mexican Chocolate.

ICED MEXICAN COFFEE

Put in skillet on medium heat
and stir until melted . . . .   1 cup **SUGAR**
Add and stir until sugar is
dissolved . . . .   1 cup **HOT WATER**
Boil 2 minutes. Add . . . .   1 cup **HALF AND HALF MILK**
                                                  4 cups **COFFEE**

Mix and pour over ice in tall glasses. Top with a scoop of **ICE CREAM.** Serve.

YIELD: 4 SERVINGS

ENGLISH WASSAIL

Boil for 5 minutes . . . .   1 cup **SUGAR**
                                                  ½ cup **WATER**
                                                  3 **LEMON SLICES**
                                                  2 **CINNAMON STICKS**
Strain into a small bowl and set aside.
Combine . . . .   2 cups **CRANBERRY JUICE**
                                                  2 cups fresh or frozen **LEMON
                                                      JUICE**
                                                  4 cups **RED WINE**

Stir in syrup and remove from heat. Serve immediately. Garnish with
LEMON SLICES.

YIELD: 20 SERVINGS

SPICED APPLE CIDER
Saint Nick's treat.

Mix in a large pan . . . .   ½ gallon **APPLE CIDER**
                                                  JUICE of 3 or 4 **LEMONS**
                                                  1½ cups **SUGAR**
                                                  2 cups **WATER**
Mix together in a six-inch
square piece of cloth, tie with
a string and drop into liquid . .   2 tsp. **CINNAMON**
                                                  1 tsp. **ALLSPICE**
                                                  1 Tbsp. **CLOVES**
                                                  2 tsp. **PICKLING SPICES**

Boil several minutes. Then turn on very low heat to just keep hot. (This will
smell so good through the entire house.) Serve in mugs while hot.

ANNIVERSARY PUNCH
Make ahead and freeze.

Combine in blender . . . . 6 **BANANAS**
Thaw and add . . . . 1 can (6 oz.) frozen **LEMONADE,**
                  undiluted
                 1 can (12 oz.) frozen **ORANGE**
                  JUICE, undiluted
Blend until smooth.
Mix in large mixing bowl . . . . . . 1 can (46 oz.) **PINEAPPLE JUICE**
                 3 cups **WATER**
                 2 cups **SUGAR**

Add the banana mixture and mix well. Pour into a plastic container or milk cartons and freeze. To serve, thaw until slightly slushy (just enough to get out of container). Add 2 bottles (64 oz. each) chilled **LEMON-LIME CARBONATED BEVERAGE.** Garnish with **ORANGE SLICES.**

YIELD: 6 QUARTS

CATAWBA CHRISTMAS PUNCH

Mix . . . . 2 quarts **CRANBERRY COCKTAIL**
                 1 quart frozen **ORANGE JUICE**
                 1 quart **GINGER ALE**
                 ½ cup **SUGAR**

Chill until ready to serve. To serve, pour over **ICE RING** in large punch bowl. Slice 1 **ORANGE** and 1 **LEMON** very thin. Add fruit just before serving, and add 1 quart chilled **CATAWBA.**

YIELD: 18 TO 20 SERVINGS

MARGIE'S APPLE SAMBA
Delicious holiday punch.

Place in the basket of a large
   coffeemaker . . . . 1 tsp. **CLOVES**
                 6 (2-inch) **CINNAMON STICKS**
Add . . . . 1½ cups **WHITE KARO**
                 3 cans (12 oz. each) **APRICOT**
                  NECTAR
                 9 cups **APPLE JUICE**

Perk. Just before serving, add ½ cup **LEMON JUICE** or **CONCENTRATE.**

YIELD: 12 TO 14 SERVINGS.

NIPPERS

HALAMICEK EGGNOG

Our good friend Emma shared this recipe with us.

Beat very well	6	**EGGS**
Add and beat again	1	cup **SUGAR**
Pour in	2	cups **HEAVY CREAM,** whipped
		BOURBON to taste

Beat until fluffy. Refrigerate until ready to serve. About 10 minutes before you are going to serve, pour mixture over ½ gallon **ICE CREAM** in a punch bowl. Add **GINGER ALE** to thin down consistency.

If you have never cared for Eggnog, try this just one time. You will love it!

YIELD: 4 SERVINGS

MARGARITA

Moisten rim of cocktail glass with.....................		**LIME** or **LEMON JUICE**
Spin rim in		**SALT**
In pitcher or shaker mix	1	jigger **TEQUILA**
	½	ounce **TRIPLE SEC**
	1	ounce **LIME** or **LEMON JUICE**

Pour into glass and sip over salty edge. (May prefer to serve over crushed ice.)

YIELD: 1 SERVING

PINA COLADAS

Recipe from Puerto Rico.

In an electric blender or tall pitcher, mix well	½	cup **CREAM OF COCONUT**
	1	cup **PINEAPPLE JUICE**
	⅔	cup **LIGHT RUM**
	2	cups **CRUSHED ICE**

Stir or shake for 1 minute. (In blender, mix ½ minute at high speed.) Pour into pre-chilled glasses. Serve with **PINEAPPLE** spear.

YIELD: 2 SERVINGS

TEQUILA SOUR

Mix .... 2 cans frozen **LEMONADE**
Using lemonade can, add....... 2 cans **TEQUILA**
2 cans **WATER**

Blend with ice in blender, or stir in pitcher with crushed ice. Pour into cocktail glasses.

YIELD: 8 TO 10 SERVINGS

SANGRIA

In a tall pitcher, combine ...... 3 cups **RED WINE**
4 Tbsp. **SUGAR**
When completely dissolved, add . 1 **ORANGE**, sliced
¼ cup **COINTREAU**
¼ cup **BRANDY**
12 ounces **CLUB SODA**
24 **ICE CUBES**

Stir well. Serve in chilled glasses.

YIELD: 6 SERVINGS

JONES'S WINE COOLER

Mix in shaker with **ICE** .... 1 part **WHITE WINE**
1 part **7-UP**
2 Tbsp. **CASSIS**
Pour into chilled glass.
Spray with .... **"ON THE ROCKS" LEMON PEEL OIL**

YIELD: 1 SERVING

STRAWBERRY DAIQUIRI

Place in blender with crushed
ICE .... 6 jiggers **DARK RUM**
2 jiggers **LIME JUICE**
STRAWBERRIES
GRENADINE and **SUGAR** to taste

YIELD: 2 SERVINGS

GOVERNOR'S COCKTAIL

Beat until stiff .... 2 **EGG WHITES**
Mix in blender .... 3 Tbsp. **HONEY**
                              6 ounces **APRICOT NECTAR**
                              6 ounces **PEACH NECTAR**
                              6 ounces **ORANGE JUICE**
                              1½ jiggers **RUM**
                              CRUSHED ICE

Blend in egg whites. Serve in large bowled glasses with **LIME JUICE** on the rims.

YIELD: 4 TO 6 SERVINGS

HAROLD JONES BLOODY MARYS FOR 8

Freeze **TOMATO JUICE** in ice cube trays. Store in plastic bags.
Combine in a large pitcher ..... 46 ounces **TOMATO JUICE**
                              ⅓ cup **WORCESTERSHIRE SAUCE**
                              8 drops **TABASCO**
                              JUICE of 2 **LEMONS**
                              CELERY SALT
                              COARSE BLACK PEPPER
                              1½ cups **VODKA**

Pour over frozen tomato ice cubes. Put a piece of **CELERY STALK** in each glass as a stirrer.

TEXAS BULLSHOT

Shake together .... 1½ oz. **VODKA**
                              6 oz. **BEEF BOUILLON**
                              1 tsp. **LEMON JUICE**
                              10 drops **WORCESTERSHIRE SAUCE**
                              2 dashes **TABASCO SAUCE**
                              SALT and **FRESHLY-GROUND PEPPER** to taste

Strain into a 10-ounce glass with ice.

YIELD: 1 SERVING

Breakfast/Brunch

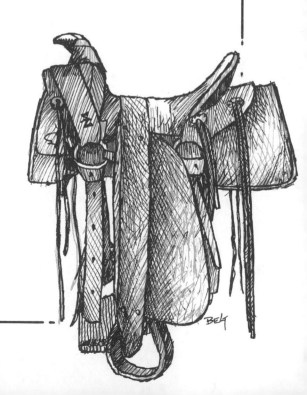

BREAKFAST CREPES

Combine and beat until smooth. . 1 cup **COMPLETE PANCAKE MIX**
                                      1 cup **WATER**
                                        2 **EGGS**

Heat an 8-inch skillet or crepe maker. Pour scant ¼ cup batter into hot skillet. Immediately tilt pan until the batter covers the entire bottom of the skillet. Cook until edges start to dry and center is set. If desired, turn to brown on other side. To serve, fill with desired **FILLING** and roll up.

To make ahead, wrap well in foil after the crepes are cooked. Store in refrigerator up to 3 days, or freezer, up to 3 months. To thaw, place in slow oven (300 degrees) for 10 to 15 minutes.

FILLINGS

Melted **BUTTER, CINNAMON,** and **SUGAR**
FRESH FRUIT and **WHIPPED** or **SOUR CREAM.**
Precooked **SAUSAGE LINKS** and hot **APPLESAUCE**
SCRAMBLED EGGS.
SCRAMBLED EGGS with **BACON** or **HAM** bits.

SUNDAY BREAKFAST CAKE

Melt in a medium saucepan . . . . 4 Tbsp. **BUTTER**
Remove from heat and cool
    slightly. Add . . . . ½ cup **MILK**
                                   1 **EGG**
Sift together and add to liquid . . ½ cup **SUGAR**
                                   1 cup **FLOUR,** scant
                                   3 tsp. **BAKING POWDER**
                                   ¼ tsp. **CINNAMON**
                                   ½ tsp. **SALT**

Stir only enough to smooth out lumps. Pour batter into a greased 8-inch square baking dish. Sprinkle with ½ tsp. **CINNAMON** mixed with 2 Tbsp. **SUGAR.** Bake in a preheated 350-degree oven for 25 minutes.

YIELD: 4 TO 6 SERVINGS

CHRISTMAS COFFEE CAKE
A tradition for Christmas morning.

Cream	1 cup **MARGARINE**
	1 cup **SUGAR**
Add	2 **EGGS**
Combine and add to creamed mixture	1 tsp. **BAKING POWDER**
	1 tsp. **SODA**
	1 tsp. **SALT**
	2 cups **FLOUR**
Add	1 cup **SOUR CREAM**
	1 tsp. **ALMOND FLAVORING**
	1 tsp. **VANILLA FLAVORING**

Pour half the batter into a greased and floured bundt pan. Spread ½ of 1 can (7 oz.) **WHOLE CRANBERRY SAUCE** over batter. Pour remainder of the batter into the pan. Top with the remainder of the cranberry sauce, and ½ cup **PECANS**. Bake in a preheated 350-degree oven for 55 to 60 minutes. When done, cool and top with **GLAZE** (2 Tbsp. warm **WATER**, ½ tsp. **ALMOND FLAVORING**, ¾ cup **POWDERED SUGAR**.) Serve warm; may be frozen.

YIELD: 18 TO 20 SERVINGS

PULL-APART COFFEE CAKE

BUTTER a tube pan heavily.

Place in pan	1 pkg. **CLOVERLEAF FROZEN ROLLS**, still frozen
(Pull each roll apart into 3 pieces.)	
Melt	1 stick **BUTTER**
Pour over rolls. Combine and sprinkle over rolls	1 pkg. (3⅝ oz.) **VANILLA PUDDING** (dry, *not* instant)
	4 tsp. **CINNAMON**
	½ cup **BROWN SUGAR**, packed
	½ cup **NUTS**, chopped

Let stand, uncovered, on cabinet top overnight. Bake at 375 degrees for 20 minutes. When done, remove from oven and let set 10 minutes. Invert on plate.

YIELD: 8 SERVINGS

VARIATION: May use 1 cup **BROWN SUGAR**, 1 package **BUTTERSCOTCH PUDDING** (use dry, not instant), 1 stick **BUTTER** and ½ cup chopped **NUTS**.

GERMAN APPLE COFFEE CAKE

Cream together	1 cup **SUGAR**
	¼ cup **MARGARINE,** softened
	1 **EGG**
Stir in	½ cup **MILK**
	¼ tsp. **LEMON EXTRACT**
Blend in	1½ cups **FLOUR**
	2 tsp. **BAKING POWDER**
	½ tsp. **SALT**

Spread mixture in a well-greased 8x8x2-inch pan.

Arrange on top of cake mixture .	3 to 4 **APPLES,** pared and sliced
Cut together with pastry blender	2 Tbsp. **MARGARINE**
	½ cup **SUGAR**
	1 tsp. **CINNAMON**
	¼ tsp. **NUTMEG**
	2 Tbsp. **FLOUR**

Sprinkle over apples.

Bake in 350 degree oven for 40 to 45 minutes, or until cake tests done with a wooden toothpick.

YIELD: 8 TO 10 SERVINGS

MAMMIE'S DOUGHNUTS
This recipe has been changed from lard to shortening to cooking oil.

Blend together and set aside	1 cup **BUTTERMILK**
	1 tsp. **SODA**
Cream together	1 cup **SUGAR**
	4 Tbsp. **OIL**
Add and beat well	2 **EGGS**
Sift	4½ cups **FLOUR**
	1 Tbsp. **NUTMEG** or **CINNAMON**
Add buttermilk mixture alternately to egg mixture.	
Stir in	1 Tbsp. **VANILLA**

This is a stiff dough. Knead 8 to 10 times. Roll and cut like doughnuts, or drop by teaspoonsful into hot cooking **OIL.** Brown on one side and turn. When underside is brown, remove from hot grease and shake in a paper bag with **SUGAR** and **SPICES.**

YIELD: 3 TO 4 DOZEN

GERMAN DROP DOUGHNUTS
Real treat for a cold day.

Sift together	2 cups **FLOUR**
	3 tsp. **BAKING POWDER**
	½ tsp. **SODA**
	½ tsp. **SALT**
Add and mix well............	1 cup **BUTTERMILK**
	1 **EGG**
	⅓ cup **SUGAR**

Heat enough **SHORTENING** in a heavy saucepan or deep-fryer, to be about 2 inches deep when melted. Drop dough by tablespoons and fry until golden brown on one side, turn and brown the underside. Drain well on paper towels. Roll in **POWDERED SUGAR,** glaze, or frost.

YIELD: APPROXIMATELY 4 DOZEN

VARIATIONS: To *Glaze:* Mix 3½ cups **POWDERED SUGAR,** 1 Tbsp. **CREAM** or **MILK,** and 1 tsp. **VANILLA.** (Add more **MILK** if too thick.) Dip cooked **DOUGHNUTS** and drain.

To *Frost:* Cook until somewhat thick, ⅓ cup **BROWN SUGAR,** ⅓ cup **BUTTER,** ⅓ cup **HONEY,** and ⅓ cup **NUTS** (chopped very fine). Cool and frost one side of cooked **DOUGHNUTS.**

DIPPED MUFFINS
Make miniatures for morning parties.

Sift together in a medium size bowl	2 cups **FLOUR**
	2 Tbsp. **SUGAR**
	2½ tsp. **BAKING POWDER**
	¾ tsp. **SALT**
Cut into dry ingredients until it resembles cornmeal	⅓ cup **SHORTENING**
Beat together and add to mixture	1 **EGG**
	¾ cup **MILK**

Stir just until moistened. Fill greased muffin tins approximately ⅔ full. Bake in a preheated 450-degree oven for 20 minutes. When done, remove from pans immediately. Dip tops of muffins into ½ cup melted **BUTTER,** then in a mixture of ½ cup **SUGAR** mixed with 1 tsp. **CINNAMON.** Serve warm.

YIELD: 12 MUFFINS

AUTUMN ALMOND MUFFINS

Make filling for muffins of . . . . .   2 pkgs. (3 oz. each) **CREAM CHEESE,** softened
1 **EGG**
1 Tbsp. **SUGAR**
Mix well and set aside.
In mixing bowl, combine . . . . 1¾ cups **FLOUR**
¾ cup chopped **TOASTED ALMONDS**
⅓ cup **BROWN SUGAR,** packed
1 Tbsp. **BAKING POWDER**
5 tsp. **PUMPKIN PIE SPICE** (or 2 tsp. each **CINNAMON, NUTMEG** and 1 tsp. **CLOVES**)
1 tsp. **SALT**
In second mixing bowl, combine . 1 cup canned **PUMPKIN**
¾ cup **MILK**
¼ cup **BUTTER,** melted
2 **EGGS,** well beaten

Stir pumpkin mixture into dry ingredients, mixing just until moistened. Fill 18 muffin tins with half of the batter, dividing equally. Spoon cream cheese filling over batter, dividing equally. Top with remaining batter to cover cheese layer. Bake in 400 degree oven for 20 to 25 minutes. Cool and remove from pans.

YIELD: 1½ DOZEN

3-WEEK BLUEBERRY MUFFINS
Karen Criswell shares this recipe.

Cream . . . . 1 stick **MARGARINE**
½ cup **OIL**
1⅓ cups **SUGAR**
Add . . . . 2 **EGGS,** well beaten
Stir in . . . . 3 cups **FLOUR**
1 tsp. **SODA**
3 tsp. **BAKING POWDER**
2 Tbsp. **BUTIVAN** (a preservative)
Mix well and add . . . . 1 cup **BUTTERMILK**
½ cup **BLUEBERRY JUICE**
Gently fold in . . . . ½ can (15 oz.) **BLUEBERRIES**

Batter will keep in refrigerator for 3 weeks. To bake, fill greased muffin tins ⅔ full. Bake in preheated 400 degree oven for 15 to 20 minutes.

"VITA" MUFFINS

In a small mixing bowl, combine
- 1 cup **BOILING WATER**
- 1 cup **ALL BRAN**
- ½ cup **OIL**

Stir and set aside. In a large
mixing bowl, combine . . . .
- 2½ cups **FLOUR**
- 2 cups **ALL BRAN**
- 1 tsp. **SALT**
- 1 cup **SUGAR**
- 2½ tsp. **SODA**

Add first mixture to dry
ingredients. Beat together and
add . . . .
- 2 **EGGS**
- 2 cups **BUTTERMILK**

Fold into the other ingredients and mix well. The batter will be lumpy. Fill
well-greased muffin tins about half full. Bake in a preheated 400 degree
oven for 15 minutes. (Batter will keep for six weeks in a covered container
in the refrigerator.)

YIELD: FULL RECIPE, 3 DOZEN

VARIATIONS:
HONEY: Omit the **SUGAR** and substitute 1 cup **HONEY.** Optional: 1 cup
RAISINS.
JELLY: Pour ¼ cup batter in muffin tin. Spoon in dab of **JELLY.** Pour ¼
cup more batter on top of jelly. Surprise the kids!

WAFFLED FRENCH TOAST

Mix in a shallow bowl . . . .
- ¾ cup **MILK**
- 2 **EGGS**
- 1 Tbsp. **BUTTER**, melted
- 1 Tbsp. **SUGAR**
- ½ tsp. **SALT**

Dip in mixture, one at
a time . . . .
- 6 slices **BREAD** (day old)

Bake in a preheated and *oiled* waffle iron until brown. Remove and serve
with hot **BUTTER** and **SYRUP.**

YIELD: 2 SERVINGS

FRENCH TOAST

Remove from bread wrapper and
   let dry out slightly . . . .   8 slices **BREAD**
Beat in a shallow bowl . . . .   2 **EGGS**
Add to egg mixture and beat
   well . . . .   ½ cup **MILK**
                                ½ tsp. **SUGAR**
                                ¼ tsp. **SALT**

Place skillet on medium heat with enough **BUTTER** or **SHORTENING** to about ½ inch deep when melted. Dip bread lightly in batter and fry until golden brown on one side, turn and brown the other side. Turn only once to prevent sogginess. Serve dusted with **POWDERED SUGAR, MAPLE SYRUP, JAM** or **JELLY.**

Or, prepare bread the night before. Place dipped bread on cookie sheet. Cover with foil and refrigerate. In the morning, cook as directed.

YIELD: 4 SERVINGS

VARIATION:
PUNKS SECRET: To above recipe, add ¼ teaspoon **MAPLE** flavoring, and ½ teaspoon **VANILLA** flavoring for a very special taste.

GRANDMOTHER VAUGHN'S OLE-TIMEY HOT CAKES

Separate . . . .   2 **EGGS**
Place the whites in a bowl and
   beat until very stiff. Lightly
   beat the egg yolks and
   combine with . . . .   2 cups **BUTTERMILK**
Add to . . . .   2 cups **FLOUR**
                                ¼ tsp. **SALT**
                                ½ cup **SUGAR**
                                3 tsp. **BAKING POWDER**
                                ¼ tsp. **SODA**
                                2 Tbsp. **OIL**

Mix well and fold in the egg whites. Pour ¼ cup batter on hot griddle. (Test with a drop of water. If it sizzles and dances around, the griddle is hot enough.) Serve with **BUTTER** and **MAPLE SYRUP.**

YIELD: 12 TO 14 LARGE PANCAKES

"TEXAS BEST" PANCAKES

Mix . . . .   2 cups **BISCUIT MIX**
                                 1 **EGG**
                                 ½ cup **OIL**
                                1⅓ cups **CLUB SODA**

Preheat griddle or heavy skillet. Use ¼ cup measuring cup for regular size pancakes, and a tablespoon for dollar size pancakes. When bubbly and a little dry around the edge, turn over and brown the underside. Serve hot with **BUTTER** and **SYRUP.** Cook any unused batter. Freeze pancakes and just reheat. They are just like fresh ones.

YIELD: 10 TO 12 REGULAR PANCAKES

YANKEE PANCAKES
Make syrup anytime, and store in refrigerator.

Blend together in a large mixing
    bowl . . . .   1 cup **FLOUR**
                                 1 tsp. **SUGAR**
                                 1 tsp. **BAKING POWDER**
                                 1 tsp. **SODA**
                                 ½ tsp. **SALT**
                               1½ cups **OATMEAL**
Beat . . . .   2 **EGGS**
Add to beaten eggs . . . .   2 cups **BUTTERMILK**
                                 ½ cup **OIL**

Add liquids to dry ingredients. Pour onto a heated griddle. Use approximately ¼ cup of batter for each pancake. This batter is slightly thick and may take longer to cook than ordinary pancakes. Serve immediately with warm **ORANGE SYRUP.**

YIELD: 12 TO 14 PANCAKES

ORANGE SYRUP

Mix in a small saucepan . . . .   ¼ cup **BUTTER**
                                 ½ cup **KARO**, white
                                 ½ cup **ORANGE JUICE**
                                 1 cup **SUGAR**

Bring to boil. Cook 3 to 5 minutes.

WAFFLES

Preheat waffle baker as manufacturer directs.
Mix in a large bowl . . . . 1¾ cups **FLOUR**
                                       1 tsp. **BAKING POWDER**
                                       1 tsp. **SODA**
                                       ½ tsp. **SALT**
Add . . . . 2 cups **BUTTERMILK**
                                       ⅓ cup **OIL**
                                       2 **EGGS,** slightly beaten

Beat until well blended. When waffle baker is ready, pour about ¾ cup batter in the middle of the waffle iron. Spread to about 1 inch from the edges. When waffle is ready, lift cover, loosen with fork, serve at once with hot **BUTTER** and **SYRUP.**

YIELD: ABOUT 5 OR 6 WAFFLES

VARIATIONS:
Try these with the recipe above, or any good **WAFFLE MIX:**
BLUEBERRY: Spoon approximately 2 Tablespoons **BLUEBERRIES** over batter. Bake and serve with **BLUEBERRY SYRUP.**
COCONUT: Stir 1 cup **COCONUT** onto the batter.
PECAN: Sprinkle chopped **PECANS** over batter.
STRAWBERRY: Stir 1 cup drained **STRAWBERRIES** into the batter. Bake.
Serve with **WHIPPED CREAM.**

EGGS A'LA GOLDENROD
So elegant, yet so simple.

Melt in a medium
   saucepan . . . . 2 Tbsp. **BUTTER**
Add and cook 1 minute . . . . 2 Tbsp. **CORNSTARCH** or **FLOUR**
Slowly add . . . . 2 cups **MILK**
                                       ½ tsp. **SALT**
                                       ¼ tsp. **PEPPER**
Bring to a boil, stirring constantly. Cook 1 more minute. Set aside.
Cook in boiling water until well
   done. . . . . 3 **EGGS**

Shell eggs and separate yolks from whites. Chop whites and add to white sauce. Season with **SALT** and **PEPPER.** Pour mixture over toasted **BREAD.** Grate yolks and sprinkle over all. Sprinkle with **PAPRIKA** and serve immediately.

YIELD: 4 TO 6 SERVINGS

CHEESE AND SAUSAGE GRITS

Brown and drain	1	pound **SAUSAGE,** scrambled
Add		**TABASCO** to taste
	⅓	clove **GARLIC,** mashed
	½	tsp. **SALT**
	⅛	tsp. **PEPPER**
Set aside.		
Cook	1	cup **INSTANT GRITS**
in	2	cups **BOILING WATER,** according to package directions
Add to sausage. Stir in	1	cup grated **SHARP CHEDDAR CHEESE**
	¼	cup **BUTTER,** melted
	2	large **EGGS,** well beaten
	1	can **GREEN CHILIES,** chopped

Mix all ingredients well. Pour into a well-buttered casserole, 13x9x2-inches. Bake in a preheated 350 degree oven for 1 hour.

YIELD: 8 TO 10 SERVINGS

TEXAS GRITS SOUFFLE

Bring to boil	6	cups very lightly salted **WATER**
Add and cook, stirring, until mixture is thick	1½	cups **GRITS**
Remove from heat and add	1	pound **GRATED CHEDDAR CHEESE**
	1½	sticks **BUTTER**
Stir until smooth. Add	3	whole **EGGS,** beaten
		Pinch of **SALT, WHITE PEPPER, GARLIC POWDER**
		Dash of **TABASCO**

Mix well. Pour into an 11x14-inch oiled baking dish. Bake one hour in preheated 250 degree oven. Serve with **MEXICAN SALSA BRAVA** and **TEXAS JALAPENO JELLY.**

YIELD: 12 TO 14 SERVINGS

BACON AND EGG LASAGNE

A change of pace for a Brunch or Supper.

Cook according to directions on box	12 **LASAGNE NOODLES**
Drain and set aside.	
In large skillet, cook until crisp	1 pound **BACON,** cut in 1-inch strips
Drain on paper towels.	
Using ½ cup **BACON DRIPPINGS,** cook until tender	1 cup chopped **ONIONS**
Add	⅓ cup **FLOUR**
	½ tsp. **SALT**
	¼ tsp. **PEPPER**
Stir until thick, then add	4 cups **MILK**
Bring to a boil, stirring constantly.	
Have ready to use	12 **EGGS,** hard boiled and sliced
	2 cups grated **SWISS CHEESE**

Grease a 13x9x2-inch baking dish. Spoon a small amount of the sauce into the bottom of the pan. Divide noodles, bacon, sauce, eggs and cheese into thirds. Layer in pan. Sprinkle with **PARMESAN CHEESE.** Bake in a preheated 350-degree oven for 25 to 30 minutes. Let stand 10 minutes before serving.

YIELD: 12 SERVINGS

EGGS BENEDICT

Easy but rather exotic.

Prepare for each person	2 **POACHED EGGS**
Butter and toast	1 **ENGLISH MUFFIN,** cut in half
Place on each half, one slice each	**CANADIAN BACON** or **HAM**
	SWISS or **AMERICAN CHEESE**

Place eggs on top of cheese. Cover with **CHEESE SAUCE.** Serve immediately.

YIELD: 1 SERVING

POACHED EGGS: Use a shallow pan, with water to cover eggs, 1 Tbsp. white vinegar and salt added. Break eggs one at a time into a saucer, slide into barely boiling water. Cook 2 to 3 minutes. Remove with slotted spoon. Can do as many at a time as you have room for in pan.

CHEESE SAUCE

Melt in a heavy saucepan over low heat	2 Tbsp. **BUTTER** or **MARGARINE**
Add and stir until smooth	2 Tbsp. **FLOUR**
Gradually add.................	1⅓ cup **MILK**
Cook over medium heat, stirring constantly until thick and bubbly. Add	1 cup grated **CHEDDAR CHEESE**
	½ tsp. **SALT**
	½ tsp. **PEPPER**

Stir until melted. Spoon over **EGGS BENEDICT.**

YIELD: 4 TO 6 SERVINGS

BREAKFAST SOUFFLE
A crowd pleaser.

Grate	1 pkg. (8 oz.) **SHARP CHEDDAR CHEESE**
Chop	2 to 3 cups **HAM**
Butter slightly and remove crusts	16 slices **BREAD**
Mix in medium bowl	8 **EGGS,** slightly beaten
	½ tsp. **DRY MUSTARD**
	½ tsp. **SALT**
	½ tsp. **WORCESTERSHIRE SAUCE**
	3 cups **MILK**

Place 8 slices of the bread in a 13x9x2-inch baking dish. Sprinkle one-half the meat and one-half the cheese on top. Add remaining slices of bread, meat and cheese; pour egg mixture over top; cover with foil; refrigerate overnight. Remove 1 hour before baking. Sprinkle with 2 cups **CORN FLAKES.** Melt ½ stick **BUTTER** or MARGARINE and drizzle over the entire casserole. Bake in a preheated 350 degree oven for 1 hour.

Cut the recipe in half, if too large, or make in two dishes and freeze the extra one. Good for a quick supper.

YIELD: 8 TO 10 SERVINGS

EARLY MORNING CASSEROLE
You can make this with one eye open.

Scramble and cook until
    brown .... 1 pound **SAUSAGE**
Drain on paper towel and put in oven-proof baking dish.
Melt in skillet .... 4 Tbsp. **BUTTER**
Scramble until slightly soft ..... 1 dozen **EGGS**
Pour over sausage and add..... 1 can **MUSHROOM SOUP,** undiluted
    1 can (4 oz.) **CHILIES,** chopped

Cover top with grated **CHEESE**. Bake in preheated oven at 350 degrees for approximately 15 minutes, or until heated through and through. Serve with **BREAD** and fresh **FRUIT.**

YIELD: 6 TO 8 SERVINGS

VARIATION: Add a small can chopped **MUSHROOMS.**

FARMER'S FARE
Hearty he-man breakfast.

In a large skillet, cook until
    crisp .... 10 slices **BACON**
Remove and drain on paper towels. Crumble.
Cut into bite-size pieces and
    brown in bacon drippings .... 3 large **POTATOES**
    1 **ONION**
Cook a few more minutes. Drain off excess fat.
Beat and add .... 8 **EGGS**
    SALT and **PEPPER**
Cook slowly, stirring, until eggs are almost done.
Sprinkle over top .... 1 cup grated **CHEDDAR CHEESE** reserved bacon bits

Cover with a lid and warm to melt cheese. Serve hot, with **TOAST** and **JELLY.**

YIELD: 6 SERVINGS

PERFECT BOILED EGGS: Cover eggs with cold water, bring to a boil, lower heat and simmer for 14 minutes. Pour off water and add cold water. Shells will come off easily.

HAM AND SWISS FRITTATA
Serve with hot bread and salad for a quick
Sunday night supper.

Melt in a one-quart
   baking dish . . . . 2 Tbsp. **BUTTER**
Combine and pour into baking
   dish . . . . 6 **EGGS,** slightly beaten
                               1 cup chopped **HAM, BACON,**
                                  SAUSAGE or **CANADIAN**
                                  BACON
                             ⅓ cup chopped **GREEN ONION**
                             ⅓ cup **MAYONNAISE**
                             ¼ cup **MILK**
                             ½ tsp. **SALT**
                             PEPPER
                             Dash of **TABASCO**
                             ¼ tsp. **WORCESTERSHIRE SAUCE**

Bake in a preheated 350-degre oven for 15 to 20 minutes. When eggs are set, remove from oven and top with 1 cup grated **MOZZARELLA** or **MONTEREY JACK CHEESE.** Return to oven until melted. Cut into wedges and serve warm.

YIELD: 4 SERVINGS

HASH BROWN SKILLET BREAKFAST

Cook in large skillet until
   crisp . . . . 6 slices **BACON**
Drain on paper towel. Crumble.
Cook in **BACON DRIPPINGS** until
   crisp and lightly browned . . . . 1 package frozen **HASH BROWN**
                                  POTATOES

Combine and pour over
   potatoes . . . . 6 **EGGS,** slightly beaten
                             ½ cup **MILK**
                             ½ tsp. **SALT**
                             ½ tsp. **PEPPER**
Top with . . . . 1 cup grated **CHEDDAR CHEESE**

Sprinkle with crumbled bacon bits. Cover and cook over low heat 10 minutes. Cut into wedges and serve warm.

YIELD: 6 SERVINGS

VARIATION:
Use frozen **POTATOES** with **ONION, RED PEPPER,** and **GREEN PEPPER.** Different taste and more colorful.

OMELET
Always make individual ones.

Beat with fork or
  wire whisk . . . .   2 **EGGS**
                                             1 Tbsp. **WATER**
                                             ¼ tsp. **SALT**
                                             ¼ tsp. **PEPPER**
Preheat 9-inch skillet on medium until water dropped on it sizzles.
Add . . . .   1 Tbsp. **BUTTER**

When Butter is melted, pour egg mixture into skillet. As omelet sets, run spatula around edge, to loosen. Tilt pan, to let the uncooked eggs run underneath. Continue loosening and tilting until omelet is almost dry on top, and golden-brown underneath. Fold and lift out onto plate.

This is only one serving. When cooking omelets for a brunch or supper, make up amount needed, but cook them *one at a time*. Place condiments on the table so that each individual may prepare according to taste. (Do not fold.) Serve with bowls of grated **CHEESE,** chopped **TOMATOES, SOUR CREAM,** chopped **CHILIES,** etc.

YIELD: 1 SERVING

ONE-SKILLET BREAKFAST
Great for cook-outs.

Cook in large skillet until
  crisp . . . .   6 slices **BACON**
Drain on paper towel.
Add to hot fat and cook for
  about 3 minutes . . . .   2 **TOMATOES,** diced
Add . . . .   ½ cup grated **CHEESE**
                                             6 **EGGS,** slightly beaten
                                             ¼ tsp. **SALT**
                                             ¼ tsp. **PEPPER**
                                             1 Tbsp. **WORCESTERSHIRE
                                                SAUCE**
                                             1 Tbsp. **CHIVES** (optional)
                                             1 Tbsp. **PARSLEY** (optional)

Cook mixture over low heat. Lift it occasionally from bottom of skillet with pancake turner or wooden spoon. When eggs are set, but still soft, stir in crumbled bacon and serve on split toasted **ENGLISH MUFFINS** or in **TOAST CUPS.** (Brush sliced **BREAD** thinly with **BUTTER;** press into muffin tins; bake at 375 degrees for 12 minutes, remove and fill toast cups with the egg mixture.)

YIELD: 2 SERVINGS

SAUSAGE EGG BAKE

Follow directions on a box of
Grits and make
enough for . . . .   2 cups cooked **GRITS**
In a medium skillet, cook until
browned, stirring to
crumble . . . .   1 pound **SAUSAGE**
Drain well and place in a lightly greased casserole. Spoon grits over top.
Make 8 indentions in the grits. Break an **EGG** into each indention. Sprinkle
with **SALT** and **PEPPER**.
Top with . . . .   1 cup grated **CHEDDAR CHEESE**

Bake in a preheated 350 degree oven for 20 to 25 minutes, or until eggs
are set.

YIELD: 4 SERVINGS

SPANISH OMELET

Heat in a heavy skillet on
medium . . . .   2 Tbsp. **OIL**
Add and cook about five
minutes, stirring
constantly . . . .   ½ cup thinly sliced **ONIONS**
                                            ½ cup thinly sliced **SWEET PEPPER**
                                            ⅓ cup chopped **TOMATOES**
                                            SALT and **PEPPER**
Set aside in a bowl.

Prepare **OMELET** recipe. (6 **EGGS,** 3 Tbsp. **WATER**) Pour one-half of the
omelet mixture in skillet. When ready to fold, add one-half of the onion,
pepper and tomato mixture. Fold and serve. Repeat with other half of egg
mixture, then tomato mixture. (Optional: Add **GARLIC** to taste.)

VARIATION:
Spanish Omelets are really best made with **POTATOES**. Grate 1 cup
potatoes. Cook in ⅓ cup **OIL** on low heat, stirring occasionally, for about
20 minutes. Add to other vegetables after they have cooked.

SHERRIED EGGS
From the kitchen of Jane Jones.

In a medium skillet melt . . . .   1 stick **BUTTER** or **MARGARINE**
Beat well and add . . . .   3 dozen **EGGS**
Cook to a soft scrambled stage. Set aside.
Grate and set aside . . . .   ½ cup **SHARP CHEDDAR CHEESE**
In a mixing bowl combine . . . . . .   1 can **MUSHROOMS**
   2 cans **MUSHROOM SOUP,**
      undiluted
   ½ cup **EVAPORATED MILK**
   ¼ cup **SHERRY**

Layer in a buttered casserole, starting with the scrambled eggs. Add liquid mixture and sprinkle with cheese. Bake in a preheated 350-degree oven for 20 minutes.

YIELD: 20 to 24 SERVINGS

THE COUNTRY GENTLEMAN'S CASSEROLE
Prepare for that overnight company.

Fry, drain, and put in a
  13x9x2-inch casserole . . . .   2 pounds **SAUSAGE,** made into 16
      patties
Put in layers over
  SAUSAGE . . . .   1 can (4 oz.) **CHOPPED CHILIES**
   1 pound **MONTEREY JACK**
      CHEESE, grated
Cover with foil and refrigerate overnight. (Or make days ahead of time and freeze.)
When ready to serve, beat and
  pour over top . . . .   8 **EGGS**
   ½ tsp. **SALT**
   ½ tsp. **PEPPER**

Put in preheated 350-degree oven. Bake until the eggs are set, about 45 minutes. Serve with **FRUIT, BREAD,** and **JELLY.**

YEILD: 8 SERVINGS

Breads

BIS-QUICKS

Blend well . . . . 2 cups **SELF-RISING FLOUR**
2 Tbsp. **MAYONNAISE**
1 cup **MILK**

Drop by teaspoonfuls onto a lightly greased cookie sheet. (May prefer to roll and cut.) Bake in a preheated 400-degree oven until golden brown, for 10 to 12 minutes. These biscuits may be made ahead of time and frozen.

YIELD: 8 TO 10 BISCUITS

FLUFFY BIS-QUICKS

Mix well with a fork
for 4 minutes . . . . 2 cups **SELF-RISING FLOUR**
2 tsp. **OIL**
¾ cup **MILK**

Pat out dough on well floured board or waxed paper, to about ½-inch thick. Cut with small biscuit cutter. Place on well oiled pan and let rise, while the oven is heating to 475 degrees. When oven is heated, place biscuits on the top rack. Bake to a golden brown, about 10 to 12 minutes.

YIELD: 18 BISCUITS

VARIATION: Add 1 cup grated **CHEDDER CHEESE**.

SNOW BISCUITS
Keeps for 2 weeks in the refrigerator.

Mix . . . . 6 cups **SELF-RISING FLOUR**
½ cup **SUGAR**
1 Tbsp. **SALT**
Cut in . . . . ½ cup **SHORTENING**
Dissolve together and add to first
mixture . . . . 2 packages **DRY YEAST**
1 cup **WATER**, lukewarm
Add . . . . 2 cups **BUTTERMILK**

Mix well. Place in a covered bowl in the refrigerator. (May bake immediately, if desired.) Pinch off and place in greased muffin tins. Bake in preheated 375-degree oven for 15 to 20 minutes.

YIELD: 2 DOZEN

OLD TIME BUTTERMILK BISCUITS

Sift dry ingredients together	2 cups	**FLOUR**
	½ tsp.	**SALT**
	4 tsp.	**BAKING POWDER**
	½ tsp.	**SODA**
Cut in with pastry blender	5 Tbsp.	**SHORTENING**
Add all at once.	1 cup	**BUTTERMILK**

Stir with a fork until dough makes a ball. Turn out on floured board and knead 5 or 6 times. Roll out on lightly floured board until about ½ inch thick. Brush with melted **BUTTER**: fold over and cut about 2-inch biscuits. Bake on a very lightly greased cookie sheet, or spray sheet with spray shortening. If you like for your biscuits to be brown all around, don't let them touch each other. If you prefer fatter biscuits, put them close together. Bake in preheated 450 degree oven for 12 to 15 minutes.

YIELD: 14 OR 15 BISCUITS

MILE HIGH FROZEN BISCUITS
Economical; use only what you need.

Combine	3 cups	**FLOUR**
	¼ cup	**SUGAR**
	4 Tbsp.	**BAKING POWDER**
	½ Tbsp.	**CREAM OF TARTAR**
	1 Tbsp.	**SALT**
Cut in with pastry blender or knives, using a scissor motion.	½ cup	**SHORTENING**
Beat and add	1	**EGG**
Stir in	1⅛ cups	**MILK**

Knead 10 to 12 times. Roll out and cut into biscuits. Place on an ungreased cookie sheet and freeze. Place in plastic bag and keep frozen until ready to use. To bake, remove as many biscuits as needed and place on a lightly greased pan. Bake in a preheated oven at 475 degrees for 12 to 15 minutes.

YIELD: 2 DOZEN BISCUITS

BISCUITS IN A HURRY: Drop instead of rolling.

BUTTERMILK CORNBREAD
Old-time recipe.

Mix in a medium bowl   1   cup **BUTTERMILK**
                               1   **EGG**
                               ½   tsp. **SALT**
                               ½   tsp. **SODA**
                             1½   cups **CORNMEAL**

Heat 2 to 3 Tablespoonsful **OIL** in a pan. (An iron skillet is best.) Pour in mixture and bake in preheated 425-degree oven for 15 to 20 minutes. Cooks very fast, so watch closely.

YIELD: 4 TO 5 SERVINGS

CORNY CHEESE MUFFINS

Combine in a medium bowl . . . . .   ¾   cup **FLOUR**
                               2½   tsp. **BAKING POWDER**
                               ¾   tsp. **SALT**
                               1   Tbsp. **SUGAR**
                               ½   cup **YELLOW CORNMEAL**
                               1   cup grated **CHEDDAR CHEESE**
Make a well in dry ingredients
    and add   1   **EGG,** beaten
                               ¾   cup MILK
                               2   Tbsp. **SHORTENING,** melted

Stir just to moisten dry ingredients. Fill greased muffin tins two-thirds full. Bake in a preheated oven at 400 degrees for 20 to 25 minutes. When done, remove from pan immediately.

YIELD: 1 DOZEN

GARLIC FRENCH BREAD
Quick.

Slice into ½-inch slices   1   loaf **FRENCH BREAD**
Soften to room temperature . . . .   ½   cup **BUTTER**

Spread each slice on one side with butter. Sprinkle with **GARLIC SALT.** Wrap in aluminum foil and heat in a preheated 350-degree oven. For crispy slices, place on a cookie sheet and place under broiler, being very careful not to burn.

YIELD: 8 SERVINGS

JALAPENO CORN BREAD
Try it, you'll like it.

In a large bowl, mix . . . .
- 3 cups **CORN BREAD MIX**
- 3 tsp. **SUGAR**
- 2½ cups **MILK**
- 3 **EGGS**
- ½ cup **SALAD OIL**

Add . . . .
- 1 large **ONION,** chopped
- 1 can **GREEN CHILIES,** chopped
- 1 cup **WHOLE KERNEL CORN,** drained
- 1½ cups grated **CHEDDAR CHEESE**
- ½ tsp. **GARLIC SALT**
- 4 or more **BACON SLICES,** fried crisp and crumbled

Stir until mixed. Heat large iron skillet or pan that has 3 or 4 Tablespoons **BACON GREASE,** and sprinkled with **CORNMEAL** and a little **SALT.** When cornmeal is light brown, add cornbread mixture. Bake in a preheated 375-degree oven until golden brown, about 30 to 40 minutes.

YIELD: 6 TO 8 SERVINGS

"MESA" HUSH PUPPIES

Combine . . . .
- ½ cup **FLOUR**
- 2 tsp. **BAKING POWDER**
- 1 Tbsp. **SUGAR**
- ½ tsp. **SALT**
- 1½ cups **CORNMEAL**
- **GARLIC SALT** (optional)

Add . . . .
- 1 **EGG**
- ¾ cup **MILK**
- ½ cup finely-chopped **ONION** (optional)

Stir only to moisten. Drop batter by teaspoonfuls into deep, hot **FAT.** Fry only a few at a time. Cook until golden brown on both sides. Drain on paper towels.

YIELD: 2 DOZEN

MAC'S WET CORNBREAD

Combine	1 cup **CORNMEAL**
	½ cup **FLOUR**
	1 tsp. **SALT**
	½ tsp. **SODA**
	1 Tbsp. **BAKING POWDER**
Add, all at one time	1 cup **BUTTERMILK**
	½ cup **SWEET MILK**
	1 **EGG**
	½ cup **OIL**

Stir well. Pour into a 8x8x2-inch pan that has been generously greased and preheated. Bake in a preheated 450-degree oven for 20 to 25 minutes.

YIELD: 6 SERVINGS

SWEET CORNBREAD

Mix in a medium bowl	1 cup **FLOUR**
	1 cup **CORNMEAL**
	1 Tbsp. **SUGAR,** heaping
	3 tsp. **BAKING POWDER**
	1 tsp. **SALT**
	2 Tbsp. **OIL**
	1 **EGG**
Stir in to make thin batter	**MILK**

Beat well and pour into an iron skillet or square cake pan that has been preheated with 3 Tablespoons **OIL** in it, and a little **CORNMEAL** sprinkled in the bottom, **SALTED** lightly, and browned. Cook in a preheated 400 degree oven until golden brown, about 20 to 25 minutes. Serve while hot with lots of **BUTTER.** So good!!

YIELD: 4 TO 6 SERVINGS

SOUR MILK: Combine 1 Tablespoon lemon juice or vinegar and enough milk to make 1 cup.

WAMPUS BREAD
This is something special.

Mix . . . .
1 cup **CORNMEAL**
½ cup **FLOUR**
1 tsp. **SALT**
1½ tsp. **BAKING POWDER**
1 tsp. **SUGAR**
½ cup **EVAPORATED MILK**
½ cup grated **ONION**
½ cup grated raw **POTATO**

Mix until smooth. Drop by teaspoonsful in pan of hot **SHORTENING** (about 1½ inches deep). Fry until golden brown. Serve warm. This is quick to make.

YIELD: 8 TO 10 SERVINGS

APACHE BREAD
Hot bread helps any meal.

Mix in a medium bowl . . . .
1 cup **FLOUR**
1 Tbsp. **BAKING POWDER**
½ tsp. **SALT**
Add to make soft dough . . . .
MILK

Pour dough on a lightly floured board or waxed paper. Knead 4 or 5 times. Roll and cut into 2-inch squares. Fry in hot, melted **SHORTENING** (about 1 to 2 inches deep). When brown on both sides, remove and drain on paper towels. Serve hot with **BUTTER, JELLY** or **HONEY.**

YIELD: 4 SERVINGS

"HOT CHEESE" GARLIC BREAD

Whip together . . . .
½ cup **MARGARINE,** softened
½ tsp. **GARLIC SALT**
⅓ cup grated **PARMESAN CHEESE**
1 tsp. **WORCESTERSHIRE SAUCE**
¼ tsp. **CAYENNE PEPPER**
Slice into ½-inch slices . . . .
1 loaf **FRENCH BREAD**

Spread both sides of each slice with mixture. Broil 1 minute on each side, or toast in the oven. May be wrapped in foil and heated on the grill, when cooking outside.

YIELD: 6 TO 8 SERVINGS

ONION SUPPER BREAD

Cook in a small skillet
    until clear................. ½ cup chopped **ONION**
                         2 Tbsp. **BUTTER** or **MARGARINE**
Prepare according to
    directions .... 1 package (6 oz.) **CORNBREAD MIX**
Spoon prepared mix into a lightly greased 8x8x2-inch pan.
Sprinkle with onion mixture.
    Combine and spread over the
    onion .... ½ cup **SOUR CREAM**
                         ½ cup grated **CHEDDAR CHEESE**

Bake in a preheated 400 degree oven for 25 minutes, or until lightly browned. Let stand a few minutes; then cut into squares. Serve warm.

YIELD: 8 SERVINGS

BREAD STICKS

Slice into sticks about the width
    of your thumb, either........ **HOT DOG BUNS, HAMBURGER BUNS,** or **WHITE BREAD**
Generously coat with .... **BUTTER,** melted
Sprinkle with .... **GARLIC SALT, ONION SALT, SEASONED SALT** or **PARMESAN CHEESE**

You may use any of the above, or any combination you like. You may also
use dried-out bread or rolls for this. Bake in a slow oven (250 degrees) until
very toasty and golden brown. Great for snacks, or to serve with soup.

YIELD: 8 TO 10 SERVINGS

VARIATION:
ONION STICKS: Cream together ½ cup **BUTTER** and 1 package **DRY
ONION SOUP MIX.** Spread mixture on **BREAD** sticks and follow above
directions.

STUFFED BREAD
Serve with spaghetti.

Slice 2 to 3 inches thick, but not
   all the way through .... 2 loaves **FRENCH BREAD**
Cut in half to make
   triangles .... 1 package **SWISS CHEESE SLICES**
Put 1 triangle of cheese in each slice of bread.
Melt .... 3 sticks **MARGARINE**
Add and cook until tender...... 1 **ONION,** diced
Add .... ¼ bottle **DRIED PARSLEY**

Spoon margarine mixture into each slice and dribble over the top. The more, the better, so be sure to use all the mixture. Place 2 slices of **BACON** on top of each loaf. Wrap in heavy foil and heat thoroughly in 350-degree oven for 15 to 20 minutes. Fold back foil and broil until bacon is brown.

This freezes well, uncooked. When ready to serve, let thaw, then follow cooking instructions.

YIELD: 10 TO 12 SERVINGS

ALL BRAN BREAD

Dissolve in large bowl .... 2 packages **YEAST**
in .... 3 cups **WATER,** warm
Add .... ¾ cup **SHORTENING,** melted
                                1 Tbsp. **SALT**
                                ½ cup **SUGAR**
                                1 cup **ALL BRAN** cereal
Gradually add................ 7 to 8 cups **FLOUR**

The dough should be fairly stiff. Let rise in a lightly greased bowl at room temperature, until double in size. Turn out on floured board and work until smooth. Divide into 3 equal parts. Mold each into a loaf and place in greased 8x4x4-inch bread loaf pans. Cover with cloth and let rise about 1 hour. Bake in a preheated 350-degree oven for 50 to 60 minutes.

YIELD: 3 LOAVES

COFFEE CANS: Make ideal baking containers for gift breads or cakes.

BRENDA'S WHEAT BREAD
Make ahead and freeze.

Dissolve together . . . .   2 packages **DRY YEAST**
                                  2 cups **WATER,** lukewarm
Add . . . .   ¾ cup **OIL**
                                    ½ cup **SUGAR** or **HONEY**
Sift together . . . .   2 cups **FLOUR**
                                    4 cups **WHOLE WHEAT FLOUR**
                                    1 Tbsp. **SALT**
                                    ½ cup **DRY MILK**

Mix well and knead 5 or 6 times. Put in a greased bowl, and cover with a cloth. Let rise at room temperature until double in size. Punch down, divide dough into two parts. Put in 2 greased loaf pans, and let rise again (about 2 hours). Bake in preheated 400-degree oven for 25 to 30 minutes.

YIELD: 2 LOAVES

BUCKET BREAD
Slice and make round sandwiches for parties.

Heat to lukewarm. . . . .   1 cup **WATER**
Dissolve in water . . . .   2 pkgs. **DRY YEAST**
                                    2 Tbsp. **SUGAR**
Set aside until mixture bubbles.
Combine in mixer . . . .   4 Tbsp. **SUGAR**
                                    4 Tbsp. **OIL**
                              2½ teas. **SALT**
                              2 cans (tall size) **EVAPORATED MILK**

Add yeast mixture, stir well. Start adding **FLOUR,** one cup at a time, until you have mixed in approximately 6 cups. With wooden spoon, add 2 more cups flour. Grease *five* 1-pound coffee cans (lids, also). Fill cans half full with batter. Put on lids and let rise. Gently remove lid, place on bottom rack of oven that has been preheated to 350 degrees. Bake for approximately 45 minutes. Remove bread from cans immediately after baking. Store extras in the freezer.

YIELD: 4½ TO 5 CANS

FEATHERWEIGHT ROLLS

Dissolve together and set
    aside . . . .   6 packages **DRY YEAST** or 4
                                                     YEAST CAKES
                                                     ½ cup warm **WATER**
In the large bowl of mixer,
    cream . . . .   1 cup **SUGAR**
                                                     1 cup **SHORTENING**
                                                     2 tsp. **SALT**
Add . . . .   4 **EGGS**
Add to the yeast mixture. . . . . . . 1½ cups lukewarm **MILK**
Combine with creamed mixture.
Add . . . .   4 cups **FLOUR**
Beat for 4 to 5 minutes on medium speed.
Remove from mixer and
    add . . . .   3 cups **FLOUR**

Cover with damp cloth and let rise for 2 hours, or until double in bulk. Turn out on a floured board. Do not knead. Handle as little as possible. Roll to ½-inch thickness. Cut into rolls. Dip in melted **BUTTER**. Fold each roll as it is placed in the pan. Let rise until double in size again. Bake in a preheated 350-degree oven until golden brown, about 20 to 25 minutes.

These freeze very well. Cool after baking and put in plastic bags.

Can refrigerate after cutting out rolls. Cover with foil. Will take longer to rise, since they will have to reach room temperature first.

YIELD: 3 DOZEN LARGE ROLLS. 6 TO 7 DOZEN PARTY-SIZE ROLLS.

"GOLIGHTLY HOTEL" ROLLS

In a large bowl, dissolve . . . . 1½ cups **WATER**, lukewarm
                                                     1 **YEAST CAKE** (not dry)
Add . . . .   1 tsp **SALT**
                                                     1½ Tbsp. **SHORTENING**
                                                     1 Tbsp. **SUGAR**, heaping
Add, one cup at a time . . . .   6 to 7 cups **FLOUR**

Add enough flour to form a stiff dough. Turn dough out on a lightly floured board and knead 4 or 5 times. Place in a greased bowl and let rise 1 hour. Punch down, return to dough-board, and roll to ½-inch thick. Brush melted **BUTTER** on one-half of the dough. Fold over and cut out with a 2-inch biscuit cutter. Place in a greased pan and let rise 2 hours. Bake in a hot oven (400 degrees) for 15 to 20 minutes.

YIELD: 3 DOZEN ROLLS

LUCILLE'S HOT ROLLS

Dissolve together . . . . 1½ pkgs. **DRY YEAST**
⅓ cup **WATER,** lukewarm
In small pan, mix . . . . 1 cup **WATER**
1 cup **MILK**
6 Tbsp. **SUGAR**
½ cup **SHORTENING**
Heat slowly until shortening is melted. Cool and add to first mixture.
Then add . . . . 2 cups **FLOUR**
Set in a warm place for 1 to 2 hours.
Stir and add . . . . 2 cups **FLOUR**
¼ tsp. **SODA**
¼ tsp. **BAKING POWDER**

Place in the refrigerator in a covered container until ready to use. Will keep 3 or 4 days.

To bake, place dough on lightly floured board and knead 5 or 6 times. Pinch off approximately 1 tablespoon of dough. Roll into ball in the palm of your hand. Place 2 balls in each muffin tin that has been well greased. Let rise 1 hour and bake in a preheated 400 degree oven for 15 to 20 minutes.

YIELD: 3 DOZEN

MONKEY BREAD
The butter is in the bread.

Mix until dissolved . . . . 2 cups **WATER,** warm
1¼ package **DRY YEAST**
Add . . . . ½ cup **SUGAR**
6 Tbsp. **SHORTENING,** heaping
6 cups **FLOUR**
1½ Tbsp. **SALT**

Knead on a floured dough board, working in enough **FLOUR** to make a fairly stiff dough. Roll out less than ½-inch thick. Cut into 2 or 3-inch triangles with a knife or pizza cutter. Dip triangles in melted **BUTTER** (about 1½ sticks of butter). Put in large tube pan in layers. Overlap the triangles. Let rise about 1½ hours. Bake in a preheated 350-degree oven for 40 to 45 minutes. To serve, turn tube pan upside down on plate. It will come out like a cake. (Don't cut, just pull apart.)

YIELD: 10 TO 12 SERVINGS

NEVER FAIL YEAST LOAF BREAD

Shamrock's best baker, Frankie Weatherby.

Fill a large glass with very hot
   WATER. When glass is warm,
     empty and replace with . . . . 1 cup slightly warmer than
                               lukewarm **WATER**
                       ½ tsp. **SUGAR**
                       3 packages **DRY YEAST**
Stir and set aside.
Place in a large mixing bowl . . . . . . 3 cups hot tap **WATER** or
                        SCALDED MILK
Add . . . . 4 rounded Tbsp. **SHORTENING**
                       6 Tbsp. **SUGAR**
                 1½ Tbsp. **SALT**
                 ½ cup **POTATO FLAKES** (optional)
Add . . . . 3 cups **FLOUR**
Mix with mixer. Pour in the yeast
   mixture and stir. Add . . . . 2 cups **FLOUR**
Mix with mixer for 5 minutes.
Remove from mixer and stir in . . . . 2 cups **FLOUR**

Spread 2 more cups **FLOUR** onto a bread board or cabinet top and pour on dough. Knead with hands until all the flour is used up. Add 1 more cup **FLOUR** and knead. Bread should be elastic by now and not easy to stick to board—should hold its shape in a large ball. (Total amount of flour used, about 10 cups, 2 of which can be **WHOLE WHEAT.**)

Place dough in a large warm greased bowl, turning dough so that it is greased on all sides. Cover with waxed paper and place in a warm area to rise until double.

Press down, pour out on slightly floured board, divide into four or five parts and let rest 5 minutes. Knead each part until all air bubbles are out of dough. Form into loaves and place in warm, greased glass loaf pans, being sure each loaf is greased on all sides. Cover with waxed paper, place in warm area and let rise until double, about 45 minutes.

Bake in preheated 375-degree oven until golden brown, about 40 to 50 minutes. Remove from loaf pans onto wire rack. With brush or paper towel, spread **BUTTER** on top of each loaf.

The secret of this recipe is: Don't let anything be cool. Bowls should be warm, and flour at room temperature.

Electric knife or saw-edged knife is best for cutting hot bread. Freezes well.

YIELD: 5 LOAVES

REFRIGERATOR ROLLS

Mix in a large bowl . . . . 2⅔ cups **HOT WATER**
                                      2 Tbsp. **SHORTENING,** rounded
                                      1½ tsp. **SALT**
                                      6 Tbsp. **SUGAR**
Set aside and cool slightly.
Dissolve in a measuring cup and
   add to first mixture . . . . ¼ cup lukewarm **WATER**
                                      1 package **DRY YEAST**
Mix well and add . . . . 5 to 6 cups **FLOUR**

Mix well and place in a large greased bowl. Cover and let rise until double in size. (Room temperature.) Punch down and store in a covered container that has been well greased. Refrigerate.

When ready to use, put amount of dough that you need on a lightly floured board or waxed paper. Knead 4 or 5 times. Make rolls into shape that you prefer. Place on a greased pan and let rise 2 hours. Bake in a preheated oven at 375 degrees for 30 to 35 minutes.

PARKERHOUSE ROLLS: Roll dough ¼-inch thick; cut with biscuit cutter; brush melted **BUTTER** on ½ of roll. Fold over. Place on pan.

CLOVERLEAF ROLLS: Pinch off dough and roll in small balls about the size of a pecan; place 3 balls in each muffin tin that has been well-greased.

DIAMOND HEAD BREAD

In a bowl cream together . . . . . . ¼ cup **BUTTER**
                                     ¾ cup **BROWN SUGAR,** packed
Add and beat well . . . . 1 **EGG**
Alternate . . . . ⅓ cup frozen **ORANGE JUICE**
                                        CONCENTRATE, thawed
with . . . . 2 cups **FLOUR**
                                     1 tsp. **BAKING SODA**
                                     ½ tsp. **SALT**
Add . . . . 1 cup **CRUSHED PINEAPPLE,**
                                      spooned from can with juice
                                      included
Stir in . . . . ½ cup chopped **PECANS**

Pour into a well greased loaf pan and bake in preheated 350-degree oven for 55 to 60 minutes. When done, cool on a wire rack.

YIELD: 1 LOAF

APRICOT NUT BREAD
Call in neighbors and serve with coffee.

Soak for 20 minutes	1 cup chopped **DRIED APRICOTS**
	1 cup warm **WATER**
Cream together	1 cup **SUGAR**
	2 Tbsp. **SHORTENING**
	1 **EGG**
Stir in	¼ cup **SUGAR**
	½ cup **ORANGE JUICE**
Add	2 cups **FLOUR**
	2 tsp. **BAKING POWDER**
	½ tsp. **SODA**
	1 tsp. **SALT**

Mix well.
Drain and stir in the apricots.

Add and mix	1 cup chopped **NUTS**

Bake in a greased and floured loaf pan. Cook in a preheated oven at 350 degrees for 60 to 65 minutes. When done, cool about 10 minutes in the pan. Remove from pan, glaze.

YIELD 8 TO 10 SERVINGS

GLAZE

Measure	½ cup **POWDERED SUGAR**
Add	**ORANGE JUICE**

Make a thin glaze. Punch holes in hot **BREAD** with toothpick and spoon glaze on, letting it run down into the holes.

BANANA BREAD
So good with coffee.

Cream together with mixer	1 cup **SUGAR**
	½ cup **SHORTENING**
Add	2 **EGGS**
	1 cup mashed **BANANAS**
	2 cups **FLOUR**
	1 cup chopped **NUTS**
Dissolve and add to above mixture	½ tsp. **SODA**
	2 tsp. **WATER**

Mix well and pour into a well-greased loaf pan. Bake in a preheated 325-degree oven for 50 minutes.

YIELD: 1 LOAF

HALLOWEEN BREAD
A spook brings this to us.

Combine and mix well . . . . 1 cup **SUGAR**
½ cup **BROWN SUGAR**
1 cup cooked **PUMPKIN**
½ cup **SALAD OIL**
2 **EGGS,** unbeaten
Sift together and add . . . . 2 cups **FLOUR**
1 tsp. **SODA**
½ tsp. **SALT**
½ tsp. **NUTMEG**
½ tsp. **CINNAMON**
¼ tsp. **GINGER**
Stir in . . . . ¼ cup **WATER**
Add . . . . ½ cup **PECANS,** chopped
1 cup **RAISINS,** optional

Mix well and spoon into greased and floured loaf pan. Bake in preheated 350 degree oven for 1 hour, or until toothpick inserted comes out clean. When done, turn out on a rack to cool.

YIELD: 1 LOAF

STRAWBERRY BREAD
Great for a brunch

Mix in a large bowl . . . . 3 cups **FLOUR**
1 tsp. **SODA**
1 tsp. **CINNAMON**
2 cups **SUGAR**
1 tsp. **SALT**
Add . . . . 1¼ cup **OIL**
4 **EGGS,** well beaten
1 tsp. **RED COLORING**
2 pkgs. (10 oz. each) **FROZEN STRAWBERRIES**
Reserve ½ cup of **STRAWBERRY JUICE.**

Mix by hand until well blended. Pour into 2 well greased and floured loaf pans. Bake in a preheated 350-degree oven for 50 to 60 minutes. When baked, cool and slice. Spread with mixture of 1 package (8 ounce) **CREAM CHEESE** and ½ cup reserved strawberry juice. Cut sandwiches into finger sandwiches. Or, cut lengthways into 3 sections, put filling on each layer. Stack together and slice like bread.

YIELD: 16 SERVINGS

OUR DAILY BREAD
Serve at any meal of the day.

Sift together .... 1¾ cups **FLOUR,** scant

                                  3 tsp. **BAKING POWDER**

                                  2 Tbsp. **SUGAR**

                                  ½ tsp. **SALT**

Add .... 1 **EGG,** well beaten

                                  1 cup **MILK**

                                  3 Tbsp. **SHORTENING,** melted

Stir only to moisten. (Use any of the following variations.) Fill greased muffin tins half-full. Bake in a preheated 425-degree oven for 20 to 25 minutes.

YIELD: 12 LARGE MUFFINS

VARIATIONS: Add any of the following ingredients:
½ cup chopped **NUTS**
1 cup **RAISINS** or **DATES**
1 cup chopped **APPLES** and ¼ cup **SUGAR** and ½ tsp. **CINNAMON**
1 cup **BLUEBERRIES,** drained, and 2 Tbsp. **SUGAR** plus 1 more Tablespoon **SHORTENING**
1 cup grated **CHEESE** and ¼ cup **MILK**
½ cup diced **HAM** or crumbled, **CRISP BACON**

MUSSY'S MUFFINS

Mix dry ingredients in a

  large bowl .... 3 cups **SUGAR**

                                  1 box (15 oz.) **RAISIN BRAN**

                                  5 cups **FLOUR**

                                  5 tsp. **SODA**

                                  2 tsp. **SALT**

Add .... 1 cup **SHORTENING,** melted and

                                      cooled slightly

                                  4 **EGGS,** beaten

                                  1 quart **BUTTERMILK**

Mix just enough to blend. Store in a tightly covered conatiner in the refrigerator. When ready to bake, fill greased muffin tins ⅔ full. Bake in a preheated 350 degree oven for 20 to 25 minutes.

YIELD: 5 DOZEN MUFFINS

PEANUT BUTTER-HONEY MUFFINS

Combine in a large bowl	1 cup	**FLOUR**
	1 cup	**QUICK-COOKING WHOLE WHEAT CEREAL**
	1½ tsp.	**BAKING POWDER**
	¼ tsp.	**SALT**
Make a well in the dry ingredients and add........	¾ cup	**MILK**
	⅓ cup	**HONEY**
	¼ cup	**OIL**
	⅓ cup	**CRUNCHY PEANUT BUTTER**
	1	**EGG**

Stir just until moistened. Spoon batter into greased muffin pans, filling two-thirds full. Bake in preheated 400 degree oven for 20 to 25 minutes.

YIELD: 1 DOZEN

PLUM MUFFINS
Bake in miniature muffin tins for parties.

Mix together in a large bowl ...	1 cup	**BUTTERMILK**
	1 cup	**OIL**
	1¾ cups	**SUGAR**
	2	**EGGS**
Add	2 cups	**FLOUR**
	1 tsp.	**SALT**
	1 tsp.	**BAKING POWDER**
	1 tsp.	**CINNAMON**
	1 tsp.	**NUTMEG**
	1 tsp.	**ALLSPICE**
Drain, chop, and add	1 can (No. 2 size)	**PURPLE PLUMS**
Mix and fold in..............	1 cup chopped	**PECANS**

Mix well. Fill greased muffin tins about ¾ full. Bake in a preheated oven at 350 degrees for 25 minutes. When baked, turn out immediately to cool.

YILED: 1½ DOZEN REGULAR MUFFINS; 3 DOZEN MINIATURE MUFFINS

Soups/Sandwiches

BLENDER GAZPACHO
A summer treat.

Combine in blender .... ½ cup **CUCUMBERS,** seeded and
  peeled
1½ cups **TOMATOES,** seeded and
  peeled
½ cup **CONSOMME,** condensed
1 tsp. chopped **PIMIENTOS**

Blend for 2 to 3 minutes,
  add .... 2 Tbsp. **OLIVE OIL**
Blend 1 more minute.
Add, but do not blend .... 1 tsp. chopped **CHIVES**
Add to taste .... **SALT** and **PEPPER**

Refrigerate, serve cold with **GARLIC CROUTONS.**

YIELD: 2 SERVINGS

SHRIMP GAZPACHO
Keep in refrigerator for an energy pick-up.

In a large container that can be
  sealed, mix .... 1 cup **BEEF BROTH**
3 Tbsp. **LEMON JUICE**
½ cup **OLIVE OIL**
1 Tbsp. **SALT**
1 Tbsp. **PAPRIKA**
1 clove **GARLIC,** pressed
1 tsp. **PEPPER**
1 tsp. **TABASCO**

Chop fine and add to
  liquid.................... 2 **CUCUMBERS,** seeded and peeled
3 **TOMATOES,** seeded and peeled
1½ cups **BELL PEPPERS,** seeded
¾ cup **SCALLIONS**
½ cup minced **PARSLEY**
Add .... 2 cups **TOMATO JUICE**
2 Tbsp. **CHIVES**
½ pound cooked **SHRIMP** (the
  frozen cocktail shrimp are just
  the right size)

This is a large recipe, but it may be cut in half. Serve cold.

YIELD: 10 TO 12 SERVINGS

TEXAS SHRIMP GUMBO

Tie ¼ cup **SHRIMP-CRAB BOIL** in a cheesecloth bag and drop into 4 quarts boiling **WATER.** Add 2½ pounds peeled and deveined **SHRIMP.** Bring to a boil, reduce heat and simmer 10 minutes. Turn off heat and let stand 10 minutes. Drain shrimp, reserving 2 cups stock.

Put in a Dutch oven	3 Tbsp. each **BUTTER** and **BACON FAT**
Add and cook until tender	1 cup each **CELERY, ONION,** and **GREEN PEPPER**
Add 2 cups shrimp stock and	1 28-ounce can **TOMATOES**
	1 tsp. dried **THYME**
	1 clove **GARLIC,** minced
	1 **BAY LEAF**
	1 tsp. **WORCESTERSHIRE SAUCE**
	1 Tbsp. **GUMBO FILE POWDER**
	1 tsp. **SALT**
	½ tsp. **PEPPER**

Simmer 45 minutes. Add shrimp, 1 ten-ounce package frozen cut **OKRA,** defrosted, and ¼ cup uncooked **RICE.** Simmer 30 minutes or until rice is tender.

YIELD: 6 TO 8 SERVINGS

CLAM CHOWDER

Cook in a saucepan	3 pieces of **BACON,** diced
Add	⅓ cup **ONIONS**
	¼ cup diced **CELERY**
Then add	1 cup **HOT WATER**
	2 cups diced **POTATOES**
	1 tsp. **SALT**
	⅛ tsp. **PEPPER**

Cook until potatoes are tender.

Then add	2 cans (6½ oz. each) drained **CLAMS**
	2 cups **MILK**
	2 tsp. **BUTTER** or **MARGARINE**

Heat but do not boil. Serve with crackers or cornbread.

OYSTER SOUP
Quick, easy and delicious.

Pour into a small pan the juice
    from...................... 1 can (8 oz.) **OYSTERS**
Add .... 2 cups **MILK**
Heat slowly to simmering point.
Add .... **OYSTERS**
    2 Tbsp. **BUTTER**
    ¼ tsp. **WORCESTERSHIRE SAUCE**
    ¼ tsp. **PEPPER**

Heat over low heat until hot. *Do not boil.* Serve with **SALTINES** or **OYSTER CRACKERS.**

YIELD: 2 SERVINGS

CASE'S BEAN SOUP
Grand Junction style.

Soak overnight in **WATER** ...... 1 cup **DRIED GREAT NORTHERN**
    BEANS or **TINY WHITE**
    BEANS
    1 tsp. **COOKING OIL**
    1 tsp. **SALT**
Drain and add .... 4 cups **WATER**
Chop and add .... 1 cup **HAM**
    2 stalks **CELERY**
    ½ cup **GREEN PEPPERS**
    1 medium **ONION**
    3 **CARROTS**
Then add.................... 1 can **TOMATO PUREE**
    1 tsp. **SUGAR**
    1 tsp. **MUSTARD**
    1 whole **CLOVE**
Add to taste .... **SALT** and **PEPPER**

Cook in a pressure cooker for about 20 minutes. Remove lid, and boil a few minutes to let juice thicken. Can also be cooked slow, covered, until beans are soft and done. Add a pan of hot **CORNBREAD** and have a hearty meal.

YIELD; 8 SERVINGS

CORN AND TOMATO SOUP
Another easy-do recipe.

Saute . . . . 1 large **ONION**
in . . . . 3 Tbsp. **BUTTER**
Add and simmer 10 to 12
    minutes . . . . 1 can **TOMATOES**
        1 can **CREAM-STYLE CORN**
        2 cups **HALF AND HALF**
        ½ tsp. **SUGAR**
Add to taste . . . . **SALT** and **PEPPER**

Do not boil, just simmer. Serve and garnish with grated **CHEESE**.

YIELD: 6 TO 8 SERVINGS

FOOTBALL SOUP
Carry to game in a thermos.

Mix all together in a large
    saucepan . . . . 1 large can **TOMATO JUICE**
        1 package **DRY ONION SOUP**
        4 to 5 shakes **WORCESTERSHIRE
            SAUCE**
        5 shakes **TABASCO**
        1 cup **WATER**
Season with . . . . **GARLIC SALT**
        SALT and **PEPPER**
        ½ tsp. **ACCENT**

Simmer for about 20 minutes or until onion soup is done. If too thick, add more **WATER**.

YIELD: 6 TO 8 SERVINGS

GREASY SOUP: Drop in a lettuce leaf to absorb grease. Then remove and discard.

FRENCH ONION SOUP
Such a quick process, you'll fix it often.

In a heavy, large saucepan,
melt . . . . 1 stick **BUTTER**
Chop and add . . . . 3 large **ONIONS**
Saute over medium heat until clear, being very careful not to burn. Stir frequently.
Add . . . . 4 cans **BEEF BROTH**
                                   5 **BEEF BOUILLON CUBES**
                                   ½ cup **MINUTE RICE**
Add to taste . . . . **SALT** and **PEPPER**

Continue to cook until rice is tender. Pour soup into individual bowls, top with toasted **ENGLISH MUFFIN** or **FRENCH BREAD** and **MONTEREY JACK CHEESE** or **SWISS CHEESE.** Broil until cheese is bubbly.

YIELD: 6 SERVINGS

QUICK ONION SOUP
From the pantry shelf to the table.

Heat thoroughly . . . . 1 can **ONION SOUP**
                                   1 can **BEEF BOUILLON**
                                   1 tsp. **WORCESTERSHIRE SAUCE**

Pour into individual bowls and
top with . . . . **GRATED CHEESE** and
                                   CROUTONS

YIELD: 4 TO 6 SERVINGS

FRESH MUSHROOM SOUP

Melt in medium saucepan . . . . . . 2 Tbsp. **BUTTER**
Add and cook for 5 minutes . . . . 1 pound **FRESH MUSHROOMS,** chopped
                                   2 Tbsp. chopped **FRESH ONIONS**
Add . . . . 2 Tbsp. **FLOUR**
Mix well and add . . . . 2 **CHICKEN BOUILLON CUBES**
                                   SALT and **PEPPER**
                                   1 pint **MILK**

Simmer 1½ hours. Serve warm. Garnish with **PARSLEY.**

YIELD: 4 TO 6 SERVINGS

FRENCH PEASANT SOUP

Heat in a small saucepan . . . . . .   1 cup **WATER**
Peel and slice thinly and add to
    the water . . . .   1 small **POTATO**
        1 small **ONION**

Boil rapidly for 8 minutes.
    Add . . . .   ½ cup **MILK**
        ½ cup **CREAM**
        1 Tbsp. **BUTTER**
        SALT and **PEPPER**

Heat just enough to be serving temperature. Top with grated **CHEESE** or chopped **CELERY LEAVES.**

YIELD: 2 SERVINGS

PEANUT BUTTER SOUP
That's right, peanut butter!

Saute until tender . . . .   1 stick **BUTTER**
        1 Tbsp. minced **ONION**
Add . . . .   1 Tbsp. **FLOUR**
        1 cup **PEANUT BUTTER**
When a smooth paste, add . . . . .   4 cups **CHICKEN BROTH**
        1 Tbsp. **SALT**
        ½ Tbsp. **PEPPER**

Cook 10 to 12 minutes on simmer.
Add before serving . . . .   1 cup **CREAM**

Be sure to try this on the kids.

YIELD: 8 TO 10 SERVINGS

QUICK SOUP: Leftover roast and gravy is a great way to start soup. Just start adding vegetables, either leftover, frozen or fresh. Just let you imagination be your guide. Don't be afraid to try new seasonings.

POTATO SOUP

Place in medium sized pan and
   cover with **WATER** . . . .   3 medium **POTATOES,** diced
Cover with lid and cook until
   tender, but not mushy. Pour
   off water and add . . . .   2 to 3 cups **MILK**
                             3 Tbsp. **BUTTER**
Add to taste . . . .   **SALT** and **PEPPER**
Mix in a cup to make
   a paste . . . .   2 Tbsp. **FLOUR**
                             ¼ cup **MILK**
Add another . . . .   ¼ cup **MILK**

Stir in with potato mixture and cook just a few minutes to thicken.

YIELD: 4 SERVINGS

VARIATION: Add ½ cup grated **VELVEETA CHEESE** and heat until cheese is melted, or add ¼ cup **ONIONS** or **DRY ONION FLAKES** while cooking potatoes.

TOMATO SOUP

Combine in a medium saucepan .   1 pkg. **ONION SOUP MIX**
                             1 cup **WATER**

Simmer 10 to 15 minutes.
   Add . . . .   1 can (32 oz.) **TOMATO JUICE**
                             Dash of **WORCESTERSHIRE**
                                 SAUCE
                             TABASCO (optional)
                             SALT and **PEPPER**
                             ACCENT and **BACON BITS**

Heat and pour in soup mugs. (Fill thermos bottle with soup and take on that hunting trip or to the game.)

YIELD: 6 SERVINGS

SOUP OR STEW TOO SALTY? Drop a peeled, quartered raw potato in and cook a few minutes. Remove potato, and taste the difference.

WHISTLE STOP STEW
Vary ingredients and seasonings to your own taste.

In a large saucepan brown	2 pounds **STEW MEAT,** cut in bite size pieces.
Salt, pepper and cover with water.	
Bring to a boil and add	2 medium **ONIONS,** chopped
	2 stalks **CELERY,** chopped, with tops
Cook until meat is tender. Add	1 large can **TOMATOES**
	3 **CARROTS,** diced
	1 pkg. (10 oz.) **FROZEN MIXED VEGETABLES**
	1 **GREEN PEPPER,** diced
Cook until vegetables are almost tender and add	2 large **POTATOES,** diced
	1 can **WHOLE KERNEL CORN**
	½ cup raw **MACARONI** (optional)
	FRESH OKRA (in season)
	1 cup chopped **BROCCOLI**
	1 cup chopped **CAULIFLOWER**
	WORCESTERSHIRE SAUCE to taste
	SALT and **PEPPER** to taste
	TABASCO (optional)

Cook until vegetables are tender. Adjust seasonings. You can't ruin vegetable soup, so don't be afraid to experiment. This is a very hard recipe to write down.

BUSY-DAY OVEN STEW

In a large oven-proof casserole with a lid, place	1 to 1½ pounds **STEW MEAT**
	1 **ONION,** diced
	4 **POTATOES,** cubed
	2 cans **VEG-ALL**
	1 can **TOMATOES**
	1 can **WATER**
	1 tsp. **WORCESTERSHIRE SAUCE**
Add to taste	**SALT** and **PEPPER**

Place covered casserole in 250-degree oven for 4 to 5 hours. Stir once during baking.

YIELD: 6 TO 8 SERVINGS

GONE-ALL-AFTERNOON STEW
Easy and good!

Place in a large dutch oven	2 pounds **BEEF STEW MEAT,** cubed
	2 medium **CARROTS,** sliced
	2 **ONIONS,** chopped
	3 **POTATOES,** quartered
	1 can **TOMATO SOUP**
	¼ cup **RED WINE**
	½ cup **WATER**
to taste	**SALT** and **PEPPER**
	1 **BAY LEAF**

Cover and cook in 275-degree oven for 5 hours. Serve with **CRACKERS** or **CORNBREAD,** add a **DESSERT,** and you have a delicious meal.

YIELD: 8 SERVINGS

NO-PEEP DINNER

Place in the bottom of a roasting pan	2 pounds lean boneless **STEW MEAT**
Pour all other ingredients on top of meat	1 can **MUSHROOM SOUP**
	1 can (4 oz.) **MUSHROOM STEMS AND PIECES**
	1 package **DRY ONION SOUP MIX**
	½ cup **RED WINE**
Season with	**PEPPER** but no salt
Add	¼ cup **WATER**

Cover and cook in oven for 3 hours at 325 degrees. Do not peep while cooking. Meat will be very tender and you will have a good rich brown gravy. Serve over **RICE.**

YIELD: 6 TO 8 SERVINGS

DINK'S FRENCH VEAL STEW

Simmer on low heat . . . .
   4 cups **WATER**
   2 pounds **VEAL STEW MEAT**
  ½ cup sliced **ONION**
  ¼ cup sliced **CARROTS**
   1 **BAY LEAF**
   3 **PEPPERCORNS**
   2 tsp. **SALT**

When meat is tender, remove
  the bay leaf and peppercorns.
    Saute . . . .
   1 cup sliced **MUSHROOMS**
   4 Tbsp. **BUTTER**

Add . . . .
  ¼ cup **FLOUR**
   2 Tbsp. **LEMON JUICE**

Add to meat and cook until thick. Serve with hot **SPICED PEACHES.** (Optional) Add ¼ cup **WHITE WINE** to flour mixture.

EASY OVEN CHILI

Heat in Dutch oven . . . .   4 Tbsp. **OIL**
Add and brown . . . .   2 pounds coarse ground **CHILI MEAT** or ground **ROUND**
                                        2 large **ONIONS,** chopped
                                        1 **GARLIC CLOVE,** minced
Cook until all blood is cooked
   out.
Drain and add . . . .   1 can (8 oz.) **TOMATO SAUCE**
                                          3 cups **WATER**
                                        1 can (14½ oz.) **STEWED TOMATOES**
                                    1½ tsp. **SALT**
Cover and cook in a 350-degree oven for 2½ hours.
Add . . . .   3 Tbsp. **CHILI POWDER**

Recover and cook for an additional hour. Adjust seasoning to taste.

HAVE A CHILI PARTY
"Easy to adjust for large or small groups."

Make your favorite **CHILI**. Make same amount of **RICE**. Start with rice on a plate, add **CHILI** and **BEANS**—then "Go Wild"! Serve with individual bowls of:

BEANS	**CHOPPED OLIVES**
TORTILLA CHIPS	**GRATED CHEESE**
CHOPPED ONION	**COCONUT**
CHOPPED TOMATOES	**RAISINS**
SHREDDED LETTUCE	**SOUR CREAM**
PECANS	**HOT SAUCE**

Fix your own.

CHILI
Given to Joy Lindley by the CHILI KING of TEXAS, Mr. Phillips.

Place in a deep saucepan ...... 10 pounds **CHILI MEAT,** very lean
Add .... **SALT**
Simmer for 30 minutes.
Add .... 2 Tbsp. **COMINO POWDER**
            WATER to cover meat
Simmer 2 hours.
Stir in .... 2 cloves **GARLIC,** crushed
            ¾ cup **MORTON'S CHILI BLEND** or
            30 crushed CHILIES

Simmer a little while longer. (The slower and longer the Chili is cooked, the better.) Stir occasionally and add **WATER** if necessary. Cool and put in cartons in the freezer. A real treat for the cook of the house for winter suppers.

YIELD: 30 SERVINGS

LARRY'S NO. 1 CHILI

Heat...................... 1 Tbsp. **OLIVE OIL**
Add .... 2½ pounds **CHILI GROUND MEAT**
            (buy 80% lean)
Cook and stir until browned, about 10 minutes.
Saute until clear.............. 2 pounds **ONIONS,** diced
Mix well in blender .... 2 cans (28 oz. each) **TOMATOES**
Add to onions, along with ...... 1 cup **WATER**
            4 Tbsp. **CHILI POWDER**
            4 Tbsp. **CELERY FLAKES**
            2 tsp. **SALT**
            1 tsp. **OREGANO LEAVES**
           GARLIC POWDER to taste
           GROUND CUMIN to taste
            ¾ tsp. **POWDERED MUSTARD**
            ½ tsp. **CURRY POWDER**
            ½ tsp. **GARLIC SALT**
            ½ tsp. **GROUND RED PEPPER**
            2 cans (4 oz. each) **GREEN**
            CHILIES, drained and chopped
            ½ to 1 tsp. **HOT CHILI PEPPERS**
            (jalapeno). chopped

Bring to a boil. Reduce heat and simmer, covered, stirring frequently, until flavors are well-blended, about 3½ to 4 hours.

YIELD: 8 CUPS

MOUNTAIN CHILI
Recipe from Ruidoso, New Mexico.

Place in a large pot . . . . 2½ pounds **GROUND BEEF**
Add . . . . 1 can (30 oz.) **TOMATOES**
                                    1 can (30 oz.) **PINTO BEANS**
                                    2 medium **ONIONS,** diced
                                    4 Tbsp. **BEEF BASE**
                                    3 Tbsp. **CHILI POWDER**
                                    1 Tbsp. **SALT**
                                    2 Tbsp. **MARJORAM**
                                    1 tsp. **GARLIC POWDER**
                                    1 tsp. **ONION POWDER**
                                    1 tsp. **COMINO (CUMIN)**
Add . . . . **WATER**

Simmer on low heat until all is cooked and flavors have blended.

YIELD: 2 GALLONS

TOUCHDOWN CHILI
Sonny's specialty for the Texas A&M Aggies.

Cook in large saucepan until
  meat loses its red color . . . . . . 3 pounds **GROUND CHUCK** or
                                    ROUND (or **CHILI MEAT**)
                                    3 Tbsp. **COOKING OIL**
Add . . . . 1 large **ONION,** chopped
                                    2 cloves **GARLIC,** minced
                                    3 cups **HOT WATER**
                                    3 Tbsp. **CHILI POWDER**
                                    1 tsp. ground **OREGANO**
                                    2 tsp. ground **CUMIN**
                                    2 tsp. **SALT**
                                    2 **JALAPENO PEPPERS,** chopped

Simmer, covered, at least 2 hours. Add more water if necessary.

YIELD: 8 TO 10 SERVINGS

NO CANNED TOMATOES?? Try substituting 1 can tomato paste plus 1 cup water. Makes very little difference.

WEST TEX CHILI

Cook until lightly browned...... 2 pounds **CHILI MEAT,** very lean
Add .... 1 large **ONION,** chopped
1 Tbsp. minced **GARLIC**

When onions are tender,
add .... 1 Tbsp. **SALT**
3½ Tbsp. **CHILI POWDER**
1 tsp. **CUMIN**
3 cups **HOT WATER**
2 cans **SNAPPY TOM**

Cook slowly for 3 hours. Why not double the recipe and freeze for later use?

YIELD: 6 SERVINGS

FRENCH FRIED PEANUT BUTTER AND JELLY
Kids loveum.

Heat in a small teflon skillet
until hot but not smoking .... 2 Tbsp. **BUTTER**
Spread between 2 pieces of
BREAD .... **PEANUT BUTTER** and **JELLY,** of
your choice
Beat together .... 1 **EGG**
⅒ cup **MILK**

Dip sandwich in egg mixture and fry in hot butter on each side until golden brown. May sprinkle with **POWDERED SUGAR** while hot. Serve hot with a glass of **MILK** for a very nutritious meal. Could also be served for breakfast, for a change of pace.

YIELD: 1 SERVING

CHICKEN DIP OR SPREAD

Mix all together .... 2 cans (5 oz. each) **SWANSON
CHICKEN**
1 carton **COTTAGE CHEESE**
1 pkg. **ONION SOUP,** dry
1 boiled **EGG,** chopped
1 cup **MAYONNAISE**
CAYENNE PEPPER to taste

Blend and refrigerate

HOT CHICKEN SANDWICHES

Combine . . . .
2 cups cooked and diced **CHICKEN**
1 cup diced **CELERY**
1 Tbsp. **LEMON JUICE**
1 tsp. **SALT**
1 tsp. **PEPPER**
½ cup **MAYONNAISE**
¼ cup **TOASTED ALMONDS**
3 **GREEN ONIONS,** chopped, with tops
¼ pound **CHEDDAR CHEESE,** grated

Stuff slit **ROLLS** of your choice with the chicken salad. Warm in 350 degree oven, or may be served cold.

YIELD: 6 TO 8 SERVINGS

DO-AHEAD SANDWICHES
Refrigerate or freeze.

Mix together . . . .
¾ cup cooked and chopped **CHICKEN**
2 Tbsp. finely chopped **ONION**
½ cup grated **SHARP CHEESE**
¼ cup chopped **ALMONDS**
¼ tsp. **SALT**
1 Tbsp. **LEMON JUICE**
½ cup **MAYONNAISE**

Place in buns, wrap in foil. Keep in the refrigerator or freeze until ready to use. If frozen, set out and let thaw slightly. Bake in 350 degree oven for 20 minutes, or until hot.

YIELD: 6 TO 8 SERVINGS

VARIATION: May use leftover **TURKEY** instead of the **CHICKEN**.

PASTRY PANS: Never need greasing. Pastry shells or crumb crusts will not stick to the sides.

MOTHER'S CHICKEN SALAD
For sandwiches or salad.

Mix together . . . . 2½ cups cooked and chopped
                                     CHICKEN
                              2 **APPLES,** peeled and diced
                              2 large **DILL PICKLES,** chopped
                              ½ to 1½ stalks **CELERY,** chopped
JUICE from . . . . 2 **LEMONS**
                              1 cup **PECANS,** chopped
                              2 hard boiled **EGGS,** chopped

Mix all together and add **MAYONNAISE** to suite taste. Add some of the
CHICKEN BROTH you have boiled the chicken in, to add flavor and moisture.

YIELD: 6 TO 8 SERVINGS

HOT TURKEY SANDWICHES
Open faced.

Place in a 13x9x2-inch
    baking dish . . . . 6 slices **BREAD**
Top each with slices of . . . . **TURKEY**
Spoon over the turkey . . . . 1 can **CREAM OF CHICKEN SOUP,**
                                    undiluted
Grate and sprinkle on top . . . . . . 1½ cups **CHEDDAR CHEESE**

Bake in 375 degree oven for 15 minutes.

YIELD: 6 SERVINGS

VARIATION: **CHICKEN** may be used instead of **TURKEY.** You may also
substitute **CREAM OF MUSHROOM SOUP.**

REUBEN SANDWICHES

Take 2 slices of . . . . **RYE BREAD**
Spread one side with . . . . **THOUSAND ISLAND DRESSING**
                              or **MUSTARD**
On bread, place a layer of . . . . . **CORNED BEEF,** thinly sliced
Top with . . . . **SWISS CHEESE** slices
Add . . . . **SAUERKRAUT,** drained

Spread top and bottom of bread with **BUTTER.** Cook in hot skillet until golden
brown on both sides and cheese is melted.

YIELD: 1 SERVING

THE MIDNIGHTER
Scrambled egg sandwich.

Melt in a medium skillet . . . .   2 Tbsp. **BUTTER**
Break in a bowl . . . .   6 **EGGS**
Add . . . .   ⅛ cup **MILK**
                                          ½ tsp. **PEPPER**
                                          1 tsp. **SALT**
Whip with whisk and pour in skillet and scramble.
When almost done, add . . . .   ½ cup cubed **CHEESE**

Finish scrambling and serve on toasted **BREAD** of your choice. Spread with **MAYONNAISE** and fresh sliced **TOMATOES**.

YIELD: 4 SERVINGS

VARIATION: FRIED BACON or slices of **ONION** may be added for a different taste.

TUNA SALAD SANDWICHES
A good reliable one.

Combine . . . .   1 can (6 oz.) **TUNA**
                                          2 boiled **EGGS**, chopped
                                          ½ **ONION**, chopped
                                          2 Tbsp. **SWEET RELISH**
                                          1 **DILL PICKLE**, chopped
To taste . . . .   **SALT** and **PEPPER**
Add . . . .   3 Tbsp. **MIRACLE WHIP**

Mix well, serve on toasted **BREAD**

YIELD: 4 SERVINGS

VARIATION: You may add almost anything to this, **APPLES, CELERY, CHEESE, PECANS, STUFFED OLIVES,** or you may omit from the above.

HARD-BOILED EGGS: Store in refrigerator, shell and chop at the last minute.

GLORIFIED SPAM SANDWICHES

Grate in medium bowl . . . .   1 can **SPAM**
Chop and add . . . .   1 large **DILL PICKLE**
                                           3 hard boiled **EGGS**
                                           1 small **ONION**
Grate and add . . . .   ½ pound **CHEDDAR CHEESE**
Mix with . . . .   3 Tbsp. **CATSUP**
                                           ¼ cup **MAYONNAISE**
Season with . . . .   **SEASONED SALT** or **SALT** and
                                           PEPPER

Serve on your choice of **BREAD** or **ROLLS**.

YIELD: 6 OR 8 SERVINGS

BACON CHEESE BUNBURGERS
Always a hit.

Fry and drain . . . .   6 slices **BACON**
Pour off bacon grease.
Add and brown . . . .   2 pounds **GROUND BEEF**
                                           1 **ONION,** chopped
Drain off grease and add . . . . . .   1 cup **CATSUP**
Slice, drain and add . . . .   1 small jar **MUSHROOMS**
Add to taste . . . .   **SALT** and **PEPPER**
Cover and simmer 10 minutes. Spread on **HAMBURGER BUNS**.
Sprinkle with . . . .   2 cups grated **CHEDDAR CHEESE**
                                           Crisp bacon, crumbled

Serve while hot.

YIELD: 6 TO 8 SERVINGS

BUNLESS LUAU BURGERS
Our favorite Leilani, Becky, makes these.

In mixing bowl, combine . . . .
- 1 **EGG,** well beaten
- 1 can (8 oz.) **TOMATO SAUCE**
- 2 Tbsp. **SOY SAUCE**
- ½ cup crushed **CRACKER CRUMBS,** extra fine
- ½ cup chopped **ONION**
- ½ cup chopped **GREEN PEPPER**
- ½ tsp. **GINGER**
- 2 pounds **GROUND ROUND,** lean

Mix well. Shape into 8 patties. Place each pattie on a 14-inch square piece of heavy-duty foil. Top each pattie with a **PINEAPPLE** slice and a **CHERRY.** Wrap securely in foil. Cook patties over medium-hot coals for 45 minutes, for medium well doneness. (May cook in 325 degree oven.)

YIELD: 8 SERVINGS

DON'S HAMBURGERS
Really great for our Texas summers!

Combine . . . .
- 4 pounds **GROUND ROUND**

Add to taste . . . .
- **SALT** and **PEPPER**
- **GARLIC SALT,** optional

Grate fine and add . . . .
- 1 medium **POTATO**

Mix well and shape into patties about the size of a hamburger bun and about ¾ inch thick. Make 3 or 4 patties per pound. Cook slow on outdoor grill basting with **BARBEQUE SAUCE** (recipe follows). The grated potato keeps the meat from shrinking and stays moist. It also keeps the patties from packing hard.

When cooking hamburgers this way, try cooking more than you need while the grill is hot, and freeze them. They are so handy to have already cooked. Just heat them in your oven, or if you have a microwave oven warm for a few seconds and you are ready to eat.

YIELD: 8 SERVINGS

FAST SEASONING: Keep a large shaker with salt and pepper mixed (six parts salt to one part pepper).

BARBECUE SAUCE

For Don's Hamburgers or anything else.

In a large saucepan, combine ...   ⅔ cup **VINEGAR**
    3 cups **TOMATO JUICE**
    ¼ cup **BROWN SUGAR**
    ¼ cup **PREPARED MUSTARD**
    2 Tbsp. **GARLIC SALT** or a little
        fresh **GARLIC**
    2 tsp. **SALT**
    ½ tsp. **PEPPER**
Chop fine and add ....   1 large **ONION**
Simmer, uncovered, for 20
   minutes. Stir in.............   ½ cup **CATSUP**
    1 Tbsp. **WORCESTERSHIRE**
        SAUCE
    1 Tbsp. **LIQUID SMOKE**

Bring to a boil, then use to brush over anything you are barbecuing.

This sauce can be refrigerated or frozen for later use. It will keep in refrigerator several months in a covered jar. I double the recipe when I make it since it keeps so well, and saves on energy (mine, that is.).

YIELD: 1 QUART

PICK POCKET TACOS

Brown in a skillet.............   1 pound **GROUND MEAT**
    1 **ONION,** chopped
Add ....   ½ tsp. **SALT**
    ½ tsp. **GARLIC SALT**
    2 tsp. **CHILI POWDER**
    ¼ cup **CHILI SAUCE** (more if
        desired)
    ½ tsp. **CUMIN**

Cook and stir until all is blended well. Warm **POCKET BREAD** and fill each with meat mixture, grated **CHEESE, LETTUCE** and **TOMATOES.** Serve with slices of **AVOCADOS,** AND **PICANTE SAUCE.**

YIELD: 6 SERVINGS

TACO BURGERS

Combine . . . . 1 pkg. **TACO SEASONING**
¼ cup **MILK**
¼ cup **CATSUP**
1½ pounds **GROUND BEEF**

Mix all together and shape into 6 patties. Grill over hot coals. Serve on **HAMBURGER BUNS** with **LETTUCE, TOMATOES, ONION,** and **TACO SAUCE.**

YEILD: 6 SERVINGS

CHILI BURGERS

Combine . . . . 1 pkg. **CHILI SEASONING MIX**
⅓ cup **MILK**
1½ pounds **GROUND BEEF**
1 cup grated **CHEDDAR CHEESE**

Mix and shape into 6 patties. Grill over hot coals. Serve on **HAMBURGER BUNS** with **GREEN PEPPER** slices and additional **CHEESE.**

YIELD: 6 SERVINGS

TOPLESS CHILI BURGERS

In a large skillet brown . . . . 1½ pounds **GROUND BEEF**
1 **ONION,** chopped
Drain off grease and stir in . . . . 1 can (8 oz.) **TOMATO SAUCE**
1 pkg. **DRY TACO SEASONING MIX**
Simmer 5 minutes.
Split and toast . . . . **HAMBURGER BUNS**
Spread with meat mixture.
Top with . . . . **CHEESE SLICES**
Place in 400 degree oven for 4 to 5 minutes.
Top with . . . . **LETTUCE**
TOMATO slices
ONION slices

Serve with **CHIPS** and **PICKLES**

YIELD: 10 TO 12 SERVINGS

WATERMELON BOWLE
Doubles as a centerpiece.

Buy a well-shaped **MELON.** Cut off the top third of the melon. Remove watermelon meat in as large pieces as possible. Fill the cavity with any combination of **FRUITS** plus the meat from the watermelon. Ball, or cut into 1-inch cubes. Place on a large serving tray and decorate with any large green leaves, fruits or flowers. (I carve a decorative motif on the side of the melon, when feeling industrious.)

When using a long melon, carve top to resemble a basket with a handle. Put flowers across handle with straight pins. Very colorful.

Suggested fruits: **FRESH PINEAPPLE, FRESH CHERRIES, SEEDLESS GRAPES, CANTALOUPE, HONEYDEW MELON,** thin slices of **ORANGE** or **APPLE,** etc.

FIX-AHEAD SALAD
Or dessert.

Mix together in a saucepan . . . .

- 2 Tbsp. **SUGAR**
- 2 Tbsp. **CORNSTARCH**
- 2 **EGG YOLKS**
- 2 cups **MILK**

Cook until thickened, stirring constantly. Remove from heat and add . . . .

- 1 bag (10 oz.) **MINIATURE MARSHMALLOWS**
- 1 can **PEARS,** drained and cut up
- 1 large can **CRUSHED PINEAPPLE,** drained
- ½ cup **BLANCHED SLIVERED ALMONDS**
- 2 cups **TOKAY GRAPES** or **QUEEN ANNE CHERRIES,** drained

Mix and cool. Fold in . . . .

- 1 cup **HEAVY CREAM,** whipped

Refrigerate for 24 hours.

QUICK CARROT SALAD: Mix grated carrots, salad dressing, raisins, and a little sugar.

BEST @#$¢% SALAD
Pat also serves this for dessert.

Mix in a bowl . . . .   1 can **CHERRY PIE FILLING**
                                              1 can **EAGLE BRAND MILK**
                                              1 large carton **WHIPPED TOPPING**
Add . . . .   1 can (8 oz.) **CRUSHED PINEAPPLE,** do not drain
                                              1 cup **NUTS,** chopped
                                              1 cup **MINIATURE MARSHMALLOWS**

Toss well and refrigerate. This will keep several days. Also good with
BLUEBERRY PIE FILLING.

YIELD: 10 TO 12 SERVINGS

JILL'S FRUIT SALAD

Combine 1 cup each . . . .   **MANDARIN ORANGES,** drained
                                              PINEAPPLE TIDBITS, drained
                                              WHITE GRAPES, drained
                                              COCONUT
                                              MINIATURE MARSHMALLOWS
                                              SOUR CREAM

Chill and serve.

YIELD: 8 SERVINGS

GREEN GAGE PLUM SALAD

Dissolve . . . .   1 package (3 oz.) **LIME JELLO**
in . . . .   ½ cup **HOT WATER**
Add . . . .   1 can (No. 2) **GREEN GAGE PLUMS** (drained, seeded and mashed)
                                              1 pkg. (3 oz.) **CREAM CHEESE,** softened
                                              1 cup **NUTS** (optional)

Pour into jello mold. When firm, unmold and serve. Garnish with **WHIP-PED TOPPING** or **MAYONNAISE.**

YIELD: 8 SERVINGS

BLACKBERRY WINE SALAD

Combine and place in the
  refrigerator overnight . . . .
1 pound small **MARSHMALLOWS**
1 jar (8 oz.) **MARASCHINO
  CHERRIES,** cut up
CHERRY JUICE from cherries
1 cup **BLACKBERRY WINE**

Remove from refrigerator
  and add . . . .
½ pint **HEAVY CREAM,** whipped
1 small can **CRUSHED PINEAPPLE**
1 cup **NUTS**

Put into a mold and freeze. For a festive look, freeze in paper muffin liners inside muffin pans and keep in the freezer until ready to serve.

YIELD: 10 TO 12 SERVINGS

FIX-IT-FAST
Orange and beet salad.

Toss together, cover and chill . . .
1 can **MANDARIN ORANGE
  SECTIONS,** well drained
1 cup **JULIENNE BEETS,** drained
1 **APPLE,** cored and sliced

In a screw-top jar,
  combine . . . .
¼ cup **OIL**
2 Tbsp. **ORANGE JUICE
  CONCENTRATE,** thawed,
  undiluted
1 Tbsp. **LEMON JUICE**
½ tsp. **DRY MUSTARD**
⅓ tsp. **SALT**

Cover, shake well, and refrigerate.

At serving time, cover a serving plate with **FRESH SPINACH.** Arrange fruit on spinach. Shake dressing well and pour over all.

YIELD: 4 SERVINGS

MELODISE'S FRUIT SALAD
Easy, easy, easy.

Mix all together, including juice .
- 1 large can **FRUIT COCKTAIL**
- 1 medium can **CHUNKED PINEAPPLE**
- 1 cup chopped **PECANS**
- 4 **BANANAS**, cut in large chunks
- 1½ packages **FRENCH VANILLA** or **VANILLA INSTANT PUDDING AND PIE FILLING**, dry

Chill and serve.

YIELD: 8 SERVINGS

THROWN TOGETHER FRUIT SALAD

Thaw . . . . 1 pkg. (10 oz.) **FROZEN STRAWBERRIES**
Add . . . . ½ cup **SUGAR**
Drain and add . . . . 1 can (8 oz.) **PINEAPPLE CHUNKS**
1 can **APRICOT PIE FILLING**
Slice and add . . . . 2 **BANANAS**

Mix together and chill overnight.

YIELD: 10 TO 12 SERVINGS

RASPBERRY SALAD
Looks like aspic.

Dissolve . . . . 1 package (6 oz.) **RASPBERRY JELLO**
in . . . . ¾ cup boiling **WATER**
Add and stir until dissolved . . . . . . 1 can (6 oz.) **ORANGE JUICE**, frozen
1 can (15½ oz.) crushed **PINEAPPLE**, well drained
1 can (20 oz.) **APPLESAUCE**

Mix well. Pour into mold. Refrigerate. When ready to serve, unmold on bed of **LETTUCE.** Garnish.

YIELD: 8 TO 10 SERVINGS

APRICOT-CHEESE DELIGHT

Drain and reserve **JUICE**
    from .... 1 large can **APRICOTS**
                          1 large can **PINEAPPLE**
Mash fruit and set aside.
Dissolve .... 1 pkg. (6 oz.) **ORANGE JELLO**
in .... 2 cups **HOT WATER**
Add .... 1 cup combined Apricot and
                           Pineapple juice
          ¾ cup **MINIATURE**
                           MARSHMALLOWS
                           Mashed fruit

Pour into a 13x9x2-inch casserole and congeal. Spread with **TOPPING.** Cut into squares and serve.

TOPPING

Combine .... ½ cup **SUGAR**
                           3 Tbsp. **FLOUR**
                           1 **EGG,** slightly beaten
Add .... 1 cup combined **APRICOT** and
                           PINEAPPLE JUICE

Cook over low heat, stirring constantly, until thick. Remove from heat. Cool completely. Fold in 1 cup **WHIPPED TOPPING.** Spread on Jello. Sprinkle with grated **CHEDDAR CHEESE.**

YIELD: 12 SERVINGS

COCA-COLA SALAD
Or, Peg's Passion Salad.

Drain and reserve **JUICE**
    from .... 1 can (16 oz.) **BING CHERRIES,**
                           pitted
                           1 can (16 oz.) **CRUSHED**
                           PINEAPPLE
Add enough **WATER** to the juice to make 1½ cups.
Bring to a boil and add .... 1 pkg. (6 oz.) **CHERRY JELLO**
Dissolve well and add .... 2 cups **COCA-COLA**
                           1 cup **NUTS,** chopped
                           drained Pineapple and Cherries

Pour into serving dish and congeal.

MANDARIN ORANGE SALAD
With Ginger dressing.

Drain and reserve liquid from ..   3 cans **MANDARIN ORANGE SEGMENTS**
Heat the juice with enough **WATER** to total 3 cups liquid.
Dissolve in the hot liquid . . . .   1 pkg. (6 oz.) **ORANGE FLAVORED JELLO**

Cool.
Combine with the mandarin
oranges . . . .   2 cans **WATER CHESTNUTS,** drained and sliced paper-thin

Chill until firm.
Combine . . . .   1 pkg. (3 oz.) **CREAM CHEESE,** softened
     ½ cup chopped **FRESH ORANGE SECTIONS**
     ½ cup chopped **CRYSTALLIZED GINGER**
Add . . . .   ¼ cup **CREAM**

Spread the dressing over the congealed salad. Dressing should be consistency of mayonnaise, so add, or take from, the cream.

YIELD: 10 TO 12 SERVINGS

CHRISTMAS SALAD

Grind . . . .   1 cup **CRANBERRIES**
     1 **ORANGE,** quarter and remove seeds (grind rind also)
Cook a few minutes with . . . .   1 cup **SUGAR**
Set aside. Dissolve . . . .   1 pkg. (3-oz.) **STRAWBERRY JELLO**
in . . . .   1 cup boiling **WATER**
Add to above mixture.
     Stir in . . . .   1 cup **PINEAPPLE JUICE**
     1 cup **PINEAPPLE TIDBITS**
     ½ cup chopped **NUTS**

Pour into a Christmas mold and congeal. Unmold onto a serving plate covered with **LETTUCE** leaves. Garnish with **MAYONNAISE**. Keep chilled until serving time. Best to make a day ahead.

YIELD: 10 SERVINGS

7-UP CONGEALED SALAD

Bring to a boil	2 cups **WATER**
Add	1 pkg. (6 oz.) **LEMON JELLO**
Dissolve well. Add	2 cups **7-UP**
	1 cup **MINIATURE MARSHMALLOWS**
	2 **BANANAS**, sliced
	1 can (20 oz.) **CRUSHED PINEAPPLE** (drain and save juice)
Put in refrigerator to congeal. Combine and cook until thick	2 Tbsp. **BUTTER**
	½ cup **SUGAR**
	2 Tbsp. **FLOUR**
	1 cup **PINEAPPLE JUICE**
	1 **EGG**

When thickened, remove from heat and let cool completely. Add 1 cup **WHIPPED TOPPING** and spread over Jello. Sprinkle with **GRATED CHEESE**.

YIELD: 10 SERVINGS

STRAWBERRY JELLO SALAD

Dissolve	1 pkg. (6 oz.) **STRAWBERRY JELLO**
in	2 cups **HOT WATER**
Add	½ cup **COLD WATER**
	1 small package **FROZEN STRAWBERRIES**
	3 **BANANAS**, mashed
	1 can (8 oz.) **CRUSHED PINEAPPLE**, with juice

Pour half of the above mixture into a serving bowl and let congeal. Cover remainder and leave sitting on the cabinet top. When firm, spread 1 cup **SOUR CREAM** over the top. Gently spoon in remainder of the Jello mixture. Return to refrigerator and congeal again.

YIELD: 10 SERVINGS

VARIATION: Put mixture in a shallow casserole pan, layering the same way, congeal, and cut into squares to serve. Place on lettuce leaves and garnish with a dab of **MAYONNAISE**.

HAWAIIAN JELLO
Buttermilk adds extra zest.

Mix in small saucepan. . . . . 1 pkg. (3 oz.) **ORANGE JELLO**
JUICE from . . . . 1 can (5¼ oz.) **CRUSHED PINEAPPLE**
Heat until mixed. Cool. Add . . . . pineapple
1 cup **BUTTERMILK**
1 carton (4 oz.) **WHIPPED TOPPING**

Pour into mold and congeal in refrigerator. Serve on a bed of **LETTUCE** leaves.

SUNNY'S STRAWBERRY JELLO
Looks as good as it tastes.

Mix together . . . . 1 box (6 oz.) **STRAWBERRY JELLO,** dry
1 can (No. 2) **CRUSHED PINEAPPLE**
1 large carton **COOL WHIP**
Fold in . . . . 1 cup small curd **COTTAGE CHEESE**

Chill and serve.

CREAMY CABBAGE SLAW

Shred fine and mix together . . . . 1 medium head **CABBAGE**
2 **CARROTS**
½ **ONION** (or ¼ cup sliced **GREEN ONION**)
1 **GREEN PEPPER**
Mix in separate bowl and stir
until sugar is dissolved . . . . . . 1 cup **MAYONNAISE** or **SALAD DRESSING**
2 Tbsp. **SUGAR**
2 Tbsp. **VINEGAR**
2 tsp. **CELERY SEED**
1 tsp. **SALT**

Drizzle over cabbage mixture and toss lightly to mix.

YIELD: 8 TO 10 SERVINGS

CABBAGE SALAD

Combine .... ½ head **RED CABBAGE**, shredded
½ head **WHITE CABBAGE**, shredded
Add .... 2 **RED ONIONS**, sliced thin
1 cup grated **CARROTS**
1 cup sliced **CELERY**
1 **GREEN PEPPER**, sliced thin
Make a dressing of .... 1 cup **OIL**
1 tsp. **SALT**
1 cup **SUGAR**
1 cup **WHITE VINEGAR**
1 tsp. **DRY MUSTARD**
1 tsp. **CELERY SEED**

Heat the dressing mixture. Pour over the vegetables while hot. Cover and refrigerate. Let set for 24 hours in refrigerator before serving. Will keep several days.

CATHERINE'S CABBAGE SALAD
With Buttermilk dressing.

Heat until boiling .... 4 Tbsp. **VINEGAR**
1 tsp. **SALAD OIL**
Pour immediately over .... 1 medium **CABBAGE**, shredded
Add .... ½ cup **BUTTERMILK**
SALT and **PEPPER**

Garnish with sliced **RADISHES** and sprinkle with sieved **HARD COOKED EGGS**.

CARROT SALAD
Make it today, serve it tomorrow.

Combine .... 2 cups shredded **CARROTS**
1 can (20 oz.) **PINEAPPLE TIDBITS**, drained
Cover and refrigerate overnight.
When ready to serve, add ...... 1 cup **COCONUT**
1 cup **MINIATURE MARSHMALLOWS**
Toss and cover with a
    dressing of .... 3 ounces **CREAM CHEESE**, softened
½ cup **MAYONNAISE**
½ cup **WHIPPED TOPPING**

CATHERINE'S CAULIFLOWER SALAD
A good make-ahead salad.

Clean and chop to the size you
    prefer ....   1 head **CAULIFLOWER**
                                   1 **GREEN PEPPER**
                                   CELERY
Add ....   **CHEDDAR CHEESE,** cubed

Cover with **HIDDEN VALLEY RANCH** dressing. Cover and store in refrigerator until ready to use. Toss and serve.

QUICK AND EASY

Toss ....   1 small head **CABBAGE,** chopped
                                   CARROTS, grated
                                   2 **APPLES,** chopped
                                   1 cup **RAISINS**
Blend and serve over salad .....   **EAGLE BRAND MILK**
Sprinkle lightly with ....   **POPPY SEED**

Serve chilled.

CHINESE VEGETABLE SALAD

Combine ....   1 can **FRENCH CUT GREEN BEANS,** drained
                                   1 can **BEAN SPROUTS** or **MIXED CHINESE VEGETABLES,** drained
                                   ½ cup chopped **ONION**
                                   2 Tbsp. chopped **PIMIENTO**
Mix and pour over
    vegetables ....   ⅔ cup **SUGAR**
                                   ⅔ cup **VINEGAR**
                                   ½ cup **OIL**
                                   ½ tsp. **SALT**

Cover and refrigerate overnight. Drain before serving.

COPPER PENNIES

Layer in serving dish . . . . 2 pounds **CARROTS,** sliced and
cooked until fork tender
1 **ONION,** sliced in rings
1 **GREEN PEPPER,** sliced in rings
Set in refrigerator.
Blend together . . . . 1 can **TOMATO SOUP**
½ cup **SALAD OIL**
1 tsp. **PREPARED MUSTARD**
1 cup **SUGAR**
¾ cup **VINEGAR**
1 tsp. **WORCESTERSHIRE SAUCE**
SALT and **PEPPER**

Pour sauce over vegetables. Refrigerate for at least 24 hours. Keeps indefinitely.

ENGLISH PEA SALAD

Combine . . . . 1 can **ENGLISH PEAS,** drained
1 small can **PIMIENTOS,** chopped
1 small **ONION,** chopped
½ pound **AMERICAN CHEESE,**
cubed
SALT

Add enough **MAYONNAISE** to moisten. Serve immediately, or make the day before.

GOOD GREEN SALAD

In a large salad bowl (4-serving
size), put . . . . 2 Tbsp. **VINEGAR**
2 Tbsp. **OIL**
SALT
GARLIC POWDER to taste

Fill bowl with broken up **GREENS (FRESH SPINACH, LETTUCE** or **RO-MAINE.)** Toss and serve.

SOUR CREAM CUCUMBERS

Peel and slice thin . . . .   6 **CUCUMBERS,** medium size
Mix and pour over
   cucumbers . . . .   ⅔ cup **SOUR CREAM**
                            2 Tbsp. **VINEGAR**
                            1 Tbsp. chopped **CHIVES**
                            SALT and **PEPPER**

Toss and refrigerate until ready to serve. Chill well.

OVERNITE SALAD

Combine . . . .   1 can **GREEN BEANS,** drained
                            1 can **YELLOW WAX BEANS,**
                              drained
                            1 can **KIDNEY BEANS,** drained
                            ½ cup **OIL**
                            ½ cup **SUGAR**
                            ½ cup **VINEGAR**
                            2 stalks **CELERY,** chopped
                            1 **GREEN PEPPER,** diced
                            1 **ONION,** diced
                            SALT, PEPPER, PIMIENTO

Mix, cover tightly and marinate overnight. Will keep several days.

SAUERKRAUT SALAD
Actually, more of a relish.

Combine . . . .   1 can (1 lb., 13 oz.) **SAUERKRAUT,**
                            Drained and cut up
                            2 cups diced **CELERY**
                            1 cup diced **ONION**
                            1 **GREEN PEPPER,** diced
                            1 large can **PIMIENTOS,** chopped
Set in refrigerator.
Make a dressing of . . . .   2 cups **SUGAR**
                            ½ cup **VINEGAR**
                            1 tsp. **SALT**

Cook dressing over medium heat until sugar is dissolved. Cool, pour over
vegetables. Store in a tightly covered container. Will keep for weeks.

SLANG JANG

Delicious served with blackeyed peas or beans.

Combine . . . . 1⅔ cups chopped **RIPE TOMATOES**
                              ½ **BELL PEPPER,** chopped
                              2 cups **CHOPPED ONIONS**
Mix well and pour over
   vegetables . . . . 2 Tbsp. **SALAD OIL**
                              ⅓ cup **SUGAR**
                              ½ cup **VINEGAR**
                              3 tsp. **ACCENT**
                              ½ tsp. **GARLIC SALT**
Add to taste . . . . **SALT** and **PEPPER**

Place in covered jar and let stand several hours. Refrigerate.

SHOE-PEG CORN SALAD

Large, but will keep for days.

Toss together . . . . 2 cans **LE SUEUR PEAS**
                              2 cans **SHOE PEG CORN**
                              1 small jar **PIMIENTOS,** chopped
                              5 **FRESH ONIONS,** chopped with
                                    tops
                              6 **CELERY STALKS,** chopped)
                              1 **BELL PEPPER,** chopped
Set aside.
In a small saucepan, mix . . . . . . ¾ cup **VINEGAR,** white
                              ½ cup **OIL**
                              1 cup **SUGAR**
                              1 Tbsp. **WATER**
                              1 tsp. **PEPPER**
                              1 tsp. **SALT**
Heat marinade until sugar is dissolved.

Cool and pour over vegetables. Refrigerate for at least 24 hours.

GREEN AVOCADOS? Place in a drawer with dish towels. Check each day until they are ripe.

VEGETABLE SALAD A'LOT

Layer in a large glass compote
   or serving dish . . . .   1 package **FRESH SPINACH,**
      chopped
   1 pound **BACON,** baked in oven,
      drained and crumbled
   1 package **FROZEN ENGLISH**
      PEAS, uncooked
   1 bunch **FRESH ONIONS,** chopped
      with tops
   1 head **LETTUCE,** chopped
   1 dozen **BOILED EGGS,** chopped

Frost like a cake with a mixture
   of . . . .   1 cup **MAYONNAISE**
   1 cup **SALAD DRESSING**

Sprinkle liberally with **PARMESAN CHEESE** or grated **MILD SWISS CHEESE.** Cover with plastic wrap and refrigerate for at least 12 hours. Will keep for about a week. Do not toss to serve.

WILTED LETTUCE SALAD

In a medium skillet, fry
   until crisp . . . .   6 slices **BACON**
Drain on paper towel. Remove all but 3 Tablespoons drippings from skillet.
Stir in . . . .   ½ cup **SOUR CREAM**
   1 **EGG,** slightly beaten
   ¼ cup **VINEGAR**
   2 Tbsp. **SUGAR**
   SALT
Cook until thickened, stirring constantly.
Add . . . .   1 head **LETTUCE,** torn in pieces
   3 **GREEN ONIONS,** chopped, with
      tops

Add crumbled bacon. Toss until well coated. Serve immediately. Garnish with **HARD COOKED EGGS** and **FRESH MUSHROOMS.**

YIELD: 6 SERVINGS

VARIATIONS:
Make with **SPINACH** or **LEAF LETTUCE,** or half lettuce and half spinach.

Dressing is good served over sliced fresh **TOMATOES.** Use crumbled bacon as a garnish.

SUPER FILL-INS

Place on a bed of **LETTUCE,** any of the following . . . .

AVOCADO HALVES, peeled
PINEAPPLE HALVES (scoop out the core)
TOMATOES (cut slits one-fourth through)
CANTALOUPE HALVES, seeded

Fill with any of the following:

CHICKEN FILL-IN: Combine . . . .

2 cups cooked, chopped **CHICKEN**
2 **EGGS,** hard boiled and chopped
1 **TOMATO,** peeled and chopped
2 Tbsp. **SWEET RELISH**
MAYONNAISE
SALT and **PEPPER**

CHEESE FILL-IN: Combine . . . . .

6 **EGGS,** hard boiled and grated
½ pound **SWISS CHEESE,** grated
½ cup **SOUR CREAM**
1½ tsp. **DRY MUSTARD**
1 tsp. **TABASCO**
½ tsp. **SALT**
½ tsp. **PEPPER**

TUNA FILL-IN: Combine . . . .

1 can **TUNA,** drained
2 Tbsp. **SWEET RELISH**
2 **EGGS,** hard boiled and chopped
¼ tsp. **PEPPER**
¼ cup chopped **APPLES**
¼ cup **PECANS**
CELERY
MAYONNAISE

CRAB MEAT FILL-IN:
Marinate . . . .
for 3 hours in . . . .
Drain and combine with . . . .

2 cups **KING CRAB**
½ cup **FRENCH DRESSING**
½ cup chopped **GREEN ONIONS,** with tops
½ cup chopped **CELERY**
2 Tbsp. **LEMON JUICE**
1 cup **MAYONNAISE**
1 tsp. **SALT**
⅛ tsp. **CAYENNE**
½ tsp. **PEPPER**

HOT POTATO SALAD WITH BACON
Supper entree for cold day.

Scrub well . . . . 9 **POTATOES**
Drop unpeeled into a large saucepan of boiling **WATER.** Cover and boil until slight resistance to knife point. Drain, peel and cut into ¼-inch slices. Set aside, tightly covered.
In medium skillet, fry until
   crisp . . . . ½ pound **BACON,** diced
Drain on paper towels. In bacon
   fat, saute . . . . ½ cup diced **ONION**
Drain. Add, stirring
   constantly . . . . ¼ cup **WHITE WINE** or **CIDER VINEGAR**
                                            ¼ cup **WATER**
                                            ½ tsp. **SALT**
                                            ¼ tsp. **PEPPER**
                                            2 Tbsp. **PARSLEY**

Pour hot sauce over potatoes, turning gently with fork to coat evenly. Gently stir in bacon. Serve at once. Serve with **VEGETABLE,** hot **BREAD,** and **DESSERT.**

YIELD: 6 TO 8 SERVINGS

POTATO SALAD

Mix . . . . 1 cup **MAYONNAISE**
                                            1 Tbsp. **SUGAR**
                                            2 tsp. **PREPARED MUSTARD**
                                            SALT and **PEPPER** to taste
Pour over and toss with . . . . 8 medium **POTATOES,** boiled, peeled and diced
                                            1 large **ONION,** minced
                                            8 hard-cooked **EGGS,** chopped
                                            1 cup **SWEET RELISH**
                                            1 small jar **PIMIENTOS,** chopped

Chill several hours. Garnish and serve.

YIELD: 10 TO 12 SERVINGS

DOT'S OVERNIGHT PASTA SALAD

Cook according to package
   directions .... 1 cup (4 oz.) tiny **SHELL
                                           MACARONI**

Drain and rinse with cold water.
In a 1½ quart salad bowl, layer
   in order given .... 2 cups shredded **LETTUCE**
                                        cooked macaroni
                                        2 hard-cooked **EGGS,** sliced
                                        2 slices (1 oz. each) cooked **HAM,**
                                            cut into thin strips
                                        1 pkg. (10 oz.) frozen **ENGLISH
                                            PEAS,** thawed
                                       ½ cup (2 oz.) shredded **SWISS
                                          CHEESE**
Combine and mix well .... ½ cup **MAYONNAISE**
                                        ¼ cup **SOUR CREAM**
                                        1 Tbsp. chopped **GREEN ONION**
                                        1 tsp. **PREPARED MUSTARD**
                                        1 tsp. **HOT SAUCE**

Spread mixture evenly over top of first mixture, sealing to edge of bowl.
Sprinkle with 1 tsp. **PAPRIKA** and chopped fresh **PARSLEY.** Cover bowl
tightly and chill overnight. Do not toss to serve.

YIELD: 6 TO 8 SERVINGS

MACARONI SALAD
Bertha Brewer's version

Cook until tender .... 1 pkg. **SHELL MACARONI**
Drain and rinse. Add .... 1 Tbsp. **LAWRY'S SEASONING
                                         SALT**
                                        1 **ONION,** diced
                                        1 tsp. **SALT**
Mix well. Set aside.
Prepare .... 8 hard boiled **EGGS,** chopped
                                        2 cups chopped **CELERY**
                                        ½ cup chopped **PIMINETOS**
                                        1 cup chopped **GREEN PEPPER**
                                        ½ **CUCUMBER,** chopped
                                        2 cans **ENGLISH PEAS,** drained

Add to the macaroni and toss lightly with **MAYONNAISE.** (Do not use Salad
Dressing.) Chill for a few hours.

YIELD: 25 SERVINGS

CHICKEN-BING SALAD

Combine . . . .   2 **CHICKENS,** cooked, boned, and
                       chopped
         1½ cups diced **CELERY**
         1 cup **MAYONNAISE**
         1 Tbsp. **LEMON JUICE**
         SALT and **PEPPER**
         1 tsp. **POPPY SEED**
         ½ cup chopped **PECANS**

Refrigerate until ready to serve. Just before serving, add 1 can **BING CHER-RIES,** *well* drained. Toss lightly and serve.

CHICKEN SALAD BRUNCH
Another of Terri Long's goodies.

Toss well . . . .   2 cans **SWANSON'S CHICKEN,**
                       white meat
         2 cans **GREEN CALIFORNIA**
                       GRAPES, drained
         1 cup chopped **CELERY**
         2 pkgs. slivered **ALMONDS**
         1 pint **HELLMAN'S MAYONNAISE**
         1 cup **HEAVY CREAM,** whipped
         dash of **SALT** (scant)
         PARSLEY

Serve in **TOMATOES** that have had seed removed.

YIELD: 10 TO 12 SERVINGS

CHINESE CHICKEN SALAD

Combine . . . .   1 **CHICKEN,** cooked and chopped
         2 hard boiled **EGGS**
         ½ cup **PICKLE RELISH**
         ½ cup chopped **CELERY**
         ½ cup **MAYONNAISE** (may need
                       more)
         2 tsp. **SOY SAUCE**
         1 can **FANCY CHINESE**
                       VEGETABLES, drained

Mix well and chill. Serve on **LETTUCE** leaves with **CRACKERS** or hot **BREAD.**

CHICKEN WILD RICE SALAD
Jayme serves this as a supper dish.

Combine	1 pkg. (6 oz.) **LONG GRAIN AND WILD RICE MIX,** cooked and cooled
	2 cups cooked and cubed **CHICKEN**
	¼ cup chopped **GREEN PEPPER**
	2 Tbsp. chopped **PIMIENTO**
	½ cup chopped **WATER CHESTNUTS**
Mix in blender	½ cup **MAYONNAISE**
	2 Tbsp. **RUSSIAN SALAD DRESSING**
	1 Tbsp. **LEMON JUICE**
	½ tsp. **SALT**

Pour dressing over rice mixture. Toss and chill. To serve, spoon chicken salad over slices of **AVOCADO.**

CRANBERRY CHICKEN SALAD
Dinner in a dish!

Chill and cut into cubes........	1 can (8 oz) **JELLIED CRANBERRY SAUCE**
In a mixing bowl, beat together	1 pkg. (3 oz.) **CREAM CHEESE,** softened
	½ cup **SOUR CREAM**
	¼ tsp. **SALT**
Stir in	¾ cup sliced **CELERY**
	½ cup **NUTS**
	2 Tbsp. chopped **GREEN PEPPER**
Fold in	1½ cups cooked and cubed **CHICKEN**
	1 can (13½ oz.) **PINEAPPLE TIDBITS,** drained

Top with cranberry cubes when ready to serve.

YIELD: 4 TO 5 SERVINGS

WINTER CHICKEN SALAD
Hot, steamy and good.

Combine . . . . 2½ cups cooked and chopped
                                       CHICKEN
                             1 can **WATER CHESTNUTS**, sliced
                             1 can **MUSHROOMS**, sliced
                             ½ cup slivered **ALMONDS**
                             2 Tbsp. **LEMON JUICE**
                             ½ cup **MAYONNAISE**
Pour into a 1½-quart buttered casserole.
Top with . . . . ¾ cup grated **CHEDDAR CHEESE**

Bake in a preheated oven at 350 degrees for 40 minutes. When done, remove from oven, top with 1 can **FRENCH-FRIED ONION RINGS**. Return to oven an additional 10 minutes.

YIELD: 6 TO 8 SERVINGS

SUMMERTIME HAM SALAD

Stir together . . . . 1 envelope **UNFLAVORED**
                                 GELATIN
                             ¼ cup **WATER**
Heat until dissolved . . . . 1 can **CREAM OF POTATO SOUP,**
                                 frozen and undiluted
Add gelatin mixture. Remove from heat and let cool.
Stir into soup mixture . . . . 1½ cups diced **HAM**
                             1 cup diced **CELERY**
                             ¼ cup diced **RIPE OLIVES**
                             2 **PIMIENTOS**, diced
                             ½ cup **SALAD DRESSING**

Mix well and pour into a 1-quart mold. Chill until firm. Cover and freeze. Use within 2 weeks. To serve, thaw in the refrigerator overnight. Unmold on **LETTUCE**. Garnish as desired. Serve with **CRACKERS** or hot **BREAD**, **DESSERT** and **DRINK**.

After meat has browned,
    add . . . . 2 cans **GOLDEN MUSHROOM**
                                 SOUP, undiluted

WILTED SALAD? Add salt just before serving time. Salt wilts and toughens salad greens.

SHRIMP SALAD
Perfect hot summer supper dish.

Mix together for dressing ......   dash **TABASCO**
2 Tbsp. **WORCESTERSHIRE SAUCE**
1 cup **MAYONNAISE**
¼ cup finely-chopped **ONION**
SALT and **PEPPER**

Pour over ....   4 hard boiled **EGGS,** sliced
2 pounds boiled **SHRIMP,** chopped
1 cup chopped **CELERY**
½ cup chopped **SWEET PICKLES**
¼ cup chopped **GREEN PEPPER**

Toss lightly and refrigerate until ready to serve. To serve, place on **LETTUCE** leaves and garnish with sliced **OLIVES** and **PIMIENTOS.**

HONEY LIME DRESSING
Keep in refrigerator for fresh FRUIT SALADS.

Mix together and beat well.....   1 cup **SUGAR**
½ cup **HONEY**
3 Tbsp. **DRY MUSTARD**
⅓ cup fresh **LIME JUICE**
1 tsp. **GINGER**
⅓ cup **PINEAPPLE JUICE**

Gradually add...............   1 cup **SALAD OIL**

Beat well and store in a closed container in the refrigerator.

YIELD: 1½ PINTS

POPPY SEED DRESSING
Great on fresh FRUIT, and so easy.

Blend together ....   1 can **EAGLE BRAND MILK**
2 Tbsp. **LEMON** or **LIME JUICE**
2 tsp. **POPPY SEED**

FRESH FRUIT DRESSING

Mix in saucepan.	2 **EGGS,** well beaten
	¼ cup **SUGAR**
	JUICE of 1 **LEMON**
Cook until thick.	
Cool and fold in	1 cup **WHIPPING CREAM,** stiffly beaten

Pour over **SALAD.**

RACHEL'S SALAD DRESSING

Mix well	1 cup **CATSUP** or **TOMATO JUICE**
	1 cup **OIL**
	1 cup **VINEGAR**
	½ cup **SUGAR**
	1 Tbsp. **LAWRY'S SEASONING SALT**
	1 tsp. **WORCESTERSHIRE SAUCE**

SOUR CREAM DRESSING
Use over fresh FRUIT SALAD,
or dip STRAWBERRIES in dressing, for dessert.

Mix	1 carton **SOUR CREAM**
	dash of **CINNAMON**
	POWDERED SUGAR to taste
	2 tsp. **POPPY SEED**

FRENCH DRESSING

Blend at high speed on blender .	½ cup **SUGAR**
	½ cup **WINE VINEGAR**
	1 cup **SALAD OIL**
	½ cup **CATSUP**
	¾ tsp. **DRY MUSTARD**
	SALT and **PEPPER**
	GARLIC SALT (optional)

Store in covered container in the refrigerator.

MEN'S FAVORITE SALAD DRESSING

Mix in large bowl of mixer at
    medium speed. . . . .   1 quart **MAYONNAISE** (Do not use
                      salad dressing.)
              ½ cup **SUGAR**
              1 large can **EVAPORATED MILK**
              1 Tbsp. **LEMON JUICE**
              1 tsp. **WORCESTERSHIRE SAUCE**
                GARLIC SALT (optional)
              ¾ cup grated **CHEDDAR CHEESE**

Store in a covered container in the refrigerator.

THOUSAND ISLAND DRESSING

I make ½ recipe at a time.

Blend at high speed . . . .   4 **EGG YOLKS**
              ½ tsp. **SALT**
              ½ tsp. **DRY MUSTARD**
              ½ tsp. **SUGAR**
              3 Tbsp. **VINEGAR**
Add and beat at low speed for
    15 minutes . . . .   1 quart **OIL**
Stir in . . . .   ½ cup **SWEET PICKLE RELISH**
              1 **ONION,** finely chopped
              1 cup **CATSUP**

Store in a tightly covered container in the refrigerator. Will keep for several weeks.

YIELD: 2 QUARTS

SALAD SUCCESS: Be sure lettuce is cold, crisp and dry. Tear, don't cut lettuce into bite-size pieces. Add dressing just before serving.

MOTHER'S CRABMEAT SALAD RAVIGOTE

Defrost	2 pounds **FROZEN CRABMEAT**

Break into bite-size pieces.

Toss with	¼ cup **TARRAGON VINEGAR**

Refrigerate 20 minutes. Drain thoroughly, pressing out with hands until fairly dry.

Combine crabmeat with . . . .   3 cups sliced **CELERY,** cut crosswise about ⅓-inch thick.
1 tsp. **CAPERS,** *well* drained
¼ cup very finely chopped fresh **GREEN ONIONS** and **TOPS**
1 cup **MAYONNAISE**
1 Tbsp. finely diced **GREEN PEPPER**

Blend well and place in a covered bowl in the refrigerator for about 30 minutes. Serve in individual clam shells, topped with **MAYONNAISE** and sieved **EGG YOLKS.**

For a buffet, mount the crabmeat on a large platter and spread entire surface with **MAYONNAISE.** Cover with grated **EGG YOLKS.** Garnish base of salad alternately with thinly sliced TOMATOES and **CUCUMBER.** Place bouquets of **PARSLEY** on each end.

This salad may be prepared hours ahead, or even a day in advance, but leave the garnishing until just before serving.

YIELD: 8 TO 10 SERVINGS

TOSSED CRAB LOUIS SALAD

Drain and flake . . . .   1 pkg. **FROZEN ALASKA SNOW CRAB,** thawed or 1 can (6½ oz.) **CRAB MEAT**

Combine with . . . .   ½ cup chopped **CAULIFLOWER**
½ cup chopped **CELERY**
½ cup chopped **GREEN PEPPER**
½ cup chopped **CUCUMBER**
½ cup **LOW CALORIE THOUSAND ISLAND DRESSING**
1 tsp. **LEMON JUICE**

On 4 individual **LETTUCE**-lined plates, place ½ cup shredded **LETTUCE** and ¼ cup of the crab mixture. Garnish plates with **TOMATO** slices and hard-boiled **EGGS** (about ½ egg per plate.)

CRAB LOUIS
So easy and so good—for lunch or dinner

Mix .... 2 cups **MAYONNAISE**
½ cup chopped **FRESH ONIONS,**
with tops
½ cup minced **GREEN PEPPER**
½ cup **CHILI SAUCE**
PARSLEY
CAYENNE PEPPER
SALT
LEMON JUICE to taste

Whip and fold into
mixture.................. ½ cup **HEAVY CREAM**

Refrigerate in a covered container until ready to serve. Arrange **CRABMEAT** on **AVOCADO** halves, on bed of **LETTUCE**. Cover with Louis Dressing. Add boiled **SHRIMP** for garnish. Nice!

YIELD: 4 SERVINGS

MA TEKELL'S TUNA SALAD
Most unusual and soooooo good.

Heat together until dissolved,
stirring constantly .... 1 pkg. (6 oz.) **LEMON JELLO**
1 can **TOMATO SOUP,** undiluted

Remove from heat and add ..... 1 cup chopped **CELERY**
1 chopped **GREEN PEPPER**
1 cup **COTTAGE CHEESE,** small
curd
1 cup chopped **ONION**
1 cup **MAYONNAISE**
1 Tbsp. **VINEGAR**
3 cans **TUNA** or **CHICKEN**
SALT and **PEPPER**

Blend well and pour into a glass casserole dish. Refrigerate. Serve with **CRACKERS** and **DESSERT.**

Main Dishes

BELT

CALF FRIES OR SWEETBREADS A LA KING

Steam 1 pound **CALF FRIES** or **SWEETBREADS** 45 minutes. Drain and remove membrane. Mince and set aside. Make **WHITE SAUCE**.
WHITE SAUCE:
In medium saucepan over low
heat melt . . . .   2 Tbsp. **BUTTER**
Stir in . . . .   2 Tbsp. **FLOUR**
                             ½ tsp. **SALT**
                             Dash of **PEPPER** and **PAPRIKA**
Gradually add . . . .   1 cup **MILK**
Cook, stirring constantly, until thickend and smooth.
Saute in small amount of
BUTTER . . . .   1 Tbsp. minced **ONION**
                             1 cup diced fresh **MUSHROOMS**
Remove from heat and add . . . . .   1 small jar chopped **PIMIENTO**
Combine meat, cream sauce and onion mixture. Serve over toast or pastry shells.

VARIATION:
Butter both sides of **PHYLLO** sheets. Place 3 sheets together and press in large muffin tins. Toast. Fill with mixture and serve warm.

BEEF BURGUNDY
A gourmet delight.

In a large skillet, brown . . . .   2 to 3 pounds boneless **BEEF,**
                             cubed
in . . . .   2 Tbsp. **COOKING OIL**
After meat has browned,
     add . . . .   **2 cans GOLDEN MUSHROOM**
                             SOUP, undiluted
                             2 packages **DRY ONION SOUP**
                             MIX
                             8 ounces **BURGUNDY**
                             4 ounces **WATER**
                             1 can **MUSHROOMS,** chopped

Simmer, covered, for 25 to 30 minutes. Serve this over **RICE** for a delicious meal.

YIELD: 6 TO 8 SERVINGS

BEEF STROGANOFF

Cut in very thin strips	1 pound **SIRLOIN**
Dip in.	⅓ cup **FLOUR**
Mixed with	1 tsp. **SALT**
	¼ tsp. **PEPPER**
Brown in	¼ cup **OIL**
Add and cook until clear	½ cup chopped **ONION**
Drain off grease and add	1 can **CREAM OF MUSHROOM SOUP,** undiluted
	1 can (8 oz.) sliced **MUSHROOMS,** drained

Cover and simmer 10 to 15 minutes. Add **SOUR CREAM** and remove from heat. Serve over **RICE.**

LARRY'S GERMAN RAGOUT

Melt in a medium saucepan	3 Tbsp. **BUTTER**
Add	1¾ pounds **SIRLOIN,** cut into ¼-inch strips

Brown well. Remove meat. Pour
  drippings into a cup.

Skim off	2 Tbsp. **DRIPPINGS** (off top)
Place in saucepan and add	3 Tbsp. **FLOUR**

Cook and stir about 1 minute. Remove from heat. Add **WATER** to drippings left in cup to make 1 cup. Add to flour mixture and blend well. Cook over medium heat, stirring constantly, until thickened.

Stir in	½ cup **WINE** (Germans use **BEER**)

Set aside.

In same skillet, melt	1 Tbsp. **BUTTER**
Add and cook until tender	¾ cup diced **GREEN PEPPERS**
	1 medium **ONION,** diced
	1½ cups **MUSHROOMS**
Add beef and gravy, plus	1 jar (4 oz.) **PIMIENTOS,** drained
	1 tsp. **SALT**
	Dash of **TABASCO**
	Dash of **WORCESTERSHIRE SAUCE**

Bring to a boil. Lower heat and simmer 20 minutes.

YIELD: 6 SERVINGS

STEAK SURPRISE
A delectable treat.

Bring to room temperature . . . . .   1 **SIRLOIN STEAK,** 2½ to 4 inches
thick

Completely cover all sides,
working into meat with the
fingers, a mixture of . . . .   1 pound **WHITE SUGAR,** superfine
¼ cup **BROWN SUGAR,** packed

Broil over a hot charcoal fire for 15 minutes on each side. Remove from
fire and place on a baking sheet in a preheated 350-degree oven. Bake approximately 10 minutes per inch of thickness of steak.

The *SURPRISE:* The sugar burns off and produces a juicy, medium rare
steak. (Don't call the fire department if the smoke alarms go off!)

YIELD: 6 TO 8 SERVINGS

BRUCE MAKES JERKY
Texas version.

Slice **BEEF** or **DEER STEAK** as thin as possible, no thicker than ¼ inch.
Cut diagonally across the grain of meat.
Put in a jar and shake until
mixed . . . .   2 tsp **SALT**
⅔ tsp. **MSG**
½ tsp. **ACCENT**
2 tsp. **LIQUID SMOKE**
½ cup **WORCESTERSHIRE SAUCE**
½ cup **SOY SAUCE**
2 tsp. **ONION POWDER**
1 tsp. **COARSE BLACK PEPPER**
(use more for hotter Jerky)
⅔ tsp. **GARLIC POWDER**

Marinate overnight. Place in 200 degree oven on cookie sheets. Bake 8 to
10 hours, turning meat several times. Store in plastic bags or covered glass
containers.

YIELD: APPROXIMATELY 3 POUNDS.

RATTLESNAKE

Skin, clean and cut into bite-size pieces. **Season** and dip in **BUTTERMILK.** Cover well with **FLOUR** or **CORNMEAL** (whichever you prefer). Fry in very hot fat until golden brown.

LOVE THAT DOVE

Thoroughly clean about 12 **DOVE BREASTS.** Brown on both sides in electric skillet with 3 Tablespoons **OIL.** Dissolve 1 **BOUILLON CUBE** in 1 cup warm **WATER.** Add 2 Tablespoons **SOY SAUCE** and ¼ cup **CLARET WINE.** Pour over birds. Cook at **220** degrees for 1 hour.

YIELD: 4 SERVINGS

QUAIL BAKED IN WINE
Allow 1 quail for each serving.

Saute in ½ cup **OIL** . . . .
  2 small **ONIONS,** minced
  2 whole **CLOVES**
  1 tsp. **PEPPERCORNS**
  2 cloves **GARLIC,** minced
  ½ **BAY LEAF**

Cook several minutes.
Add and brown well . . . .
  6 **QUAIL,** cleaned and trussed
Add . . . .
  2 cups **WHITE WINE**
  ½ tsp. **SALT**
  ⅛ tsp. **PEPPER**
  Dash of **CAYENNE**
  1 tsp. minced **CHIVES**

Simmer until tender, about 30 minutes. Remove quail to hot serving dish. Strain sauce, add 2 cups **CREAM** and heat to boiling point. Pour over quail.

YIELD: 6 SERVINGS

HEAT-PROOF GLASS: Lower oven 25 degrees to insure even baking.

PERFECT ROAST BEEF
This really works.

Use either .... **PRIME RIB, ROLLED** or **RUMP ROAST,** any size
SALT and **PEPPER**

Place in a roasting pan on a rack, uncovered, in a *preheated* 375-degree oven for *1 hour.* (Do this in mid-afternoon.) After 1 hour, turn off the oven, but *do not open* the oven door.

FOR RARE ROAST BEEF:
45 minutes before serving time, turn oven to 300 degrees.

FOR MEDIUM ROAST BEEF:
50 Minutes before serving time, turn oven to 300 degrees.

FOR MEDIUM WELL ROAST BEEF:
55 minutes before serving time, turn oven to 300 degrees.

Just follow the instructions and *Don't Peep, Don't Peep!*

ROAST AND GRAVY
Makes gravy while cooking.

Tear foil large enough to
   completely wrap .... 3 or 4 pound **CHUCK** or **SHOULDER ROAST**
Sprinkle with a little .... **SALT** and **PEPPER**
Place roast on foil and spread
   with .... 1 can **CREAM OF MUSHROOM SOUP,** undiluted
Sprinkle with .... 1 package **DRY ONION SOUP MIX**

Wrap tightly and place in pan. Bake in preheated 300 degree oven for 2½ to 3 hours.

YIELD: 6 TO 8 SERVINGS

SUNDAY DINNER POT ROAST
Old faithful.

Sprinkle generously . . . . 4 pound **ROAST** of your choice
with . . . . **SEASON SALT**
Place in uncovered, heavy, deep pan. Place in hot oven and sear, turning
to brown all sides.
When very lightly browned,
   pour in . . . . 2 cups **WATER**
Reduce heat to 300 degrees and cover with lid. Cook 1½ to 2 hours.
Add . . . . 3 **POTATOES,** quartered
                             3 **ONIONS,** quartered
                             3 **CARROTS,** quartered
Season vegetables with . . . . **SALT** and **PEPPER**

Continue cooking for 1 hour or longer. Remove roast and vegetables to a
platter and make **ROAST GRAVY.**

ROAST GRAVY

Mix . . . . 2 to 3 Tbsp. **FLOUR**
                             ½ cup **WATER**
                             SALT and **PEPPER**
                             ¼ tsp. **CHILI POWDER**

Stir into liquid from **ROAST.** Cook and stir until slightly thickened. This is
one that you will need to taste to get the flavor you want.

YIELD: 8 SERVINGS

COKE STEAK
Very tender.

Cut in serving pieces . . . . 1 pound **ROUND STEAK**
Mix and dip steak into . . . . ½ cup **FLOUR**
                             ½ tsp. **SALT**
                             ¼ tsp. **PEPPER**
Brown in . . . . ¼ cup **SHORTENING**
Cover with . . . . 1 medium **ONION,** sliced
Add . . . . 4 Tbsp. **CATSUP**
                             2 cups **COCO-COLA**

Simmer on low heat until meat is tender. If it gets too dry, add more **COKE**
or a little **WATER,** and continue cooking, for about 45 to 50 minutes, or
until done.

YIELD: 4 SERVINGS

INDIVIDUAL BAKED STEAKS
So you're cooking for yourself tonight??

For each serving, cut a piece of aluminum foil large enough to completely wrap up meat. Place on foil . . . .   1 serving **ROUND STEAK,** about the size of a saucer

or . . . .   ⅓ pound **GROUND ROUND**

Cover with . . . .   1 large **POTATO,** sliced in ¼-inch slices

   1 medium **ONION,** sliced

Season with . . . .   **SALT** and **PEPPER**

   GARLIC SALT (optional)

Wrap in foil and crumple ends together. Place on flat pan, just in case it leaks. Bake at 350 degrees for 1 hour.

YIELD: 1 SERVING

SON-IN-LAW STEAK IN A CROCK
Jack's specialty for Brenda, Colby, and Christopher, too.

Spray crock pot with **OIL.** Cut into 4 serving pieces . . . .   1 pound **ROUND STEAK**

Season meat by wetting both sides with . . . .   **WORCESTERSHIRE SAUCE**

Then sprinkle with . . . .   **SEASON ALL**

and a dash of . . . .   **GARLIC SALT**

Peel and slice into ½-inch slices . . . .   2 medium **POTATOES**

Slice into ¼-inch slices . . . .   ½ **BELL PEPPER**

Slice thinly . . . .   ½ medium **ONION**

Open . . . .   1 can **VEG-ALL**

Start layering with about one-fourth of the vegetables, then top with meat. Repeat until all ingredients are used.

Then pour in . . . .   1 cup **RED BURGUNDY WINE**

If needed, add **WATER** until all is covered by 1 to 2 inches of liquid. Cook on *High* for 4 hours, or *Low* for 6 to 8 hours.

YIELD: 4 SERVINGS

"A REAL MAN'S" CHEESEBURGER QUICHE

Make favorite quiche **PASTRY**, or use frozen **PASTRY SHELL**. Prepare by brushing with a very small amount of **EGG WHITE**. Bake 10 minutes at 425 degrees. Cool.

Melt in skillet over high heat ...   2 Tbsp. **BUTTER**
When very hot, fry until
browned .... ¾ pound **GROUND MEAT,** very
                          lean
Drain well. Season with .... **SALT** and **PEPPER**
Place in prepared pastry.
   Sprinkle over meat.......... ½ cup grated **SHARP CHEDDAR**
                            CHEESE
Make a custard of .... 1 cup **CREAM**
                            1 **EGG**
                            2 **EGG YOLKS**
                            ¼ tsp. **SALT**
                            ⅛ tsp. **CAYENNE**
                            ⅛ tsp. **NUTMEG**

Pour custard over cheese and meat. Bake in preheated 375-degree oven for 35 to 45 minutes, or until custard is puffed and tests completely done, and pastry is nicely browned. Allow to rest 5 minutes before serving. Serve warm with **SALAD** and **DESSERT**.

YIELD: 4 TO 6 SERVINGS

VARIATION:
CHILIBURGER QUICHE: Follow recipe above. Sprinkle 1 teaspoon **CHILI POWDER** over the grated cheese. Pour on custard, bake as directed.

TEXAS FRIED STEAK
Also for chicken or chicken livers.

Cut into convenient serving
   portions .... **ROUND STEAK** (have your
                            butcher tenderize)
Sprinkle with .... **SALT** and **PEPPER**
Dip into a shallow bowl of ..... **BUTTERMILK**
Mix together in separate bowl .. **FLOUR**
                            SALT and **PEPPER,** scant

Dip steak in buttermilk and then flour. Fry in hot **SHORTENING** and drain on paper towels.

VARIATION:
1 beaten **EGG** with **SWEET MILK** added may be used instead of the **BUTTERMILK.** Use just sweet milk for a thinner crust.

ANKIE'S MEAT BALLS

Have in deep freeze ready for guests.

Combine and mix well	1 pound **GROUND BEEF**
	1 **EGG**
	1 tsp. **SALT**
	¼ tsp. **PEPPER**
	½ cup crushed **CRACKERS**
Form into 1½-inch balls and sprinkle with	**GARLIC SALT**

Brown in hot **OIL.** Make **SPAGHETTI SAUCE** and add meatballs; simmer a few minutes. Serve over cooked **SPAGHETTI.** Grate **CHEESE** and sprinkle on top.

YIELD: 8 SERVINGS

SPAGHETTI SAUCE

Saute	1 cup chopped **ONION**
	1 clove **GARLIC,** crushed
in	¼ cup **OIL**
Add	1 can (2 lb. 3 oz.) **ITALIAN TOMATOES**
	2 cans (6 oz. each) **TOMATO PASTE**
	¼ tsp. dried **OREGANO LEAVES**
	1 tsp. **SALT**
	⅛ tsp. **PEPPER**
	1 tsp. dried **BASIL LEAVES**
	2 Tbsp. **SUGAR**
	2 Tbsp. chopped **PARSLEY**
	½ cup **WATER**

Bring to a boil, reduce heat and simmer, covered, 1½ hours. Stir occasionally. Add **MEAT BALLS** and simmer a few minutes. Serve over cooked **SPAGHETTI.** Top with grated **CHEESE.**

STICKY PASTA? Add 1 to 2 Tablespoons salad oil to the cooking water.

BIRDWELL CASSEROLE

Saute until clear in a small amount of **MAZOLA OIL**	3	medium **ONIONS**, chopped
	2	cups chopped **CELERY**
Add	2	pounds **GROUND MEAT**
Cook until meat is done.		
Add to taste		**SALT** and **PEPPER**
Heat separately	3	cans **MUSHROOM SOUP**
	1½	soup cans **WATER**
	1	small can pitted and chopped **RIPE OLIVES**
	½	pound **AMERICAN CHEESE**
When cheese and soup are blended, add	1	can **ENGLISH PEAS**, drained
	1	can **PIMIENTOS**, chopped
When heated, add meat mixture and season with plenty of		**LAWRY'S SEASONED SALT**
Cook according to directions	16	oz. **EGG NOODLES**

Grease 2 large casseroles and layer with noodles, then meat mixture. Repeat. Top with **PARMESAN CHEESE** and **PAPRIKA**. Bake at 350 degrees for 30 minutes or until completely hot. This recipe freezes well.

YIELD: 18 SERVINGS

CHEESY MEATY BROCCOLI

Super easy supper

Cook according to directions	1	pkg. frozen **CHOPPED BROCCOLI**
Brown separately	1	pound **GROUND BEEF**
	1	small **ONION**, chopped
Add to taste		**SALT** and **PEPPER**

Spread broccoli in greased 6x9-inch baking dish. Top with meat and onion mixture.

Cover with	1	can **CREAM OF MUSHROOM SOUP**, undiluted
Grate and sprinkle on top	½	pound **AMERICAN CHEESE**

Bake in 350 degree oven until hot through and through. (Or microwave until hot.)

YIELD: 6 SERVINGS

GOULASH
Excellent for a cold night.

In a large skillet brown
   together . . . . 1½ pounds **GROUND BEEF**
                                 1 large **ONION,** chopped
Season with . . . .   **GARLIC SALT** and **PEPPER**
                                   1 tsp. **CHILI POWDER** (optional)
Add . . . . 1 can **TOMATOES**
Cook separately in salted water
   until tender . . . . ½ box **MACARONI**

Drain, add to meat mixture and simmer on low for 15 minutes. Pour into individual bowls. Serve with **CORNBREAD** or **CRACKERS.**

YIELD: 6 SERVINGS

HAMBURGER CORNPONE PIE
A one-dish meal.

Brown in skillet . . . . 1 pound **GROUND MEAT**
                                   ½ cup chopped **ONION**
Add . . . . 2 Tbsp. **CHILI POWDER**
                               1½ tsp. **SALT**
                               1 Tbsp. **WORCESTERSHIRE SAUCE**
                               ½ tsp. **PEPPER**
                               1 cup **TOMATOES**
Cover and simmer over low heat
   for 15 minutes. Add . . . . 1 cup **PINTO BEANS,** cooked or canned
Pour into greased baking dish.
Top with . . . . 1½ cups **CORNBREAD BATTER**

Carefully spread with a wet knife. Bake in a preheated 425 degree oven for 20 to 30 minutes, or until cornbread is browned.

YIELD: 6 SERVINGS

CHOPPED ONIONS: Added to a casserole have best flavor if browned first.

JAMBALAYA
Karla's treat.

Brown in skillet until crumbly... 1 pound **GROUND BEEF**
½ cup chopped **ONION**
⅓ cup chopped **BELL PEPPER**
Add . . . . 1 clove **GARLIC,** chopped
⅓ cup uncooked **RICE**
1 tsp. **SALT**
½ tsp. **BLACK PEPPER**
OTHER SEASONINGS to taste
1 can **TOMATO SOUP**
1 soup can **WATER**

Stir all together. Cover tightly with lid and simmer on medium-low for 35 minutes. *Do not pick up lid until the time is up.*

YIELD: 6 SERVINGS

MAMA'S OLE COUNTRY ITALIAN SAUCE
Double and freeze so you will always have it on hand.

Slightly brown, drain and set
aside . . . . 1½ pounds **GROUND CHUCK,** very
lean
SALT to taste
Heat. . . . . ¼ cup **OLIVE OIL**
Add and brown slightly . .   . . 1 clove **GARLIC,** crushed
1 medium **ONION,** chopped
Add . . . . 1 can **ITALIAN TOMATOES**
1 can **HUNT'S TOMATO SAUCE**
1½ cups **WATER**
Add meat, and simmer slowly 1½ hours.
Add the last 15 minutes of
cooking . . . . 1 cup chopped **CELERY**
1 cup **MUSHROOMS**

Cook **SPAGHETTI, LASAGNA,** or **NOODLES** while the sauce is cooking. This stores very well in the refrigerator, if you omit the meat.

YIELD: 8 SERVINGS

MARVELOUS MEAT LOAF

Combine in a bowl . . . . 2 pounds **GROUND ROUND STEAK**
2 **EGGS**
1½ cups **BREAD CRUMBS**
¾ cup **CATSUP**
1 tsp. **MONOSODIUM GLUTAMATE**
½ cup **WARM WATER**
1 package **DRY ONION SOUP MIX**

Mix thoroughly and place in a loaf pan.
Cover with . . . . 2 strips **BACON**
Pour over all . . . . 1 can (8 oz.) **TOMATO SAUCE**

Bake at 350 degrees for 1 to 1½ hours. This will slice easier if allowed to cool slightly.

YIELD: 8 SERVINGS

MEAT 'N' BEAN BAKE
Super easy!

Cook until crumbly . . . . 2 pounds **GROUND MEAT**
2 slices **BACON,** cut up
1 small **ONION,** chopped
Add . . . . ½ cup **CATSUP**
½ tsp. **WORCESTERSHIRE SAUCE**
½ tsp. **SALT**
¼ tsp. **DRY MUSTARD**
2 cans **PORK AND BEANS**

Mix all together and pour into a greased casserole. (If desired, make ahead and place in refrigerator until ready to heat for serving. Use a baking dish that will go from refrigerator to oven.) Bake in 350-degree oven for 20 to 30 minutes.

YIELD: 8 TO 10 SERVINGS

QUICK MEAT LOAF: Bake in muffin tins. Top with catsup or tomato sauce, bake in 350 degree oven for 20 minutes.

QUICK SCRAMBLE
Couldn't be easier.

Brown in large skillet .... 1½ pounds **GROUND MEAT**
Add .... 1 can **PINTO BEANS**
1 can (16 oz.) **TOMATO JUICE**
1 small **ONION**, chopped
1 Tbsp. **CHILI POWDER**
Add to taste .... **SALT** and **PEPPER**

Simmer for 20 minutes. Serve over cooked **RICE**. Add a **TOSSED SALAD** and **CORNBREAD**. *Super!*

YIELD: 8 SERVINGS

MINER'S DELIGHT
The family will cheer for these.

1 recipe **PANCAKES:** Beat 6 **EGGS**, 1 cup **MILK**, 1½ cups **FLOUR** and ½ teaspoon **SALT** together. Bake on a lightly greased, moderately hot crepe pan on one side only. Makes 16.

1 recipe **MEAT FILLING:** Cook 2 cups chopped **ONION** and 1 minced clove **GARLIC** in 1 tablespoon **OLIVE OIL**; add ½ pound chopped **MUSHROOMS**; remove from heat. Stir in 1½ pounds ground **BEEF**, 1½ cups diced **MOZZARELLA** or **SWISS CHEESE**, 1 cup soft **BREAD CRUMBS**, 1 **EGG**, 1½ teaspoons **SALT**, and ¼ teaspoon each **OREGANO** and **PEPPER**.

1 recipe **CHEESE FILLING:** Combine 1½ cups **RICOTTA CHEESE**, ½ cup grated **ROMANO CHEESE**, ¼ cup chopped **PARSLEY**, 2 **EGGS**, 1½ teaspoons **SALT** and ⅛ teaspoon **PEPPER**.

Spoon meat filling on 8 pancakes; cheese filling on remainder. Roll and place seam side down in a greased 13x9x2-inch baking dish. Spoon 1 16-ounce jar **SPAGHETTI SAUCE** with **MUSHROOMS** over all. Sprinkle with 1 cup shredded **MOZZARELLA** or **SWISS CHEESE**. Bake in a 350 degree oven for 30 to 40 minutes.

YIELD: 8 SERVINGS

MINER'S PIES

A Colorado miner's wife gave this recipe to Mrs. Noble.
The miner's carry them in their lunch pails.

PIE DOUGH:

Dissolve in ½ cup **WATER**	1 **YEAST CAKE**
	1 Tbsp. **SUGAR**
Let set 5 to 10 minutes.	
Heat to lukewarm.	2 Tbsp. **BUTTER**
	½ cup **MILK**
Remove from heat and add	½ cup more **MILK**
	½ scant tsp. **SALT**

Stir in yeast mixture. Add 3 cups **FLOUR.** (one-half cup at a time). Dough will be slightly thicker than for rolls. Let rise until double in bulk. Make dough into balls about 1-inch in diameter. Roll as thin as possible. Spread mixture in middle of circle. Wet edges and fold. Seal with finger tips. Place on greased cookie sheets. Bake 15 to 18 minutes at 425 degrees.

YIELD: 12 TO 15 PIES.

MEAT MIXTURE:

Brown in heavy saucepan	1 pound **GROUND MEAT**
	1 large **ONION,** diced
Add	**SALT** and **PEPPER** to taste
	Dash of **CAYENNE**
	3 Tbsp. **WORCESTERSHIRE SAUCE**
	2 Tbsp. **SOY SAUCE**
In separate pan, stir fry	½ head **CABBAGE,** shredded
	1 Tbsp. **OIL**

Combine cabbage and meat. Let completely cool before putting in pastry.

SHERI'S SMOTHERED HAMBURGER STEAKS

Combine and mix lightly . . . . 2 pounds lean **GROUND BEEF**
SEASONED SALT, PEPPER, and
GARLIC POWDER to taste
2 Tbsp. **WORCESTERSHIRE**
SAUCE
¼ large **ONION,** finely chopped

Separate mixture into 4 equal patties, about 1 inch thick. Brown in skillet, adding **OIL** if needed. Drain and set aside while making **GRAVY:**
Remove meat from skillet and
replace with . . . . 2 Tbsp. **COOKING OIL**
Saute until clear . . . . ¾ large **ONION,** sliced into rings
Add and cook until light brown,
stirring constantly . . . . 2 Tbsp. **FLOUR**
SALT and **PEPPER**
Add while stirring . . . . 1 large can (8 oz.) **MUSHROOM**
STEMS AND PIECES, with
liquid
1 cup **BEEF BOUILLON** (or 1 cup
WATER with 1 **BEEF**
BOUILLON CUBE)
1 tsp. KITCHEN BOUQUET

Return meat patties to skillet. Cover and simmer about 20 minutes, stirring occasionally, until meat is done and gravy thickens. (Add more **BEEF BOUILLON** or **WATER,** if gravy becomes too thick.

YIELD: 4 SERVINGS

VARIATION: *SURPRISE HAMBURGER STEAKS.* Divide meat mixture into 8 patties, ½-inch thick. Place a chunk of **CHEDDAR CHEESE** between 2 patties, sandwich-style. Moisten fingers and press edges together. sealing well. Repeat with remaining patties. Brown and cook as above, being careful not to pierce meat while cooking. (Also good with **GREEN CHILIES** inside double patties, with or without the cheese.)

FREEZING: Meat patties, steaks, or chops, separate with two thicknesses of wrapping paper for easy separation.

STUFFED CABBAGE
Fit for a king.

Bring 1 cup **WATER** to a boil
and steam for 5 minutes . . . . .   8 to 10 **CABBAGE LEAVES**
Drain and reserve liquid for
sauce.
Combine . . . . 1½ pounds **GROUND BEEF**
    ½ **GREEN PEPPER,** chopped
    1 large **ONION,** chopped
  1½ tsp. **SALT**
    ½ tsp. **GARLIC SALT**
    ½ tsp. **PEPPER**
    3 **EGGS,** beaten
    ¾ cup regular **RICE,** uncooked
    2 Tbsp. grated **ROMANO CHEESE**
      (optional)

Mix well. Place about ¼ cup meat mixture on each cabbage leaf; roll up, turning edges in, and secure with toothpicks. Place rolls in a dutch oven, and cover with **SAUCE.** Cover and simmer 45 minutes.

YIELD: 8 TO 10 ROLLS

SAUCE

Saute . . . .   2 cloves **GARLIC,** minced
in . . . .   ¼ cup **OIL**
Remove from heat and
blend in . . . .   2 Tbsp. **FLOUR**
Gradually add . . . .   reserved **CABBAGE LIQUID**
Stir until smooth. Add . . . .   2 cans (15 oz. each) **TOMATO**
    SAUCE
    2 tsp. **SUGAR**
    1 tsp. **PAPRIKA**
    ½ tsp. **PEPPER**
    ⅛ tsp. **BASIL** (optional)
    SALT to taste

TOM'S BACHELOR PARTY SPAGHETTI SAUCE
Men love this robust meal.

Slightly brown in a medium-size
    skillet . . . .   1 pound **GROUND ROUND,** lean
                                    1 **ONION,** diced
                                   ½ **GREEN PEPPER,** diced
Stir in . . . .   1 can (15 oz.) **TOMATO SAUCE**
                                    1 can (12 oz.) **TOMATO PASTE**
                                    1 pkg. **ITALIAN STYLE**
                                         SPAGHETTI SAUCE MIX
                                   ½ Tbsp. **SUGAR**
                                   1 cup **WATER**
                                   ½ cup **RED WINE**
                                    SALT and **PEPPER**

Bring to a rolling boil. Reduce heat, cover, and simmer 1½ hours. Stir occasionally to pervent burning on bottom. Serve hot over 1 package cooked **SPAGHETTI.**

YIELD: 8 SERVINGS

STUFFED GREEN PEPPERS
Easy and yummy.

Cut tops from . . . .   4 **GREEN BELL PEPPERS**
Remove seeds and membrane. Pre-cook in boiling water for 5 minutes and
    drain.
In medium skillet, brown . . . .   1 pound **GROUND BEEF**
                                    ⅓ cup minced **ONION**
Add . . . .   1 **EGG,** slightly beaten
                                   1 cup soft **BREAD CRUMBS**
                                   1 tsp. **SALT**
                                   ½ tsp. **POULTRY SEASONING**
                                   ¼ tsp. **PEPPER**
Add enough to moisten of . . . . . .   1 can (8 oz.) **TOMATO SAUCE**

Stuff peppers with mixture and arrange in a baking dish. Top with grated **CHEESE.** Pour remaining tomato sauce around the peppers. Cover and bake for 30 to 40 minutes at 350 degrees.

YIELD: 4 SERVINGS

✓ SUE'S HAMBURGER STEAK WITH MUSHROOM GRAVY
Quick and easy.

Mix .... 2 pounds **GROUND MEAT**
½ package **DRY ONION SOUP MIX**
1 **EGG**
Make into thick patties. Brown in skillet. Pour off grease.
Combine and pour over
meat .... 1 can **MUSHROOM SOUP**
½ package **DRY ONION SOUP MIX**
½ can **WATER**

Cover and simmer until done. Very good served with **RICE**.

YIELD: 8 SERVINGS

WEDNESDAY NITE POKER PARTY STROGANOFF
A winner every time.

Cook in large skillet until all
redness is gone .... 2 pounds **GROUND MEAT**
Add .... 1 cup chopped **ONION**
Stir in .... ½ tsp. **SALT**
½ tsp. **PEPPER**
1 tsp. **MONOSODIUM
GLUTAMATE**
2 cups **CREAM OF MUSHROOM
SOUP,** undiluted
Simmer about 10 minutes. Just
before serving, add .... 1 carton **SOUR CREAM**
Serve this over .... **FRITO CORN CHIPS**

Add a tossed **SALAD, DESSERT** and you have a great meal. This can be
halved if need be.

YIELD; 8 SERVINGS

I.G. HOLMES'S SPICED TONGUE

Menu for husband who's late for dinner: Hot Tongue & Cold Shoulder.

Wash and remove any visible fat
and small bones . . . . 1 or 2 **BEEF TONGUES** (2½ to 3
pounds each)

Place in pressure cooker and
add . . . . 1 cup **CIDER VINEGAR**
½ cup **WINE VINEGAR** or
COOKING SHERRY
2 cloves **GARLIC**
2 **BAY LEAVES**
2 Tbsp. **DRIED MINCED ONION**
½ tsp. **DRIED RED PEPPERS**
(optional)
½ tsp. each any combination, or all
**TARRAGON, DILL SEED,
ROSEMARY, MARJORAM,
THYME**
1 tsp. each **OREGANO, SWEET
BASIL**
¼ tsp. **CAYENNE PEPPER**
1 tsp. **SALT**

Add **WATER** to bring liquid level in pressure cooker to about ⅔ full. Cook
at 15 pounds pressure (or with pressure gauge just rocking slightly) for 45
minutes for 1 tongue, to 1 hour and 15 minutes for 2 tongues. After all
pressure has gone down in cooker, remove tongues and peel tough skin off.
(Skin will come off in large pieces.) Slice meat and serve hot with some of
cooking liquid as dip or gravy. Or, slice and serve warm on dark **BREAD
(RYE, PUMPERNICKEL, etc.)** with **HORSERADISH SAUCE.** Delicious served cold as sandwiches or tongue salad.

LIVER AND ONIONS

Pour boiling water over sliced **CALVES' LIVER.** Let set for 10 minutes. Heat
small amount of **SHORTENING** in heavy skillet. Saute at least 1 large
ONION, sliced. Remove and keep onions warm. Remove calve's liver from
water. Drain on paper towel. Season with **SALT** and **PEPPER. FLOUR** the
pieces. Saute until lightly brown and top with onions.

BARBECUED RIBS
A hearty cold-weather dish!!

Sear well . . . . 2 pounds **RIBS (STEW MEAT** may
be used)
Sprinkle with . . . . **SALT**
Mix and pour over meat . . . . 1 Tbsp. **VINEGAR**
1 Tbsp. **WORCESTERSHIRE SAUCE**
¼ cup **CATSUP**
2½ cups **WATER**

Bake in tightly covered pan in 350-degree oven. Add a little **WATER** if necessary. When tender, remove lid and brown under broiler for a few minutes.

YIELD: 6 TO 8 SERVINGS

BARBECUED SPARERIBS

Cut into serving pieces . . . . 4 to 5 pounds **SPARERIBS**
Place in shallow pan, meaty-side-up. Roast at 450 degrees for 30 minutes.
Drain and discard fat.
Meanwhile, combine and simmer
15 to 20 minutes . . . . 1 cup **CATSUP**
2 tsp. **SALT**
½ tsp. **PEPPER**
¼ cup **WORCESTERSHIRE SAUCE**
1½ cups **DR. PEPPER**
¼ cup **VINEGAR**
2 tsp. **PAPRIKA**
2 tsp. **CHILI POWDER**
1 cup finely chopped **ONION**

Spoon sauce over ribs. Reduce oven temperature to 250 degrees and roast ribs, basting frequently, until tender.

YIELD: 4 TO 6 SERVINGS

CLEAN GRILL: Turn gas barbecue grill to high for 10 minutes to clean rock.

BONELESS BEEF BRISKET
Smells as good as it tastes.

Take a . . . .   4 to 5 pound **BRISKET**
Mix and pour over brisket . . . . .   1 tsp. **CELERY SALT**
    1 tsp. **ONION SALT**
    1 tsp. **GARLIC SALT**
    4 ounces **LIQUID SMOKE**
    ½ cup **WORCESTERSHIRE SAUCE**

Cover tightly and marinate overnight. Place in a covered pan and bake at 275 degrees for 5 hours. Uncover and drain.
Pour over brisket . . . .   6 ounces **KRAFT HICKORY BAR-B-QUE SAUCE**

Cook 1 hour longer. Slice and serve.

YIELD: 8 TO 10 SERVINGS

BRISKET BAR-B-QUE
When time allows, Bruce V. uses the smoker.

Sprinkle . . . .   1 **BRISKET**
    1 tsp. **ONION SALT**
with . . . .   1 tsp. **CELERY SALT**
    2 Tbsp. **WORCESTERSHIRE SAUCE**
    2 Tbsp. **LIQUID SMOKE**

Place on rack with pan underneath it. Baste 3 or 4 times during cooking with drippings. Bake at 250 degrees for 5 hours. This will slice easier if allowed to cool. Slice thin and serve.

YIELD: 10 TO 12 SERVINGS

QUICK MEAL: Split frankfurters nearly in half and fill with thin slices of Cheddar cheese. Then broil . . . ready in 10 minutes.

BASTING SAUCE
Use for charcoal grilled steaks.

Melt in small saucepan . . . .   1 stick **BUTTER**
Add . . . .   2 Tbsp. **GARLIC SALT**
                    ¼ tsp. **BLACK PEPPER**
                    1 Tbsp. **WORCESTERSHIRE SAUCE**
                    1 Tbsp. **SOY SAUCE**
                    1 Tbsp. **HEINZ 57 SAUCE**

Mix all together, brush over **STEAKS** as they cook. Will keep indefinitely in refrigerator in covered container. Melt slightly when ready to use.

BEER BAR-B-QUE SAUCE
Tom Hunter's "no longer secret" recipe.

Blend . . . .   3 bottles **HEINZ BAR-B-QUE SAUCE**
                    1 package **HIDDEN VALLEY ITALIAN DRESSING MIX**

Thin to good spreading consistency with **BEER.** Cook **MEAT** on charcoal grill. Baste several times during cooking. Serve extra sauce with meal. Will keep in the refrigerator for several weeks.

SONNY'S BARBECUE SAUCE

	For 20-25 pounds meat		For 250 pounds meat	
Melt	¾	pound **BUTTER**	6	pounds **BUTTER**
Add	1	cup **VINEGAR**	1	gallon **VINEGAR**
	4	Tbsp. **BLACK PEPPER**	1	pound **BLACK PEPPER**
	1	Tbsp. **RED PEPPER**	2	ounces **RED PEPPER**
	9	ounces **PREPARED MUSTARD**	5	quarts **PREPARED MUSTARD**
	2	Tbsp. **CHILI POWDER**	1	bottle **CHILI POWDER**
	1	ounce **LEA & PERRINS SAUCE**	3	pounds **LEA & PERRINS SAUCE**
	1½	cups **SUGAR**	5	pounds **SUGAR**
	2	Tbsp. **SALT**	2	pounds **SALT**
	2	ounces **LEMON JUICE**	18	ounces **LEMON JUICE**

Simmer 3 to 4 minutes. Baste meat often during cooking.

CHICKEN FRIED BACON
A real treat.

Dip . . . .   thick sliced **BACON**
in . . . .   **BUTTERMILK**
then in . . . .   **FLOUR**
seasoned with . . . .   **SALT** and **PEPPER**

Fry in hot **VEGETABLE OIL** until golden brown. Drain on paper towels.

BAKED HAM WITH APRICOTS

Peel skin and trim excess fat from a 12 to 14 pound "ready-to-eat" **HAM.**
Score fat in a diamond pattern with a sharp knife. Place in a shallow baking pan. Place a whole **CLOVE** in the crossed point of each diamond. Spread
prepared **DIJON-STYLE MUSTARD** over top and sides. Sprinkle with about
1 cup **BROWN SUGAR.** Pour 3 cups **APPLE JUICE** into the bottom of the
pan. Bake 1½ hours at 350 degrees. Baste frequently. (Meantime, make
GLAZED APRICOTS.)

YIELD: 24 SERVINGS

GLAZED APRICOTS

Combine in a small saucepan . . .   1 pound **DRIED APRICOTS**
    1 cup **MADEIRA WINE**

Bring to a boil, cover and remove from heat. Let set until the last 30 minutes
of baking time of **HAM.** Add to ham and continue to bake and baste. Transfer
ham to serving dish. Decorate with apricots, securing them with toothpicks.
Skim fat from pan juices and pour sauce into a gravy dish. This will serve
approximately 24 people. Freeze leftovers. Use for sandwiches, casseroles,
canapes, etc. The possibilities are endless for uses of ham.

BACON TRICK: Coat bacon with flour to keep from curling.

COMPANY FARE PORK CHOPS

Ask butcher to cut 8 2-rib **PORK CHOPS,** with pocket slit for stuffing.

Mix together	2 cups **FROZEN CORN**
	2 cups **WHITE BREAD CRUMBS**
	1 tsp. **SALT**
	¼ tsp. **PEPPER**
Saute	1 Tbsp. chopped **ONION**
	2 Tbsp. chopped **PARSLEY**
	1 Tbsp. **BUTTER**
Add to corn mixture with	1 **EGG,** beaten
	1 cup chopped **APPLE**
Stir in	½ cup **CREAM**
	1 tsp. **POULTRY SEASONING**

Stuff pockets in pork chops. Brown on both sides in a heavy skillet. Sprinkle with **SALT** and **PEPPER.** Add 1 cup **WATER.** Cover and bake at 350 degrees for 1½ to 2 hours. Add more liquid, if necessary.

YIELD: 8 SERVINGS

EASY CHOPS
'N' Rice.

Melt in a large skillet	3 Tbsp. **SHORTENING**
Add and brown	6 to 8 **PORK CHOPS**
Remove, set aside and add to grease	1 cup chopped **ONION**
	2 cups chopped **CELERY**
When tender, add	1 cup regular **RICE**
	1 can **BEEF CONSOMME**
	1½ cups **WATER**

Pour into a greased casserole dish and place pork chops on top. Bake in 350 degree oven for 45 to 60 minutes, or until rice is tender.

YIELD: 6 TO 8 SERVINGS

WILD RICE AND PORK CHOP BAKE

Brown in skillet	6	**PORK CHOPS** (¾-inch thick)
in	3	Tbsp. **BUTTER**
Remove chops and stir in	1	pkg. (6 oz.) **LONG GRAIN AND WILD RICE (UNCLE BEN'S)**
	1	cup chopped **CELERY**
	1	cup chopped **ONION**
	1	can **CREAM OF CHICKEN SOUP**
	2½	cups **WATER**
	¼	cup **PIMIENTOS**
	½	tsp. **SALT**

Mix, heat and stir until bubbly and liquids are dissolved. Pour into a greased 2-quart baking dish. Arrange chops on rice, brown side up. Sprinkle with **SALT,** cover with foil. Bake in 375 degree oven for 1 hour.

YIELD: 6 SERVINGS

VARIATION:
Substitute **CHICKEN BREASTS,** brown and place on rice. Sprinkle with **PAPRIKA** and **ALMONDS.**

ROBERTSONS GLAZED TENDERLOIN

Cover 2 to 3 pound **TENDERLOIN** with a mixture of **BROWN SUGAR** and **HONEY.** (May prefer to use a small jar of **APRICOT** or **PEACH PRESERVES.**) Wrap tightly with foil. Place in a pan that has 1 cup **WATER** in the bottom. Bake 2 to 3 hours at 350 degrees until tender.

CAJUN CHICKEN
Passed from a CAJUN to a TEXAN.

Cut into serving pieces .... | 1 **CHICKEN** (or use 6 **CHICKEN BREASTS**)
Sprinkle with .... | **SALT**
| **PEPPER**
| **GARLIC SALT**
Beat together .... | 1 **EGG YOLK**
| 1½ Tbsp. **HONEY**

Baste chicken with honey and egg mixture. Place in a baking dish and dot with **BUTTER**. Bake at 350 degrees for 45 minutes. Keep it moist while it is baking with additional butter.

YIELD: 6 SERVINGS

CHICKEN-ALMOND CASSEROLE

Mix and place in a large
casserole .... | 2 cooked **CHICKENS**, boned and chopped
| 1 package **UNCLE BEN'S WILD RICE** with **HERBS**, cooked in 2½ cups **BROTH** from chicken
| 2 cans **FRENCH STYLE GREEN BEANS**, drained
| 1½ cups **HELLMAN'S MAYONNAISE**
| 1 jar (2 oz.) **PIMIENTOS**
| 1 **ONION**, chopped
| 1 can **WATER CHESTNUTS**, sliced
| 1 can **CREAM OF CELERY SOUP**
| 1 cup slivered **ALMONDS**

Sprinkle generously with **PARMESAN CHEESE** and **PAPRIKA**. Bake uncovered in a 350 degree oven for 30 to 40 minutes.

YIELD: 8 TO 10 SERVINGS

CHICKEN: Freeze dejointed fryers or parts on a cookie sheet; the wrap. It's easier to thaw.

CHICKEN ALPINE

Combine and pour into a greased
    casserole . . . .   4 cups cooked and chopped
                                  CHICKEN
                                2 cups chopped **CELERY**
                                ¼ cup chopped **ONION**
                                1 cup **MAYONNAISE**
                                2 cups **PEPPERIDGE FARM**
                                    STUFFING
                                1 cup **MILK**
                                1 tsp. **SALT**
                                PEPPER to taste
Top with . . . .   8 ounces **SWISS CHEESE,** sliced
                                ¼ cup slivered **ALMONDS**

Bake in a preheated 350 degree oven for 30 to 40 minutes.

YIELD: 6 SERVINGS

CRANBERRY CHICKEN
Different and good!

Parboil until tender . . . .   1 **CHICKEN** or **CHICKEN PARTS**
Meanwhile mix . . . .   1 can **WHOLE CRANBERRY**
                                  SAUCE
                                1 bottle **WISHBONE FRENCH**
                                  DRESSING
                                ½ cup **WATER**
                                1 package **LIPTON ONION SOUP**
                                MIX

Drain chicken well and dip each piece in mixture. Place in a greased casserole dish and pour rest of mixture over chicken. Cover and bake in 325 degree oven for 1 hour.

YIELD: 6 SERVINGS

FREEZING CASSEROLE: Line dish with heavy-duty foil, then fill and cover with foil. Place in freezer. When frozen, remove from dish, mark and date. Return to same dish when ready to heat and serve.

CHICKEN BREASTS SUPREME

Place each on a square of heavy- duty aluminum foil	4 **CHICKEN BREASTS**
Combine	1 can **CREAM OF MUSHROOM SOUP,** undiluted
	1 package **DRY ONION SOUP MIX**

Spread on each chicken breast. Wrap foil securely and place on cookie sheet to bake at 350 degrees for 1 hour.

YIELD: 4 SERVINGS

CHICKEN TETRAZZINI

Handy to make ahead and have in the freezer for surprise guests or for a dinner party.

Cook in boiling **SALTED WATER** until done, then set aside	1 box **SPAGHETTI,** small elbow kind
Melt in pan	1 stick **BUTTER**
Chop and add	½ cup **ONION**
	½ large **BELL PEPPER**
	1 small jar **PIMIENTO**
Add	3 cans (5 oz. each) **BONED CHICKEN**
	SALT and **PEPPER**
	1 can **CREAM OF MUSHROOM SOUP**

Drain and add spaghetti. Mix all ingredients together, and place in a large greased baking dish. Top with . . ½ pound **AMERICAN CHEESE,** grated

Bake in 350-degree oven until hot through and through.

YIELD: 6 TO 8 SERVINGS

CREAM GRAVY: Heat in skillet, 3 Tablespoons drippings from fried foods. Add and brown, 3 Tablespoons flour, ¾ teaspoon salt, ¼ teaspoon pepper. Then add 3 cups milk. Stir until thickened to right consistency.

MAMMIE GURLEY'S CHICKEN AND DUMPLINGS

Mammie uses a 3-finger pinch of baking powder.
We converted it to ½ teaspoon.

Wash and trim off excess
    fat from . . . .   1 large **CHICKEN,** cut into pieces
Place in a heavy pan. Fill halfway full with **WATER.** Cook until done. Remove
    from pan. Skin, bone and return to pan.
Season with . . . .   **SALT** and **PEPPER**
Slowly simmer and drop in **DUMPLINGS.**

DUMPLINGS

Mix together . . . . 1½ cups **FLOUR**
                                         ½ tsp. **BAKING POWDER**
                                         ½ tsp. **SALT**
                                         ½ tsp. **PARSLEY**
                                         2 Tbsp. **SHORTENING**
                                         1 **EGG**
Moisten with . . . .   **WATER**

Roll dough very thin. Cut with knife to desired size. Leave on top of the
cabinet, covered with wax paper. Let dry out for at least 2 hours. (It doesn't
harm the dumplings to leave all day. They will dry up and curl, but will
be good.) Drop into rapidly boiling broth. Cover with a lid and cook 20 to
30 minutes, or until dumplings are done.

YIELD: 8 SERVINGS

DEBORAH'S BUSY-DAY DUMPLINGS

Add 1 stick of **BUTTER** to hot **CHICKEN BROTH.** Cut **FLOUR TORTILLAS**
into 6 pieces each. Drop into hot liquid. Boil until tender, only about 3 to
5 minutes.

Or, buy **FLAKY REFRIGERATOR BISCUITS,** peel each layer from biscuit
(about 6 or 8 per biscuit). Pat each side in **FLOUR.** Drop in hot **BROTH.**

Or, buy cheap brand canned **BISCUITS.** Roll thin and drop in hot **CHICKEN
BROTH.**

KENNY'S KASSEROLE
An unusual combination, but very good.

Boil in large saucepan until tender	1 **CHICKEN,** cut in pieces

Remove chicken, bone and chop.

Add to chicken stock and cook	4 ounces **NOODLES,** very thin
Grate and set aside	1 cup **SHARP CHEDDAR CHEESE**
Mix together and heat	1 can **CREAM OF MUSHROOM SOUP**
	1 can **CREAM OF CHICKEN SOUP**
	½ cup **MAYONNAISE**
	1 tsp. **MUSTARD**
	1 Tbsp. **PICANTE SAUCE**

Cover bottom of 3-quart casserole with half of chicken.

Layer with	1 can (14½ oz.) **ASPARAGUS,** cut
	½ cup **ALMONDS,** toasted, slivered
	1 can (3 oz.) **MUSHROOMS,** sliced

Add noodles and the rest of the chicken. Pour the sauce over all of casserole. Sprinkle with grated cheese. Put **PAPRIKA** on top. Cover and bake in a preheated 350-degree oven for 45 minutes.

YIELD: 8 SERVINGS

MYNA'S CHICKEN LIVERS
Serve over Rice Pilaf.

Season with **SALT** and **PEPPER**	1 pound **CHICKEN LIVERS**
Dredge in	**WONDRA FLOUR**
Saute until done in	**REAL BUTTER**

Remove from skillet. Add more **BUTTER** if necessary, and

saute	1 cup chopped **FRESH MUSHROOMS**
	1 bunch **FRESH GREEN ONIONS,** chopped

Stir livers and vegetables

together and add	1 can flat **BEER**
	1 cup **BEEF BONE GLAZE** or **CHICKEN BROTH**

Simmer a few minutes. Add more **SALT** if needed and a dash of **SWEET BASIL** for seasoning. Serve over **RICE.**

YIELD 6 TO 8 SERVINGS

RICE PILAF

In saucepan, brown . . . .   2 cups uncooked **RICE**
                                1 stick **MARGARINE**
Add . . . .   2 cans **ONION SOUP**
                                2 cans (3 ounces each) whole **MUSHROOMS** with juice

Simmer, covered until done, about 45 minutes.

ONE-POT PAELLA
Louisiana fare.

Melt in skillet . . . .   4 Tbsp. **SHORTENING** or **BUTTER**
Shake in a paper bag . . . .   8 **CHICKEN LEGS** (or 4 **LEGS** and 4 **THIGHS**)
                              ½ cup **FLOUR**
                              SALT and **PEPPER**
Shake off excess flour and brown in the melted butter. Remove and set aside.
Slice and brown in same
   skillet . . . .   4 ounces **CHORIZO** or **ITALIAN SAUSAGE**
Drain on paper towels.
Put into skillet and cook until
   clear . . . .   1 medium **ONION,** chopped
                              1 **GREEN PEPPER,** chopped
                              1 clove **GARLIC,** minced
Stir in . . . .   ¾ cup **LONG GRAIN RICE,** uncooked
                           1½ tsp. **INSTANT CHICKEN BOUILLON**
                           ¼ tsp. **TUMERIC**
                           3 cups **HOT WATER**
Add sausage, and 4 sliced **BABY CARROTS.** Arrange chicken on top. Cover and bake 20 minutes at 375 degrees. Remove from oven.
Add . . . .   1 package **FROZEN PEAS**
                            ¼ cup **RIPE OLIVES**
                           6 **CHERRY TOMATOES,** halved

Bake uncovered 20 minutes longer. Serve warm.

YIELD: 8 SERVINGS

SWEET AND SOUR CHICKEN
Marinade is good to use on pork chops, too.

Cut into serving pieces, or into
   halves .... 2 **CHICKENS,** or use 6 **CHICKEN
      BREASTS**

Soak in the following marinade
   for 1 or 2 hours or
   overnight .... 1 medium jar **APRICOT
      PRESERVES**
      1 bottle **RUSSIAN DRESSING**
      1 package **ONION SOUP MIX**

Place in lightly greased baking dish. Spoon remaining marinade over chicken and bake at 350 degrees for 60 minutes. Serve over **RICE.**

YIELD: 6 SERVINGS

√ TEXAS' MOST POPULAR OVEN FRIED CHICKEN
Easy and delicious.

Cut up .... 1 **CHICKEN** (or use 6 **CHICKEN
      BREASTS)**
Mix together .... ¾ cup **FLOUR**
      ¼ cup **YELLOW CORNMEAL**
      1 tsp. **CHILI POWDER**
      ¼ cup **PARMESAN CHEESE**
      1 cup **BUTTERMILK**
      ½ cup **BUTTER**

Dip chicken in mixture and place in baking dish. Cook in preheated 375-degree oven for 1 hour.

YIELD: 6 SERVINGS

POLSTON'S PAPRIKA CHICKEN
An easy-do recipe.

Season with **SALT** and
   PEPPER .... 1 cut-up **CHICKEN** or **CHICKEN
      PARTS**

Place in **BUTTERED** baking dish. Sprinkle with **PAPRIKA.** Bake in 350-degree oven. Turn, skin side up, and bake until done, about 30 to 45 minutes.

YIELD: 4 SERVINGS

SPECIALTY OF THE HOUSE

A quick, easy casserole.

Melt in a 13x9x2-inch casserole	1 stick **BUTTER**
Sprinkle with	1 cup regular **RICE**
and	1 package **DRY ONION SOUP MIX**
Mix	1 can **CHICKEN BROTH**
plus enough.................	**WATER** added to make 4 cups liquid
	1 can **MUSHROOM SOUP**
Mix and pour over rice. Arrange on top	6 **CHICKEN THIGHS,** skinned, or 1 **CHICKEN,** cut up
Sprinkle chicken with	**SALT** and **PEPPER**

Bake in preheated 325 degree oven until chicken is done, 1 hour to 1 hour and 15 minutes.

YIELD: 6 SERVINGS

TURKEY SPAGHETTI

Melt in saucepan	½ cup **BUTTER** or **MARGARINE**
Add	½ cup **FLOUR**
Stir and cook until blended.	
Add	2 cups or 1 can **CHICKEN BROTH**
	½ cup **WHITE WINE** (Chablis is good)
Cook until thickened. Remove from heat and add	1 cup **HALF & HALF CREAM**
	1 small can chopped **GREEN CHILIES**
	⅛ tsp. **POWDERED GARLIC**
	¼ tsp. **CUMIN POWDER**
	Pinch of **DRIED TARRAGON**
Return to heat and bring to boil.	
Add	2 cups diced **TURKEY** or **CHICKEN,** cooked
	1 can **MUSHROOMS**
Remove from heat.	
Cook according to package	1 small package **SPAGHETTI**
Drain and add to turkey mixture.	

Pour into buttered 13x9x2-inch casserole. Top with grated **MONTEREY JACK CHEESE.** Cook in 350 degree oven for 30 minutes, or until bubbly.

TURKEY AND DRESSING

A favorite Thanksgiving and Christmas tradition at the Vaughns.

Thaw a . . . . 10 to 12 pound **TURKEY**
Rub with . . . . **BUTTER**
and . . . . **SALT**
Place in a roasting pan with a
    lid, and add . . . . 2 quarts **WATER**

Cover and bake according to directions with turkey, or bake at 325 degrees for 30 minutes per pound, or until done. This will not be a real pretty bird, but will be very tender. Slice and place on a platter and serve with **DRESSING** and **GIBLET GRAVY.**

DRESSING

Crumble together . . . . 9 cups **CORNBREAD**
                                                       7 cups **BISCUITS**
Add and mix with dry
    ingredients . . . . 2 cups chopped **ONIONS**
                                                       3 tsp. **SAGE**
                                                       2 tsp. **SALT**
                                                       2 tsp. **BLACK PEPPER**
                                                       ¼ tsp. **RED PEPPER**
Use liquid the turkey was
    cooked in . . . . 5 cups **TURKEY BROTH**
                                                       1 can **CHICKEN BROTH**
                                                       2 **EGGS,** slightly beaten

Stir all together and cook in a greased 13x9x2-inch pan at 325 degrees for about 1 hour. (Don't let it cook until dry.)

GIBLET GRAVY

Combine . . . . 2 cups **BROTH**
                                                       2 hard boiled **EGGS,** chopped
                                                       LIVER, GIZZARD and **NECK OF**
                                                            TURKEY, cooked and chopped
                                                       SALT and **PEPPER**
Bring to a boil and thicken
    with. . . . . ¼ cup **FLOUR**
                                                       ½ cup **SWEET MILK**

This can be prepared ahead of time. Freeze the dressing before it is cooked; just let thaw and cook when needed. Cook turkey, slice and freeze. Let thaw and warm in slow oven, covered. Wait to make the gravy the day you want to serve it. This is so easy you can enjoy the family.

YIELD: 16 TO 18 SERVINGS

LES POLSTON'S EASY TURKEY FOR A BUNCH
Les is a great cook.

Cook on top of the stove with a
   lot of **WATER** . . . .   1 10-pound **TURKEY**
When done, lift out and add . . . .   4 **ONIONS,** quartered
                                    2 cups sliced **CELERY**

When vegetables are done, add a little **FLOUR** to thicken broth. Season with **SALT** and **PEPPER.** Cut turkey into bite size pieces and add to broth. Serve over **RICE.**

YIELD: 15 to 18 SERVINGS

CHILIPITIN DOVES
Small, very hot chili peppers that grow wild in South Texas.

Sprinkle 6 **DOVES** inside and out with **SALT** and **PEPPER.** Place 2 **CHILIS** in they body cavity of each. (May use any hot peppers.) Wrap each bird in a slice of **BACON,** taking care to cover the breast. Place in a baking dish side by side. Add ½ cup **WATER.** Cover and bake at 350 degrees for 1½ hours. Uncover and cook until birds are browned (about 20 minutes longer). Remove to platter and garnish. Serve immediately.

YIELD: 3 TO 6 SERVINGS

DUCKS
Mr. Drew Mouton also cooks dove this way.

Prepare **DUCKS,** planning ¼ duck per person. **SALT** and **PEPPER** ducks, roll in **FLOUR.** Brown quickly in about ½ inch of **BACON GREASE.** Remove from skillet.
Fry in grease . . . .   1 **ONION,** chopped
Place ducks back in pan and
   add . . . .   1 cup **WATER**
                                   1 cup **BURGUNDY**
                                   2 Tbsp. **WORCESTERSHIRE**
                                          SAUCE
                               Few drops **TABASCO**

Add **WATER** until ducks are about half covered. Cover pan and boil at a rolling boil for about 20 minutes, then simmer for 2 hours. Serve with **WILD RICE.**

CHINESE TUNA
A Swinney favorite.

Melt in a medium skillet	2 Tbsp. **BUTTER**
Add and saute until tender	½ cup chopped **CELERY**
	½ cup chopped **ONION**
Add	1 can **TUNA,** drained
	1 can **CREAM OF MUSHROOM SOUP,** undiluted
	⅔ cup **MILK**
	½ can **CHINESE NOODLES**

Mix all together and transfer to a greased casserole dish suitable to serve in.

Top with remaining	½ can **CHINESE NOODLES**
	1 small can **CASHEW NUTS**

Bake in 350 degree oven for 20 to 25 minutes, or until hot.

YIELD: 6 TO 8 SERVINGS

CREVETTES MOUTON
Drew's "savory" shrimp.

Clean, rinse and drain	1 pound **SHRIMP**
Put in saucepan with	½ cup **PINET BLANC WINE**
	1½ cups **CHICKEN BROTH**
	½ tsp. **CELERY SALT**
	½ tsp. **BASIL**
	½ tsp. **PAPRIKA**

Cover and simmer 10 minutes.

Add	1 cup sliced **FRESH MUSHROOMS**
Simmer 5 minutes, then add	½ cup sliced **GREEN ONIONS**
	1 cup chopped **CELERY**

Simmer 5 more minutes.

In a small bowl, blend	1 Tbsp. **LEMON JUICE**
	2 Tbsp. **CORNSTARCH**
	2 Tbsp. **DRY SHERRY**

Stir into sauce mixture. Cook and stir until thickened. Taste. Add more **SALT** if necessary. Add 1 Tbsp. **PARSLEY.** Serve over **RICE PILAF.**

RECIPE FOR *Vermicelli Pie*

FROM THE KITCHEN OF *Abbie O*

1/2 - 12 oz PKG Vermicell

2 T Butter or MARG

1/3 C GRATED PARMESAN

2 Eggs - well Beaten

1 lb ground beef

1/2 C Chopped onion

1/4 C Chopped green pe

1 - 8 oz con stewed tom

1 - 6 oz con tomato paste

3/4 teasp oregano

1/2 teasp garlic salt

RICE PILAF

Melt in a medium saucepan .... ¼ cup **BUTTER** or **MARGARINE**
Add and cook until brown ...... ½ cup chopped **ONION**
                                 ½ tsp. **CURRY POWDER**
Stir in and cook until brown
   (about 5 minutes) .... 1½ cups **LONG GRAIN RICE**
Add .... 1½ tsp. **SEASON SALT**
                                 2½ cups **CHICKEN BROTH**
                                 ½ cup **PINET BLANC WINE**

Simmer, covered, until liquid is absorbed (20 minutes). Add 2 Tbsp. **PIMIEN-TO.** Fluff rice before serving.

YIELD: 8 SERVINGS

BAKED FISH
Easy for the calorie counter.

Start with cold or frozen .... **FISH FILLETS**
Rub with .... **BUTTER**
                              SALT and **PEPPER**
                              PAPRIKA
Roll in .... **BREAD CRUMBS**

Wrap in foil and bake 40 minutes to 1 hour at 325 degrees. Open foil and brown under broiler.

YIELD: ½ POUND PER PERSON

H.G.'S BACKYARD SHRIMP

Shell and devein .... 2 pounds **JUMBO SHRIMP,** fresh
Marinate for 2 to 3 hours
   in .... ½ pound **BUTTER,** melted
                              JUICE of 1 **LEMON**
                              ½ tsp. **SALT**
                              1 Tbsp. **WORCESTERSHIRE SAUCE**
                              1 Tbsp. **SOY SAUCE**
                              3 to 4 dashes **TABASCO**

Remove shrimp from marinade and place over a hot charcoal fire. Cook 2 to 3 minutes per side, or just until barely cooked. Baste with marinade 1 time per side. Serve with leftover sauce.

SALMON CROQUETTES
A family favorite.

Drain, remove bones and
   mash well . . . .   1 can **SALMON**
Add . . . .   1 **EGG**
                                            1 small **ONION,** chopped fine
                                          ½ tsp. **SALT**
                                          ¼ tsp. **PEPPER**
                                          ¼ cup **CRACKER CRUMBS**

Mix well and form into patties, using about ⅓ cup for each. Flatten and roll pattie in crushed **CRACKER CRUMBS** or **CORN MEAL.** Fry quickly in ½ cup **OIL** or **SHORTENING.** Drain on paper towel, and serve.

YIELD: 4 TO 6 SERVINGS

SALMONETTES
A seafood lover's delight.

Drain and reserve juice from . . .   1 can (15 oz.) **PINK SALMON**
Add and stir together . . . .   1 **EGG**
                                          ½ cup **FLOUR**
                                          ½ **ONION,** chopped (optional)
Set aside and mix
   separately . . . .   ¼ cup salmon juice
Add . . . .   1 heaping teaspoon **BAKING POWDER**

Beat with a fork and stir into salmon mixture. Mix well. (It will be thin.) Drop ½ teaspoonful at a time into hot **SHORTENING** and fry until brown.

YIELD: 6 SERVINGS

TEXAS SEAFOOD BATTER
Use to dip your favorite seafood.

Mix . . . .   ½ cup warm **WATER**
                                            1 tsp. **DRY YEAST**
Let set a few minutes. Add . . . . .   1 **EGG**
                                            SALT and **PEPPER**

Add enough **FLOUR** to thicken. Dip **SEAFOOD** in batter and fry in hot **OIL.** May also add **CORNMEAL** if you prefer.

Tex-Mex

FLIPOS

Brown in skillet	½ pound **GROUND MEAT**
	2 **ONIONS,** chopped
Add	1 cup **REFRIED BEANS**
	GARLIC POWDER
	SALT
	CHILI POWDER, to taste
Grate	½ pound **CHEESE**
Have ready	8 **FLOUR TORTILLAS**

Melt small amount of **MARGARINE** in skillet. Place 1 tortilla in hot skillet, and cover half with mixture of beans and meat. Sprinkle **ONIONS** and cheese on top of meat. Flip over uncovered side. Brown; then, flip over, and when golden brown, serve with **HOT SAUCE.**

GUACAMOLE

Mix in a blender until smooth. . .	2 **AVOCADOS,** peeled and chopped
	3 Tbsp. **PICANTE SAUCE**
	2 Tbsp. **MAYONNAISE**
	1 Tbsp. **LEMON JUICE**
	½ tsp. **WORCESTERSHIRE SAUCE**
	Dash **GARLIC**

MEXICAN CHEESE DIP
Make a meal of this dip and fried FLOUR TORTILLAS.

In a medium saucepan scramble and brown	1 pound **GROUND MEAT,** very lean
Add and cook until clear	1 small **ONION,** chopped
Add and stir until melted	1 pound **VELVEETA CHEESE**
Add	1 can **RO-TEL TOMATOES AND GREEN CHILIES**
	2 **TOMATOES,** chopped

Mix well and serve with crisp **TORTILLAS.** This is good made ahead of time and put in the refrigerator. Just reheat before using.

To make in microwave, melt cheese; brown meat according to manual. Add rest of ingredients. Serve.

GOURMET NACHOS

Melt in a 3-quart saucepan or
  heatproof casserole . . . .   2 Tbsp. **BUTTER** or **MARGARINE**
Add and cook until
  transparent . . . .   1 clove **GARLIC,** minced
                                1 cup diced **ONION**
Add . . . .   1 can (4 oz.) **GREEN CHILIES,**
                                  chopped
                                1 **TOMATO,** chopped
                                1 Tbsp. **FRESH CILANTRO** or 1
                                  tsp. **DRIED** (optional)
Simmer until tender. Add . . . . . .   2 cans **REFRIED BEANS**
Mix well and stir in . . . .   6 ounces **MOZZARELLA CHEESE,**
                                  cubed
Cook until cheese melts. Cool; cover and chill well.

To serve: Place small **TORTILLA CHIPS** on a cookie sheet. (Try the cheese-flavored ones for a change in taste.) Top each with a heaping teaspoonful of bean mixture. Sprinkle with grated **CHEDDAR CHEESE.** Top with a slice of **JALAPENO PEPPER.** Broil until the cheese melts. (Be careful not to burn the Nachos.) Remove from broiler and top with **GUACAMOLE.** Unused bean mixture may be frozen for later use.

YIELD: 12 DOZEN NACHOS

NACHOS GRANDE

Spread in a 13x9x2-inch
  casserole . . . .   2 cans (16 oz. each) **REFRIED**
                                  BEANS
In a small skillet, brown . . . . 1½ pound **GROUND MEAT**
                                  1 **ONION,** chopped
Season with . . . .   **SALT** and **PEPPER**
Layer over beans.
Sprinkle with . . . .   1 can **GREEN CHILIES,** chopped
                                  3 cups grated **CHEDDAR CHEESE**
Cover with . . . .   3 cans (4 oz. each) **TACO SAUCE**

Bake in a preheated 400 degree oven for 30 minutes. Remove from oven and spread with chopped **GREEN ONIONS** and sliced **RIPE OLIVES.** Garnish with **GUACAMOLE** and **SOUR CREAM.** Serve with **TOSTADO CHIPS** for dipping.

YIELD: DIP TO SERVE 12 AS APPETIZER

MEXICAN SALSA BRAVA

Combine in large saucepan . . . . . 2 cups peeled, chopped ripe **TOMATOES**
1 cup thinly sliced **GREEN TOMATOES**
½ **ONION,** minced
¼ tsp. **OREGANO**
½ tsp. **SALT**
½ tsp. **SUGAR**
3 tsp. chopped **CILANTRO**

Simmer over low heat until tomatoes are liquefied.
Strain and add . . . . ¼ cup **VINEGAR**
1½ tsp. **JALAPENO VINEGAR**
1½ **CHILI JALAPENOS,** chopped fine

Mix well, cool, and pour into four 8-ounce jars.

MARY NELL'S MEXICAN RELISH
Mary Nell has shared this relish with us for years.
We eat it on practically everything.

Chop following ingredients into a
large saucepan . . . . 8 cups **RIPE TOMATOES** (use canned if necessary)
4 cups **BELL PEPPERS**
3 cups **ONIONS**
2 cups **CELERY**
2 Tbsp. **SALT**
1½ cups **SUGAR**
3 cups **VINEGAR**
1 tsp. **CINNAMON**

????? **HOT** **PEPPERS**
Mary Nell uses a lot of hot peppers. Adjust to your own taste.

Mix all ingredients and simmer slowly for approximately 1 hour. Stir often.
Pour into sterilized jars. Seal. Will keep for at least a year.

TAKEETAS

Brown in a medium skillet. . . . . . 1 pound **GROUND MEAT**
Cool and combine with . . . . ½ pound **CHEESE,** grated
        SALT and **PEPPER** to taste

Dip **TORTILLAS** in **HOT SHORTENING,** one at a time. (Count to four, turn, count again.) Remove from skillet, put a small amount of meat-cheese mixture in the middle of the tortilla. Roll into small roll (like a cigarette). Pin with a toothpick and fry in deep fat. Dip in **HOT SAUCE.**

YIELD: APPROXIMATELY 18 TO 20 TAKEETAS

TAKEETA HOT SAUCE

Mix together . . . . 1 can **TOMATO SAUCE**
        1 can **PIMIENTOS,** chopped
        1 can **ORTEGA PEPPERS,** chopped

BREAKFAST TACOS

In a medium size skillet, cook for
  5 minutes . . . . 1 Tbsp. **MARGARINE**
        ½ **TOMATO,** chopped
        4 **GREEN ONIONS** with tops,
          chopped
Remove from skillet. Crumble
  into same skillet and cook
  until done . . . . 1 **CHORIZO SAUSAGE**
Drain well on paper towel. Pour off any remaining grease in skillet, then
Melt . . . . 1 Tbsp. **MARGARINE**
Beat well in small bowl . . . . 4 **EGGS**
        ½ tsp. **SALT**
        ½ tsp. **PEPPER**

Cook, stirring eggs until done. Be careful not to cook too dry. Add rest of ingredients.

Heat 4 **FLOUR TORTILLAS** in a medium oven, 350 degrees, for about 10 minutes. **BUTTER** lightly. Spoon mixture on tortilla and fold like an enchilada. Serve with bowl of grated **CHEESE** and **PICANTE SAUCE.** Good with **BLOODY MARY'S.**

YIELD: 2 SERVINGS

LOS HUEVOS Y LAS PAPAS
Eggs and potatoes.

In a small skillet heat	1 cup **OIL** (olive oil preferred)
Add	1 cup very thinly-sliced **POTATOES**

Turn to coat with oil. Cover and reduce heat. Cook until done, about 20 minutes. In a medium skillet,

cook about 5 minutes........	½ cup sliced **ONIONS**
	½ cup sliced **GREEN PEPPERS**
Add and cook 15 more	
minutes...................	½ cup peeled, seeded, drained and chopped **TOMATOES**
	½ tsp. **SALT**
	½ tsp. **PEPPER**
	GARLIC to taste

Add potatoes and keep mixture hot. Make an **OMELET,** according to favorite recipe, for 2 people. When omelet is done, *do not fold.* Gently slide onto serving plate. Cover with vegetable mixture. Serve with **TOAST, JELLY,** and **MEXICAN COFFEE.**

YIELD: 4 SERVINGS

JANIE MARTINEZ FLOUR TORTILLAS
Making tortillas is a Mexican art. They take practice.
Work the dough very fast.

Combine	4 cups **FLOUR**
	2 tsp. **SALT**
	¼ tsp. **BAKING POWDER**
Add	⅔ cup **SHORTENING** or **LARD**
Mix well with your hands.	
Add.....................	1 cup **HOT WATER**

Knead well with your hands until the mixture forms a smooth ball and leaves the side of the bowl. (Add more warm **WATER** if you need to.) Place in a bowl and cover with dish towel for 10 minutes before making tortillas.

Pinch off dough about the size of a heaping tablespoon. Work to a circle about the size of a saucer. (Janie uses the palms of her hands, but you may prefer to roll them out on waxed paper.) Cook on a hot griddle, turning often. The dough should be stiff enough to turn with your hand and not require an egg turner. Keep tortillas warm in towels after cooking.

YIELD: 20 TO 24 TORTILLAS

JANIE MARTINEZ CORN TORTILLAS

Combine . . . .   2 cups **MASA HARINA**
                                1½ cups **HOT WATER**

Mix well with hands. Roll or pat by hand to circles the size of a saucer. Cook on lightly greased griddle until browned on both sides. (Be sure to knead dough quickly and firmly after adding hot water.)

YIELD 12 TO 14 TORTILLAS

CORN TORTILLA SOUP

In a large saucepan melt . . . .   3 Tbsp. **BUTTER**
Add to butter and cook until
   clear . . . .   ¼ cup diced **ONION**
Stir in . . . .   3 Tbsp. **FLOUR**
                                  1½ tsp. **SALT**
                                  PEPPER to taste
Add . . . . 2½ cups **CREAMED CORN**
                                  2½ cups **MILK**
                                  ½ cup **CREAM**

Simmer about 15 minutes. *Do not boil.* Break crisp **CORN TORTILLAS** into the bottom of each soup bowl. Pour warm soup over tortillas. Top with **CHOPPED CHIVES** or **PARSLEY.**

YIELD: 8 SERVINGS

MEXICAN SOUP

Brown . . . .   2 pounds **GROUND LEAN MEAT**
                                  1 large **ONION,** chopped
Add . . . .   3 medium **POTATOES,** diced
                                  2 cans (No. 303) **TOMATO SAUCE**
                                       WITH TOMATO BITS
                                  1 Tbsp. **CUMIN**
                                  1½ cups **WATER**
                                  SALT and **PEPPER** to taste

Simmer for 1 hour. Add more water if necessary.

YIELD: 12 SERVINGS

TACO BEEF SOUP

This chunky soup is like a taco in a bowl.

In a large saucepan cook until
browned . . . . ½ pound **GROUND BEEF**
¼ cup chopped **ONION**
Drain off excess fat. Add . . . . . . 1½ cups **WATER**
1 can (16 oz.) **STEWED
TOMATOES,** cut up
1 can (16 oz.) **KIDNEY BEANS**
1 can (8 oz.) **TOMATO SAUCE**
½ envelope (2 Tbs.) **TACO
SEASONING MIX**
Simmer, covered, 15 minutes.
Add . . . . 1 small **AVOCADO,** peeled, seeded
and chopped

Pour into individual bowls and pass grated **CHEESE, CORN CHIPS** and **SOUR
CREAM** to top each serving with.

YIELD: 6 SERVINGS

GUACAMOLE TEX-MEX COLESLAW

Combine in large bowl,
mixing well. . . . . 3 ripe **AVOCADOS,** mashed
2 Tbsp. **LEMON JUICE**
Add . . . . 6 cups shredded **CABBAGE**
1 cup finely chopped **ONION**
1 cup finely chopped **GREEN
PEPPER**
Mix well. Combine . . . . ½ cup **MAYONNAISE** or **SALAD
DRESSING**
1 Tbsp. **SUGAR**
1 Tbsp. **TARRAGON VINEGAR**
½ tsp. **SALT**
¼ tsp. **GARLIC POWDER**
¼ tsp. **PEPPER**
Dash of **HOT SAUCE**
Dash of **WORCESTERSHIRE
SAUCE**
Stir into mixture. Sprinkle
with. . . . . ¼ tsp. **PAPRIKA**

YIELD: 8 TO 10 SERVINGS

LA ENSALADA
Salad

Dressing:
Mix and chill . . . .   ½ cup **MAYONNAISE**
    ½ cup chopped **ONION**
    2 Tbsp. **CHILI SAUCE**
    2 tsp. **CIDER VINEGAR**
    1 tsp. **SALT**
    ½ tsp. **CHILI POWDER**
    4 drops **HOT SAUCE**

Combine and toss gently . . . .   1 can (12 oz.) **WHOLE KERNEL CORN,** drained
    1 can (8½ oz.) **KIDNEY BEANS,** drained
    1 can (6 oz.) **RIPE OLIVES,** drained, sliced
    1 head **LETTUCE**

When ready to serve, pour dressing over the vegetables. This is a large recipe. Make only one-half, if necessary.

YIELD: 6 TO 8 SERVINGS

VARIATION: Brown 1 pound of **GROUND MEAT.** Drain well. Add to vegetables just before adding the dressing.

MEXICAN CHEF'S SALAD

Brown in a medium skillet . . . . . .   1 pound **GROUND MEAT**
Add and simmer for 10
    minutes . . . .   1 can **KIDNEY BEANS,** drained
    SALT and **PEPPER** to taste
Set aside.
Chop . . . .   1 **ONION**
    4 **TOMATOES**
    1 head **LETTUCE**
    2 large **AVOCADOS**
Toss with . . . .   8 ounces **FRENCH DRESSING**
    HOT SAUCE to taste
    1 bag (6 oz.) **TORTILLA CHIPS,** crushed

Add meat mixture. Mix well. Decorate with extra **CHIPS, AVOCADO** and **TOMATO.** Serve *pronto!*

YIELD: 6 SERVINGS

SALAD
Serve with Enchiladas.

Mix in blender	1 **GARLIC CLOVE,** crushed
	¼ cup **VINEGAR**
	3 Tbsp. **SALAD OIL**
	3 Tbsp. **FRENCH DRESSING**
	2 Tbsp. **SUGAR**
	¼ tsp. **PEPPER**
	½ tsp. **SALT**
Mix well. Pour over	3 cups shredded **CABBAGE**
	1 **GREEN PEPPER,** diced

Store in covered container in refrigerator. Drain before serving.

YIELD: 6 SERVINGS

SOUTH OF THE BORDER SALAD

Cut up into a large salad bowl	1 head **LETTUCE**
	1 **ONION**
	2 **TOMATOES**
Add	1 can **RANCH STYLE BEANS** with juice
Mix together. Season with	**PEPPER** to taste
	¼ tsp. **GARLIC SALT**
Just before serving, add and toss well	1 bag **FRITOS** (regular size)
	1 small bottle **CATALINA DRESSING**

Serve as a salad, or very good as a quick supper dish.

YIELD: 8 SERVINGS

FRIED RELLENOS

Prepare **CHILES** as for Baked Chile Rellenos. Stuff with **CHEESE,** secure with toothpick.

Prepare a batter of . . . . ½ cup **FLOUR**
1 cup **MILK**
1 **EGG**

Beat until smooth. Hold **CHILE** by stem and dip into the batter. Place immediately into **HOT FAT.** Brown, turning only once. Drain on paper towel.

CHILI RELLENOS QUICHE

Add Egg Topping for puffy effect for a special "Fiesta".

Buy frozen or prepare 1 (9-inch) **PASTRY SHELL.** Bake at 475 degrees for 5 minutes.

Sprinkle in partially baked
crust . . . . 1 cup grated **MONTEREY JACK CHEESE**
Layer with *half* of . . . . 1 can (4 oz.) **CHILIES**
Sprinkle with . . . . 1 cup grated **MONTEREY JACK CHEESE**
Add rest of . . . . chilies, more if you like it hot
Mix together and pour over
mixture in crust . . . . 4 **EGGS**
1 cup **HALF-AND-HALF**
¼ tsp. **PEPPER**

Bake in a preheated 375 degree oven for 30 minutes. Serve with **TACO SAUCE.** Or, add **EGG TOPPING,** bake and serve.

YIELD: 6 SERVINGS

EGG TOPPING

In small bowl, beat until very
stiff . . . . 2 **EGG WHITES**
Fold in, just until blended . . . . . . 2 **EGG YOLKS,** slightly beaten

Spoon over *baked* **QUICHE.** Be sure to seal to edge of crust. Return to oven and bake at 375 degrees for 15 minutes or until golden brown.

BAKED CHILE RELLENOS
Stuffed green chiles.

Place fresh **GREEN CHILES** on a cookie sheet and bake at 350 degrees until they look blistery. (Turn often.) Put a damp cloth over them for a few minutes to steam them. Then peel carefully. Split lengthwise and remove seeds.

Stuff with . . . .   Grated **MONTEREY JACK CHEESE**
    SALT
Spread on each **CHILE** . . . .   1 tsp. **PICANTE SAUCE**

Place **CHILES** on a greased cookie sheet. Cook in a preheated 350 degree oven until cheese is melted, about 20 minutes. Serve hot.

YIELD: PREPARE 2 CHILES PER PERSON

CHALUPAS

Drop **FLOUR** or **CORN TORTILLAS** into deep **FAT.** Using a large spoon, hold down center in order to form a cupped tortilla. Drain.

Cover bottom of tortillas
with . . . .   1 cup **KIDNEY BEANS,** mashed
Layer with . . . .   1 can **TOMATOES,** drained and chopped
    ½ cup chopped **ONIONS**
    1 cup grated **CHEESE**

Place in preheated 300-degree oven until heated thoroughly. To serve, top with **GUACAMOLE.**

YIELD: 4 SERVINGS

CREME DE LA TORTILLA
Margaret's San Francisco treat

Combine in saucepan . . . .   1 can (14½ oz.) **TOMATOES**
1 can (4.11 oz.) chopped **CHILES**
1 clove **GARLIC,** minced
1 **ONION,** diced

Cook until very thick (almost dry). Approximately 1 to 1½ hours. Soften about 10 **CORN TORTILLAS** in small amount of hot oil. Drain on paper towels. Shredd about ½ pound **CHEDDAR CHEESE.** Grease cookie sheet. Starting with a tortilla, layer and stack with 1 tablespoon tomato mixture, cheese, and 1 tablespoon **SOUR CREAM.** Repeat. Should have about 5 tortillas in each stack. Place in oven until cheese is bubbly on top. To serve, cut in wedges.

JALAPENO GRITS
A good side dish for sandwiches.

Cook according to directions on
   package. . . . .   1 cup **GRITS**
Add . . . .   2 rolls **JALAPENO CHEESE**
1 stick **BUTTER**
1 can **GREEN CHILES,** chopped
2 **EGGS,** well beaten
GARLIC to taste

Put mixture into a well-greased casserole and bake in a preheated 350 degree oven for 40 minutes.

YIELD: 4 TO 6 SERVINGS

MEJICO HOMINY

Drain and pour into a saucepan .   1 can (16 oz.) **HOMINY**
Add and cook over low heat 5
   minutes . . . .   1 cup **SOUR CREAM**
1 can (4 oz.) **CHILES,** chopped
1 cup grated **CHEDDAR CHEESE**
SALT

Place in an ungreased 1-quart casserole and bake uncovered in a preheated 375 degree oven for 20 minutes.

YIELD: 6 SERVINGS

JALAPENO SQUASH

Cook until tender . . . . 6 or 7 **SQUASH,** large
  ½ cup chopped **ONION**
Drain *well.* Add . . . . 3 Tbsp. **BUTTER**
  1 large jar **CHEEZ-WHIZ**
  1 can **CREAM OF CHICKEN SOUP**
  1 can **GREEN CHILES,** chopped
    (more if you like it hot)
  2 **EGGS,** well beaten

Put into a buttered casserole and top with **BUTTERED BREAD CRUMBS.**
Bake at 300 degrees until set, approximately 40 minutes.

YIELD: 6 SERVINGS

RICE ORTEGA

Mix . . . . 3 Tbsp. **BUTTER,** melted
  ½ cup chopped **ONION**
  4 cups cooked **RICE** (do not use
    instant)
Add . . . . 1 **JALAPENO PEPPER,** chopped
  2 cans **GREEN CHILES,** diced
  2 cups **SOUR CREAM**
  1 cup **COTTAGE CHEESE**
  1 **BAY LEAF,** crushed
  SALT and **PEPPER** to taste

Mix well. Pour mixture into a buttered casserole. Bake in a preheated 375 degree oven for 30 minutes. Remove from oven and sprinkle with ½ pound grated **SHARP CHEDDAR CHEESE.** Return to oven and bake 10 minutes more. Serve warm.

YIELD: 6 TO 8 SERVINGS

WARM RICE: Place in a colander and run hot water over it.

SPAGHETTI MEJICANO
Put into two casseroles, freeze one.

Cook according to directions on
    package.................. 1 package (10 oz.) **SPAGHETTI**
Drain. Set aside.
Brown in a medium skillet...... 2 **ONIONS,** chopped
                               1 **GREEN PEPPER,** chopped
                               ¾ pound **GROUND MEAT,** very
                                     lean
                               2 Tbsp. **CHILI POWDER**
                               2 Tbsp. **BACON DRIPPINGS**
Stir in .... 1 can **TOMATOES**
                               1 can **MUSHROOMS,** chopped
                               1 Tbsp. **WORCESTERSHIRE**
                               TABASCO to taste
                               SALT and **PEPPER**
                               ½ pound **SHARP CHEDDAR,** grated

Mix sauce with cooked spaghetti. Place in a buttered baking dish. Top with
grated **CHEESE,** ½ cup **CATSUP** and ½ cup **BUTTERED BREAD CRUMBS.**
Bake in a preheated 350 degree oven for 30 to 45 minutes.

YIELD: 10 SERVINGS

FAJITAS
Specialty of Bruce Franklin.

Purchase from butcher .... 2 pounds **BEEF SKIRTS**
Season meat *generously* with ... **SALT**
                               COARSELY GROUND PEPPER
                               ACCENT or **MSG**
Sprinkle lightly with.......... **GARLIC POWDER**

Place on medium-hot charcoal grill. Open a 16-oz. bottle of **ZESTY ITALIAN
SALAD DRESSING** and cover meat generously with dressing. Cook approximately 5 minutes. Turn and cover underside with Italian dressing. Turn
and dress each side every 10 minutes. Cook until the right doneness, ac-
couding to your taste. (Bruce cooks approximately 1 hour. The thickness
of the meat determines the cooking time.)

To serve, slice beef skirts into ¼ to ½-inch slices and roll in warmed **FLOUR
TORTILLAS.** Serve as an appetizer, or with **BEANS** and **HOT SAUCE,** as
an entree.

YIELD: 10 TO 12 SERVINGS

BEEF STEAK SALSA FRIA

Mix . . . .   1 cup chopped **TOMATOES**
½ cup sliced **ONIONS**
1 can (4 oz.) **CHILIES,** chopped
1 Tbsp. **OIL**
1 Tbsp. **VINEGAR**
1 tsp. **CORIANDER**
¼ tsp. **SALT**
¼ tsp. **PEPPER**
Store in the refrigerator at least 3 hours.
Grill . . . .   4 boneless **RIB EYE STEAKS**

Grill steaks at moderate temperature. For one-inch steaks, grill 2 to 3 inches from heat, for approximately 10 to 15 minutes for rare and 15 to 20 minutes for medium. Grill 2-inch steaks 3 to 5 inches from heat, approximately 25 to 30 minutes for rare and 30 to 35 minutes for medium. When one side of steak is browned, turn, season with **SALT** and **PEPPER,** and finish cooking the second side. Turn and season. Serve steaks with well-chilled sauce.

YIELD: 4 SERVINGS

MANUELITA'S ENCHILADAS

Brown, drain and set aside . . . . .   **GROUND MEAT,** seasoned with **SALT** and **PEPPER**
Warm . . . .   **CANNED ENCHILADA SAUCE,** hot or mild
Brown slightly in skillet . . . .   1 Tbsp. **CHILI POWDER**
1 Tbsp. **FLOUR**
1 Tbsp. **OIL**
SALT

Add **WATER** and simmer to make a fairly thick mixture. Cool to just warm, and dip **CORN TORTILLAS** into mixture, one at a time, then dip them into the enchilada sauce, just long enough to make them soft.

Fill dipped tortillas with 2 Tbsp. meat, grated **CHEESE,** and chopped **ONION.** Roll up and secure with toothpick. Place in a long pan and sprinkle with more **CHEESE.** If desired, pour a can of **ENCHILADA SAUCE** over top. Cook in 350-degree oven until very hot and cheese has melted. Serve with a **GREEN SALAD** and pot of **BEANS** for good eating.

PANCAKE ENCHILADAS

Combine and mix until smooth ..   1 cup **PANCAKE MIX**
       1 cup **MILK**
       1 Tbsp. **OIL**
       1 **EGG**

Lightly grease griddle before baking each pancake. Pour ⅓ cup batter onto hot greased griddle, bake until bubbles appear. Turn and brown the underside.

FILLING

Have ready to use . . . .   1 can (10 oz.) **ENCHILADA SAUCE**
In small skillet, brown . . . .   ½ pound **GROUND MEAT**
       ⅓ cup finely-chopped **ONION**
Drain well. Add . . . .   2 tsp. **CHILI POWDER**
       2 cups grated **CHEDDAR CHEESE**

Pour ½ cup enchilada sauce in an 8-inch square baking dish. Place ⅓ cup meat mixture on each pancake. Roll up and place seam-side down in dish. Pour remaining sauce over pancakes and sprinkle with ½ cup **CHEESE.** Bake in a preheated 350-degree oven for 20 to 25 minutes. Serve hot.

YIELD: 6 SERVINGS

TACOS
Have a Taco Party and let each guest choose their own topping.

In a medium skillet, cook but do
    not brown . . . . 1½ pounds **GROUND CHUCK**
       2 medium **ONIONS,** chopped
       1 clove **GARLIC,** mashed
(May substitute ½ pound **CHORIZO** for ½ pound ground chuck.)
Season with . . . .   **SALT** and **PEPPER** to taste

Drain the mixture well. Use prepared **TORTILLA SHELLS,** or prepare your own. (Dip each **TORTILLA** in hot **OIL.** While still soft, fold in half with a fork or tongs to make a half-circle pocket. Hold in oil until crisp but not brown. Drain on paper towel.) Fill tortilla shells with the hot meat filling. Top with your choice of the following:
CHOPPED JALAPENOS   GRATED CHEESE   CHOPPED ONIONS
CHOPPED TOMATOES SHREDDED LETTUCE GREEN TOMATO SALSA

YIELD: 10 TO 12 TACOS

TACO TWISTS

In a large skillet, brown . . . . 1 pound **GROUND MEAT,** very
lean

Drain well.
Mash . . . . 1 can (15½ oz.) **KIDNEY BEANS,**
drained

Add . . . . 2 Tbsp. **ONION FLAKES**
1 tsp. **GARLIC SALT**
2 tsp. **CHILI POWDER**

Add to meat mixture.
In medium bowl, mix
together . . . . 1 cup grated **CHEESE**
½ cup crushed **CORN CHIPS**

On a piece of waxed paper or dough board, sprinkle ¼ cup **CORNMEAL.**
Place 2 rows of 5 **CANNED BISCUITS** together; press to form an 8x16-inch
rectangle. Spread meat mixture over dough. Roll up like jelly roll. Cut into
10 slices and place in a greased 13x9x2-inch baking dish. Sprinkle with
the cheese and corn chips. Bake in a preheated 350 degree oven for 35
minutes.

YIELD: 6 TO 8 SERVINGS

VARIATION:
Add 2 Tbsp. chopped **JALAPENO PEPPER** to meat and bean mixture.

CHICKEN TACOS

Grease baking dish and
line with . . . . **CORN CHIPS**
Cover with mixture of . . . . 1 3-pound **CHICKEN,** cooked and
boned
1 large can **ENCHILADA SAUCE**
1 can **MUSHROOM SOUP,**
undiluted
1 **ONION,** chopped
½ tsp. **GARLIC SALT**
⅛ tsp. **PEPPER**
Sprinkle with . . . . 1 cup grated **CHEESE**

Cover the entire casserole with crushed **CORN CHIPS.** Pour over mixture
1 can **CHICKEN BROTH** (or use broth from cooked chicken). Bake in a
preheated 350 degree oven for 30 minutes. Serve warm with **HOT SAUCE.**

YIELD: 8 SERVINGS

SPANISH DELIGHT

Melt in a medium skillet	4	Tbsp. **BUTTER**
Add and brown	2	pounds **GROUND BEEF,** lean
	1	cup chopped **ONION**
	1	clove **GARLIC,** crushed
Drain off excess fat and set aside.		
In saucepan, mix and heat	1	can **TOMATOES**
	1	can **TOMATO SOUP**
	1	can **TOMATO SAUCE**
	1	can **WHOLE KERNEL CORN**
	1	can **MUSHROOMS**
		RIPE OLIVES (Optional)
Cook according to directions on package.	1	package **LARGE NOODLES**
Drain and add	2	Tbsp. **MARGARINE**
	1	tsp. **SALT**
	¼	tsp. **CAYENNE**

Mix all ingredients together and pour into a very large buttered casserole. Top with 1 pound grated **AMERICAN CHEESE**. Bake in a preheated 350 degree oven for 20 to 25 minutes. This is a good recipe to make ahead of time. You may also freeze it.

YIELD: 10 TO 12 SERVINGS

SONORA CASSEROLE

This is an old favorite.

Brown in medium skillet	2	pounds **GROUND MEAT**
	1	**ONION,** chopped
Add	1	can **MUSHROOM SOUP**
	1	can **CHICKEN SOUP**
	1	can **GREEN CHILIES,** chopped
	1	small can **EVAPORATED MILK**
Grate	1	pound **AMERICAN CHEESE**

Tear 1 package **TORTILLAS** (10 to 12) into pieces. Starting with meat mixture, layer twice in a 2-quart casserole. (Tortillas, meat, cheese, etc.) End with the cheese. This dish may be made ahead of time and either refrigerated or frozen. Bake in preheated 350 degree oven for 30 minutes, or until bubbly.

YIELD: 6 TO 8 SERVINGS

FRIJOLES CON PUERCO
Beans and Pork

Soak overnight	2 pounds **PINTO BEANS**
Cut into small chunks	4 pounds **PORK ROAST**
Cover with **WATER**	
and add	2 **JALAPENO PEPPERS,** whole
	2 cloves **GARLIC,** whole
	1½ tsp. **OREGANO**
	1½ tsp. **COMINO POWDER (CUMIN)**
	2 Tbsp. **CHILI POWDER**
	SALT and **PEPPER** to taste

Cook all day on "simmer". Check often to see if more water is needed. When done, mixture should be almost paste consistency. Serve over **CORN CHIPS** and sprinkle with **GRATED CHEESE.** Make at least two layers. Top with chopped **LETTUCE, AVOCADO** and **TOMATOES.**

YIELD: 14 TO 16 SERVINGS

VARIATION:
YUCATAN STYLE: Use **BLACK BEANS** in place of pinto beans. (A real treat, if you've never tried them.)

BURRITOS

Brown in a medium skillet.	1 pound **GROUND MEAT**
	1 pound **SAUSAGE**
	1 **ONION,** chopped
Stir in	2 Tbsp. **FLOUR**
	1 cup **WATER**
	½ tsp. **CUMIN SEEDS,** or **POWDER**
Cook until thickened.	
Remove from heat and add	4 ounces **CHILIES,** chopped

Heat **FLOUR TORTILLAS** over low heat until they are soft and pliable. Spread ½ cup or less of the meat mixture on tortilla. (Work quickly so the tortillas won't get hard.) Fold the 2 sides together toward the center and then fold the top edge down over the rest. Secure with a toothpick. Fry burrito in ½ inch **OIL.** Let tortilla get lightly brown.

YIELD: 8 SERVINGS

MEXICAN FRIED CHICKEN

Combine in paper sack	¼	cup **FLOUR**
	1½	tsp. **CHILI POWDER**
	½	tsp. **SALT**
Shake in above mixture........	1	**CHICKEN** (2½ to 3 pounds), cut up and skinned
Fry in......................	⅓	cup **OIL**
When brown, remove chicken from skillet.		
Put in skillet and cook until tender	¼	cup chopped **ONION**
	¾	cup chopped **GREEN PEPPER**
Stir in	¾	cup **RICE** (regular, uncooked)
	1	can **RO-TEL TOMATOES AND GREEN CHILIES**
	1½	cups **WATER**
	1	tsp. **CHILI POWDER**
	½	tsp. **SALT**

Arrange chicken over the rice and tomato mixture. Cover and simmer for 35 to 40 minutes, or until chicken is tender and rice is done.

YIELD: 4 SERVINGS

CHIMICHANGAS

In medium saucepan combine ...	2	pounds **BEEF STEW MEAT**
	1½	cups **WATER**
	2	cloves **GARLIC**, minced
	2	Tbsp. **CHILI POWDER**
	1	Tbsp. **VINEGAR**
	2	tsp. dried **OREGANO**, crushed
	1	tsp. **SALT**
	1	tsp. ground **CUMIN** opt.
	⅛	tsp. **PEPPER**

Cover; reduce heat and simmer about 2 hours or till meat is very tender. Uncover and boil rapidly about 15 minutes or until water has almost evaporated. Watch closely and stir near end of cooking time so meat doesn't stick. Remove from heat and using 2 forks, shred meat very fine. Wrap stack of **TORTILLAS** in foil; heat in oven at 350-degrees for 15 minutes. Spoon ¼ cup mixture onto each tortilla, near one edge. Fold edge nearest filling up and over filling just till mixture is covered. Fold in the two sides envelope fashion, then roll up. Fasten with toothpick. Fry filled tortillas in ½ inch hot fat about 1 minute on each side or till golden brown. Drain on paper toweling. Keep warm in 300-degree oven. Garnish with **LETTUCE** and **GUACAMOLE**.

BARRACHITOS
Little Drunkards cookies.

Cream . . . .   1 cup **BUTTER**
⅔ cup **SUGAR**
Add . . . .   2 **EGG YOLKS**
½ tsp. **SALT**
Mix well. Add . . . .   3 cups **FLOUR,** sifted

Alternate flour with enough **CLARET WINE** to moisten all of the mixture to a soft cookie dough. Drop from a teaspoon onto an ungreased cookie sheet. Bake in a preheated 375 degree oven for 8 to 10 minutes. When cookies are done, but still hot, sprinkle with **SUGAR** and **CINNAMON.** Serve with **COFFEE.**

YIELD: 6 DOZEN

CHOCOLATE CREAM
Mexican refrigerator dessert.

Melt in medium saucepan . . . . . .   1 package (12 oz.) **CHOCOLATE CHIPS**
2 Tbsp. **WATER**
1 tsp. **INSTANT COFFEE**
Stir until smooth and remove from heat. *Cool.*
Add, one at a time, and beat
well after each . . . .   6 **EGG YOLKS**
In separate bowl, beat until
frothy . . . .   6 **EGG WHITES**
Add . . . .   ¼ tsp. **CLOVES**
2 tsp. **CINNAMON**
Add and beat until stiff . . . .   6 Tbsp. **SUGAR**
Fold into chocolate mixture.
Fold into above mixture . . . .   1 carton (large) **WHIPPED TOPPING** (Reserve small amount.)

Put into individual serving bowls or glass container. Refrigerate. To serve, top with more **WHIPPED TOPPING** and serve with plain **COOKIES.** (Make the day before you plan to serve.)

YIELD: 6 TO 8 SERVINGS

DOWN EL PASO WAY
Flan.

Dissolve and brown over medium
    heat . . . . ½ cup **SUGAR**
Pour into individual molds and rotate to coat sides. (When using only one
    mold, use a 3-cup size.)
Beat well . . . . 2 large **EGGS**
Stir in . . . . 1 can (13 oz.) **EVAPORATED MILK**
                                    ¼ cup **SUGAR**
                                    SALT
                                    1 tsp. **VANILLA**

Pour into mold or molds. Set into a larger pan of hot **WATER.** Bake in a preheated 325 degree oven for 50 to 55 minutes, or until a knife inserted halfway comes out clean. Chill and unmold.

YIELD: 4 TO 6 SERVINGS

JOSIE'S BUNUELOS

Mix . . . . 4 cups **FLOUR**
                                    ½ cup **OIL**
                                    2 tsp. **SALT**
                                    1 cup **WARM WATER**

Turn out on floured board and knead until very smooth. Divide dough into 24 balls and roll each into a 5-inch circle. (Josie uses her hands.) Fry in deep, hot **FAT.** Sprinkle with **CINNAMON** and **SUGAR.** Or use with **DIPS (CHILI CON QUESO, GUACAMOLE,** etc.)

YIELD: APPROXIMATELY 24 BUNUELOS.

MEXICAN PRALINES

Mix in heavy saucepan . . . . 2½ cups **SUGAR**
                                    1 can (5.33 oz.) **EVAPORATED MILK**
                                    2 Tbsp. **WHITE KARO**
                                    2 Tbsp. **BUTTER**
Bring to a boil. Add . . . . 2 cups **PECANS**

Cook on high to 238 degrees on candy thermometer (soft ball). Remove from heat. Beat until creamy, Drop by teaspoons on waxed paper.

YIELD: 24 PRALINES

MICRO PRALINES

In 3-quart casserole combine
  and mix well.............. 1½ cups **BROWN SUGAR,** packed
                             ⅔ cup **CREAM**
                             ⅛ tsp. **SALT**
                             2 Tbsp. **BUTTER**

Microwave on "High" for 5 minutes. Stir. Cook 4 to 5 more minutes, to soft ball stage (238 degrees on candy thermometer).
Add .... 1½ cups **PECANS**

Cool 1 minutes, then beat until creamy (about 3 minutes). Drop by teaspoons on waxed paper.

YIELD: 24 PRALINES

JOSIE'S EMPANADAS DULCE
Little pies.

Mix .... 1 can **PUMPKIN,** solid pack
                          ¾ cup **SUGAR**
                             Grated **ORANGE** and **LEMON**
                                RIND
                          ½ tsp. **CINNAMON**
                             Dash of **ANISE** (Optional)
Set aside.
Put in medium bowl .... 1¼ cups **FLOUR**
                             ⅛ tsp. **SALT**
                             1½ Tbsp. **SUGAR**
                             1 tsp. **BAKING POWDER**
Cut into dry ingredients until it
  resembles cornmeal .... 5 Tbsp. **SHORTENING**
Add .... 2 to 3 Tbsp. **ICE WATER**

Make pastry into a ball. Pull off balls the size of marbles. Roll in circles about the size of your hand. prick half of circle with a fork. Place a heaping teaspoon of pumpkin mix on pastry circle. Fold in half. Dampen edges and seal together with fork. Sprinkle with **SUGAR** and bake in preheated 350 degree oven until golden brown.

YIELD: ABOUT 15 EMPANADAS

NORTH OF THE BORDER DESSERT
Flan with caramelized topping.

Place in a saucepan and melt
    until golden brown . . . . ¾ cup **SUGAR**
Pour into bottom of 8x8x3-inch glass baking dish, or individual baking dishes.
    Let cool.
Put in mixer or blender . . . .   1 can **EAGLE BRAND MILK**
                               1 can **EVAPORATED MILK**
                               6 **EGGS**
                               2 tsp. **VANILLA**

Mix thoroughly. Pour over melted sugar. Place dish, or dishes, in a larger
pan. Pour 1 cup hot **WATER** into the larger pan. Place in a preheated 350
degree oven. Cook for one hour, or until a toothpick inserted comes out clean.
When done, remove from oven and cool slightly. Turn onto a serving plate,
or individual serving plates.

YIELD: 6 SERVINGS

SOPAIPILLAS
Good as a bread or dessert.

Sift together in medium bowl . . .   2 cups **FLOUR**
                               2 tsp. **BAKING POWDER**
                               1 tsp. **SALT**
Beat together and add to dry
    ingredients . . . .   1 **EGG**
                               3 Tbsp. **OIL**
                               ½ cup **WATER**

Stir with fork until blended. Knead dough until smooth. Roll dough, cut into
3-inch squares. Melt enough **SHORTENING** in deep skillet or saucepan to
make a depth of 2 to 2½ inches. Heat to 380 degrees (hot). Fry 2 to 3
Sopaipillas at a time. They will puff and float to the top. Turn and fry until
golden brown. Serve with **HONEY.**

YIELD: 16 TO 18 SOPAIPILLAS

VARIATIONS:
Sprinkle with **CINNAMON** and **SUGAR.**
Sprinkle with **POWDERED SUGAR.**

QUICK METHOD: Thaw frozen yeast dough. Pinch off pieces the size of
walnuts. Fry as above.

MEXICAN WEDDING CAKES

Cream together . . . .   ½ cup **BUTTER**
                                            2 Tbsp. **POWDERED SUGAR**
Add . . . .   1 cup, less 2 Tbsp., **FLOUR**
                                            1 cup **PECANS,** chopped
                                            1 tsp. **VANILLA**

Roll dough into 1-inch balls. Place on a greased baking sheet. Flatten with bottom of a glass that has been dipped in **POWDERED SUGAR.** Bake in a preheated 300-degree oven for 15 to 20 minutes. When done, roll in powdered sugar while still warm.

YIELD: 2 TO 2½ DOZEN

SWEET TOOTH: Butter a flour tortilla, sprinkle with cinnamon and sugar. Fold over and place in oven or microwave until warm.

Vegetables

BEANS, BEANS, AND MORE BEANS

Serve the "Grandstand Quarterbacks" after the game.

Use ovenproof skillet to brown . .	1	pound **GROUND MEAT**
	½	pound **BACON,** chopped
Drain off grease. Stir in	1	can (14 oz.) **BAKED BEANS**
	1	can (14 oz.) **KIDNEY BEANS**
	1	can (14 oz.) **BUTTER BEANS**
	1	can (14 oz.) **PORK AND BEANS**
	½	cup **CATSUP**
	1	**ONION,** chopped
	1	tsp. **MUSTARD**
	1	cup **BROWN SUGAR**
	4	Tbsp. **VINEGAR**

Bake in a 350-degree oven, *covered,* for 1 hour. Serve with **SALAD** and hot **BREAD.** (I prefer **CORNBREAD.**)

YIELD: 12 TO 14 SERVINGS

DRIED PINTO BEANS

1 cup dried beans serves approximately 4 people.

Wash and soak	3 cups **DRY BEANS**
Cook over low heat with lid on until beans begin to get soft, probably about 2 hours.	
Add	**SALT PORK, HAM HOCK,** leftover **HAM,** or 4 to 5 strips **BACON,** cut up
	SALT and **PEPPER**
	SUGAR, just a dab

Continue cooking until beans are done. If the bean juice is not thick enough, remove lid and boil rapidly for a few minutes. If you need to add more **WATER,** always add hot water; it helps to cook the beans soft. (A pinch of **SODA** added helps the gas situation.) When cooking beans, it is good to cook more than you need and freeze leftovers for future use.

YIELD: 12 SERVINGS

VARIATION: *Carter's Tasty Hot Pinto Beans* After first 2 hours of cooking, add 1 large **ONION,** chopped, 1 large **GREEN PEPPER,** chopped, and 1 can **RO-TEL TOMATOES AND GREEN CHILIES** to beans, and simmer until beans are done.

DAFFERN'S BAKED BEANS
Serves a multitude at Lake Brownwood.

Mix together . . . . 3 cans **PORK AND BEANS**
¾ cup **BROWN SUGAR**
¾ cup **CATSUP**
1½ tsp. **MUSTARD**
3 Tbsp. **SYRUP**
1 large **ONION,** chopped

When mixed, pour into a large,
greased casserole and top
with . . . . **BACON** slices

Bake in 325 degree oven for 2 hours. This is a large recipe, but it can easily be cut in one-third or two-thirds.

YIELD: 12 TO 14 SERVINGS

BAR-B-QUE BUTTER BEANS

Wash and put in a large
saucepan with lid, and cover
with **WATER** . . . . 1 pkg. **LARGE DRIED BUTTER**
BEANS (large limas)
1 **HAM HOCK**

Cook until beans are a little soft.
Add . . . . ½ cup **CATSUP**
1 tsp. **CHILI POWDER**
1 tsp. **WORCESTERSHIRE SAUCE**
2 Tbsp. **BROWN SUGAR**
½ cup chopped **ONION**
SALT, if needed

Cover and continue cooking until beans are soft and done. It will take about 3 hours. These will need to just simmer slowly. Add more **WATER** when necessary.

YIELD: 8 TO 10 SERVINGS

VARIATION: To beans and ham
hock, add . . . . 2 tsp. **SALT**
1 **BOUILLON CUBE**
1 **ONION,** chopped
1 jar (4 oz.) **PIMIENTOS**

Use same method to cook.

MARINATED BEANS
Looks as good as it tastes.

Drain	3 cans **GREEN BEANS**
Slice and add	2 **PURPLE ONIONS**
	½ cup **RIPE OLIVES**
Add	2 cups **WHOLE CHERRY TOMATOES**
Mix and pour over bean mixture	½ cup **VINEGAR**
	½ cup **OIL**
	¼ cup **SUGAR**
Add to cover	1 bottle **ZESTEE ITALIAN DRESSING**

Refrigerate at least 24 hours or longer.

YIELD: 10 TO 12 SERVINGS

RED BEANS AND RICE
And SAUSAGE, too.

Sort, wash, and soak overnight in **WATER**	1 pound **PINTO BEANS**
The following day, drain and rinse beans and combine with	2 **ONIONS,** chopped
	2 stalks **CELERY,** chopped
	1 **GREEN PEPPER,** chopped
	1 clove **GARLIC,** mashed

Put in heavy saucepan and cover with **WATER.** Bring to a boil. Reduce heat, cover and simmer for 1 hour.

Add	1 pound **SMOKED SAUSAGE,** cut into pieces

Continue cooking for 1½ hours, or until beans are tender and a thick gravy is formed. If necessary, add **WATER** to prevent beans from sticking. Stir in **SALT, PEPPER, TABASCO** and **PARSLEY** as mixture simmers. Add 2 cups cooked **RICE** last 30 minutes.

YIELD: 10 SERVINGS

NEW YEARS DAY BLACK-EYED PEAS
Great for those football fans.

Sort and wash .... 2 pounds **DRIED BLACKEYED PEAS**
Place in a large saucepan
    and add .... 1 **HAM HOCK** or 1 to 2 cups
                           left over **HAM**
                         3 tsp. **SALT**
                         1 tsp. **PEPPER**

Cover with **WATER** to about 2 inches above ingredients. Boil gently with lid on. Cook about 1½ hours, or until peas are done. Check **WATER** periodically.

YIELD: 10 TO 12 SERVINGS

VARIATION: Try adding 3 to 4 cups cooked **RICE** for something different.

"BUNDLES" OF GREEN BEANS

Drain 2   cans **WHOLE GREEN BEANS**
Divide into individual servings and wrap each serving with ½ slice uncooked
    BACON. Place in a baking dish.
Mix together and pour over
    beans .... ⅓ cup **BROWN SUGAR**
                         ⅓ cup **MARGARINE**, melted
                         Dash **GARLIC SALT**

Bake in 350-degree oven for 30 minutes.

YIELD: 8 SERVINGS

GREEN BEANS WITH ALMONDS

Heat in a saucepan .... 2 cans **FRENCH STYLE GREEN**
                         BEANS
Season with.................... **SALT** and **PEPPER**
Drain and place in a bowl.
Saute .... ½ cup **MARGARINE**
                         ⅓ cup **ALMONDS**

Pour over hot green beans.

YIELD: 8 SERVINGS

BROCCOLI CASSEROLE

Cook according to directions on
    package . . . .   2 packages frozen chopped
                                           BROCCOLI
Have ready . . . .   2 cups grated **CHEESE**
Drain broccoli and add . . . .   1 can **CREAM OF MUSHROOM**
                                           SOUP, undiluted
                                       1 can **MUSHROOMS,** chopped
                                       ½ cup chopped **ALMONDS**
                                       1 cup grated **CHEESE**

Pour in a greased casserole and top with 1 cup grated cheese; bake in
350-degree oven until hot and cheese is melted. (May be warmed in the
microwave.)

YIELD: 6 TO 8 SERVINGS

BROCCOLI AND RICE CASSEROLE

Nell always fixes this for the Vaughns' holiday dinners.

Cook according to directions on
    package for about
    6 minutes . . . .   2 pkgs. frozen chopped **BROCCOLI**
Melt in saucepan . . . .   ¼ cup (½ stick) **BUTTER** or
                                         MARGARINE
Add and saute until clear . . . . . .   1 small **ONION,** chopped
                                       2 stalks **CELERY,** chopped
Add . . . .   1 cup **INSTANT RICE,** raw
                                       1 can **CREAM OF MUSHROOM**
                                         SOUP, undiluted
                                       1 can **CREAM OF CHICKEN SOUP,**
                                         undiluted
                                       1 large jar **CHEEZ WHIZ**
To taste . . . .   **SALT** and **PEPPER**

Mix all together and put in a medium casserole that has been well greased. Bake in a 350-degree oven for 20 minutes.

YIELD: 8 SERVINGS

COUNTRY CABBAGE

Saute until tender . . . . 2 **ONIONS,** chopped
in . . . . 3 Tbsp. **BUTTER**
Add . . . . 1 **CABBAGE,** cut into wedges
                                           2 **TOMATOES,** chopped
Sprinkle with . . . . **SALT** and **PEPPER**

Cover and cook over low heat for 20 to 30 minutes, or until cabbage is tender.

YIELD: 6 SERVINGS

APRICOT-GLAZED CARROTS

Cook until tender in
    salted water . . . . 2 pounds **CARROTS,** scraped and
                                                     cut diagonally
Drain well. Set aside.
Melt in medium saucepan . . . . . . 3 Tbsp. **BUTTER**
Add . . . . ⅓ cup **APRICOT PRESERVES**
Remove from fire and add . . . . . . ¼ tsp. **NUTMEG**
                                            ¼ tsp. **SALT**
                                            1 tsp. freshly grated **ORANGE PEEL**
                                            2 tsp. **LEMON JUICE**

Blend well. Toss carrots with the apricot mixture until they are well coated. Serve.

YIELD: 6 TO 8 SERVINGS

HOMINY CASSEROLE

Drain . . . . 1 large can **HOMINY**
Add . . . . 1 can **MUSHROOM SOUP,** undiluted
                                            1 can **JALAPENO PEPPERS,** drained & chopped
Top with . . . . ½ pound **VELVEETA CHEESE,** grated

Place in greased 1-quart casserole. Cook in a 325 degree oven for 20 minutes.

YIELD: 6 SERVINGS

JACK BUSH JR. COOKS CELERY CASSEROLE

Cover with **WATER** and **SALT**
   and cook until tender . . . .   4 cups sliced **CELERY** (slice
                            ½-inch thick)
Drain and combine with . . . .   1 can **CREAM OF CHICKEN SOUP,**
                            undiluted
                        ½ cup sliced **WATER CHESTNUTS**
                        ¼ cup sliced **BLANCHED**
                            ALMONDS
                        2 Tbsp. **PIMIENTO**
Pour into a buttered casserole.
Top with . . . .   ½ cup **BREAD CRUMBS**
                        2 Tbsp. **BUTTER,** melted

Cover and bake in 350 degree oven for 30 minutes.

YIELD: 4 TO 6 SERVINGS

TOMATO-CORN CASSEROLE

Cut in half . . . .   8 slices **BACON**
Place *half* of bacon in bottom of
   shallow 2-quart casserole. Top
   with . . . .   1 cup **BREAD CRUMBS**
Layer . . . .   1 cup chopped **TOMATOES**
                        ½ can (3 oz.) chopped **GREEN**
                            CHILIES
                    1½ cups **CORN**
Sprinkle with . . . .   **SALT** and **PEPPER** to taste
Layer . . . .   1 cup chopped **TOMATOES**
                        ½ can chopped **GREEN CHILIES**
                    1½ cups **CORN**
Sprinkle with . . . .   **SALT** and **PEPPER** to taste

Mix 1 cup **BREAD CRUMBS** with ¼ cup melted **MARGARINE,** and spoon over casserole. Top with remaining bacon. Cook at 350 degrees for 45 minutes.

CORN FRITTER FAVORITES

Combine in medium bowl . . . .   1 can (8½ oz.) **WHOLE KERNEL CORN**
  ½ tsp. **SALT**
     PEPPER
  ¼ cup **FLOUR**
Add . . . .   1 **EGG YOLK**
Beat until stiff . . . .   1 **EGG WHITE**
Fold into corn mixture.

Mix well. Drop by teaspoonful into hot **OIL** or **SHORTENING** (about 1½ to 2 inches deep, when melted). When brown, remove from pan, place on paper towel to drain. Serve warm.

YIELD: 4 SERVINGS

EASY BAKED CORN

Pour into small greased
  casserole . . . .   1 can **CREAM STYLE CORN**
Add . . . .   1 Tbsp. **CORNSTARCH**
  1 **EGG,** beaten
  1 Tbsp. **SUGAR**
  ¼ cup **MILK**
Add to taste . . . .   **SALT** and **PEPPER**
Top with . . . .   1 Tbsp. **BUTTER,** cut in small chunks

After you have emptied corn into dish, mix remaining ingredients in the can and add to corn. (Saves on dirty dishes.) Bake until thick and slightly brown in a 350 degree oven (about 20 to 30 minutes).

YIELD: 4 SERVINGS

MICRO CORN: Leave corn on cob. Remove shucks and silks. Place corn, one layer deep, in a microwave safe dish or plastic bag. Cook on High for about 2 minutes per ear.

FRITO GRIT CASSEROLE
Good for a crowd.

Bring 6 cups **WATER** to a rolling
   boil in a large saucepan.
     Add . . . . 1½ cups **QUICK GRITS**
                            1 tsp. **SALT**
Cook 10 minutes.
Add and mix well . . . . 1 stick **MARGARINE**
                                 1 roll **GARLIC CHEESE** (or 1 pound
                                    CHEESE and a dash of
                                    GARLIC SALT)
                               Dash **TABASCO SAUCE**
                               SALT and **PEPPER**
Add . . . . 3 **EGGS,** well beaten

Pour into a greased 13x9x2-inch pan. Top with crushed **FRITOS**. Bake in
a 350-degree oven for 45 minutes.

YIELD: 10 TO 12 SERVINGS

FRITO SOUFFLE
Dresses up soup or sandwiches to look
like Sunday dinner.

Layer, in order given, in a
   buttered 13x9x2-inch baking
   dish . . . . 1 medium **ONION,** chopped
                                   1 can (4 oz.) **GREEN CHILIES,**
                                   chopped
                                   1 small bag **CORN CHIPS,** crushed
                                   1 can **CREAM OF CHICKEN SOUP,**
                                   undiluted
                                   1 large can **EVAPORATED MILK**

Cover top generously with grated **AMERICAN CHEESE.** Bake in a 400-degree
oven for 20 to 30 minutes, or until cheese is melted. (Good with **HAM** and
PINTO BEANS.)

YIELD: 6 TO 8 SERVINGS

GRANNY'S MACARONI AND CHEESE
Everyone loves it.

Cook in **SALTED** water that has
    come to a rolling boil . . . .   1 box **MACARONI**
Boil until the macaroni is tender.
Drain. Cut in chunks
    and add . . . .   1 pound **OLD ENGLISH** or
                                      VELVEETA CHEESE
                                1 Tbsp. **BUTTER**
                                ½ tsp. **SALT**
                                ¼ tsp. **PEPPER**

Melt cheese and stir; add a little **MILK** or **WATER** if it is too dry. The secret is to keep it moist. This is good to serve with almost any menu.

YIELD: 6 TO 8 SERVINGS

MACARONI AND TOMATOES

Cook in hot water until tender . .   ½ package **MACARONI**
                                ½ tsp. **SALT**
Drain water off and add . . . .   1 can **TOMATOES,** chopped, with
                                     juice
                                2 Tbsp. **BACON GREASE**
Season with . . . .   **SALT** and **PEPPER**
                                ¼ tsp. **SUGAR**

Heat on high until bubbly, then reduce heat and simmer for about 15 minutes.

YIELD: 4 TO 6 SERVINGS

VARIATION: ¼ cup **CHEESE** may be added to this.

BAKED ONION SUPREME

Bake according to microwave
    manual (or in oven) . . . .   6 medium **ONIONS,** sliced
Remove and stir in . . . .   **CHEEZ WHIZ,** half regular and
                                    half **JALAPENO**

Mix well. **SALT** and **PEPPER** to taste. Serve warm. A great condiment with **ROAST.**

YIELD: 6 SERVINGS

POTATO CAKES
Good way to use leftovers.

Mix .... 1½ to 2 cups **CREAMED POTATOES**
                                                   2 **EGGS**
                                                      PEPPER
Add .... 1 **ONION,** chopped fine
Crush and add .... 2 dozen **SALTINE CRACKERS**

Mix well. Batter should be very stiff. (May need to add more crackers.) Make into 2-inch patties and roll in **CORNMEAL.** Fry in hot **GREASE** in a medium skillet. When brown, turn and cook the under side. Drain on paper towel. Serve warm.

YIELD: 4 SERVINGS

POTATO SUPREME
Can make ahead and freeze.

Peel, cut in ¼ inch slices and
   arrange in buttered casserole
   in layers .... 5½ cups **POTATOES**
                                                   1 cup **ONION**
Mix in separate bowl.......... 1 can **CREAM OF MUSHROOM
                                                      SOUP,** undiluted
                                                   1 can **CHEDDAR CHEESE SOUP,**
                                                      undiluted
                                                   1 can **WATER** or **MILK**
Pour over vegetables in
   casserole and dot with ...... 1 stick **BUTTER**
Add to taste .... **SALT** and **BUTTER**

Bake in a 350-degree oven for 1½ hours. Serve hot. For small families, put in two casseroles, bake one, freeze one.

YIELD: 8 SERVINGS

HANDY POTATOES: Boil a few extras and have in refrigerator for a quick dish. Makes good potato salad. Slice for scalloped or grate for hash browns.

TATORS AND TOPPINGS

Freeze toppings in small amounts. Microwave or heat for a quick meal.

Scrub large **POTATOES** thoroughly and rub skins with **OIL,** wrap in foil. Bake at 400 degrees for 1 to 1½ hours, or until done. When done, cut in half. Place several condiments in bowls and serve with hot potatoes.

GRATED CHEESE	CHOPPED FRESH ONIONS	CUBED HAM
DICED RIPE OLIVES	STUFFED OLIVES	CRUMBLED BACON
SOUR CREAM	COCKTAIL SHRIMP	FRESH MUSHROOMS
DICED GREEN PEPPER	CHOPPED CHILIES	CORN

CREAMY SHRIMP TOPPING: Heat 1 can **CREAM OF SHRIMP SOUP,** undiluted, ¼ teaspoon **SALT** and ⅛ teaspoon **PEPPER.** Spoon over potato and sprinkle with shredded **CHEDDAR CHEESE.**

CHEESY BACON TOPPING: Combine 6 slices **BACON,** (cooked and crumbled) ⅓ cup chopped **GREEN ONION,** ⅓ cup shredded **CHEDDAR CHEESE,** 1 cup **SOUR CREAM,** 1 teaspoon **SALT** and ½ teaspoon **PEPPER.** Spoon over hot potato halves. Sprinkle with **PAPRIKA.**

JALAPENO-HAM TOPPING: Combine ½ cup diced **HAM,** 1 cup **SOUR CREAM,** ½ teaspoon **CELERY SALT** and ½ teaspoon **PEPPER.** Spoon over potatoes and top with shredded **MONTEREY JACK CHEESE** with **JALAPENO PEPPERS.**

TERIYAKI-CHICKEN TOPPING: Brown 2 teaspoons **ONION** in 1 tablespoon **MARGARINE.** Add 1 can **CHICKEN CHUNKS,** dash of **GARLIC, SALT** and 1 tablespoon **SOY SAUCE.** Spoon over potatoes.

PIZZA BURGER TOPPING: Brown ½ pound **GROUND ROUND,** ⅛ cup chopped **ONION,** ½ teaspoon **SALT,** ⅛ teaspoon **PEPPER.** Drain and add ⅛ cup **CATSUP,** 5 chopped **RIPE OLIVES** and ⅛ cup **PARMESAN CHEESE.** Spoon over potatoes. Top with **MOZZARELLO CHEESE.**

SUNDAY POTATOES

The more onion soup, the more flavor.

Butter a medium casserole and layer	3 **POTATOES,** sliced
Sprinkle with	**SALT** and **PEPPER**
	2 Tbsp. **ONION SOUP,** dry
Slice on top	1 stick **BUTTER**

Cover and bake in 325 degree oven for 1 hour.

YIELD: 4 SERVINGS

POTATOES O'BRIEN
A 50-year-old recipe.

Peel and cut fine	4 **POTATOES**
	1 **ONION**
Add	1 **GREEN PEPPER,** seeded and chopped
Cook for 5 minutes in a shallow pan in	2 Tbsp. **BUTTER**
Add	1 cup **MILK**

Cook 15 minutes more. Mince with a knife while cooking. Add more **MILK** as it cooks away. When finished, this should be a rich, creamy mass. Add **SALT** and **PEPPER** to taste. Stir in ½ cup grated **CHEESE** and brown the top under the broiler.

YIELD: 6 SERVINGS

SWEET POTATO BALLS

Cook in large saucepan until soft	1 can **SWEET POTATOES**
	½ cup **SUGAR**
Drain, cool and mash.	
Form mixture around	**LARGE MARSHMALLOWS**
Roll in	**COCONUT**

Place these in a baking dish and bake in 350 degree oven until coconut is lightly browned. Watch very closely, the coconut will burn quickly. You may make these ahead and freeze before they are baked. Remove from freezer when ready to cook.

YIELD: 6 SERVINGS

SWEET POTATO CHIPS

Peel and slice into very thin slices	**SWEET POTATOES** (as many as desired, approximately ½ potato per person)

Soak in cold water overnight, or in ice water a few hours. Drain and dry well. Fry in hot deep **OIL** (375 degrees) until crisp and slightly brown. Drain on paper towels. Sprinkle with **SALT** or **POWDERED SUGAR.**

MARSHMALLOW SWEET POTATOES
A must for Thanksgiving.

Peel and boil until tender . . . . . . 2 large **SWEET POTATOES** (or use
                                      1 can)
Drain, mash and add . . . . ½ cup **SUGAR**
                                        3 Tbsp. **MARGARINE**
                                        2 tsp. **VANILLA**
                                        1 can **COCONUT**

Place in a buttered 1-quart casserole. Bake in a 350 degree oven for 20 minutes. When done, take from oven and place **MARSHMALLOWS** on top. Return to oven and toast to a golden brown.

YIELD: 4 SERVINGS

VARIATIONS: Add ½ cup chopped **PECANS.**

FRIED RICE
A delicious choice.

Cook crisp, crumble and
    set aside . . . . 2 slices **BACON**
In **BACON GREASE**, fry until
    yolk is hard . . . . 1 **EGG**
Remove egg, chop and set aside.
Saute in drippings until
    tender . . . . ½ cup chopped **GREEN PEPPER**
                                   ½ cup chopped **ONION**
Add . . . . 1¾ cups cooked **RICE**

Add crumbled bacon and chopped egg to the other ingredients. Cover with a lid and warm.

YIELD: 6 SERVINGS

MELODISE'S QUICK RICE

Bring to a boil . . . . 1 stick **MARGARINE**
                                        1 can **ONION SOUP,** undiluted
Drain, chop and add . . . . 1 can **MUSHROOMS**
Stir in . . . . 2 cups **MINUTE RICE,** raw

Set aside for 10 minutes with a lid on tight. Serve warm with your favorite **MEAT.**

YIELD: 6 TO 8 SERVINGS

RICE DRESSING

Mix together in mixing bowl ...... 2 cups cooked **RICE**
2 Tbsp. **DEHYDRATED ONION**
2 cups **MILK**
½ pound **VELVEETA CHEESE,**
    grated
2 **EGGS,** beaten
½ cup **COOKING OIL**
GARLIC SALT
SALT
1 **ONION,** chopped fine

Pour in greased, covered baking dish. Bake in preheated oven at 350 degrees for 45 minutes.

YIELD: 6 SERVINGS

SQUASH CASSEROLE

In a saucepan, cover with water
and cook until tender .... 4 or 5 medium **SQUASH**, diced
Drain and add .... ¼ cup **ONION**, minced
2 Tbsp. **BUTTER**
¾ cup **VELVEETA CHEESE**, cubed
SALT and **PEPPER** to taste

Place in a buttered baking dish. Sprinkle with ¼ cup grated **CHEESE**. Bake at 350-degrees for 30 minutes or may be cooked in microwave until thoroughly hot and cheese is melted.

YIELD: 4 to 6 SERVINGS

SPINACH SOUFFLE
Pat's treat for "after-the-game."

Beat until smooth . . . .   4 Tbsp. **FLOUR**
                                     3 **EGGS**
Add . . . .   1 pkg. frozen **SPINACH** (thaw and
                                            squeeze out juice)
                                 ½ pound **COTTAGE CHEESE**
                                 ½ pound **CHEDDAR CHEESE,**
                                            grated
                                 ½ tsp. **SALT**

Place in a greased 8x8x2-inch baking dish. Bake in a preheated 350-degree oven for 1 hour, or until slightly browned. Let set a few minutes before cutting.

YIELD: 6 SERVINGS

BAKED STUFFED SQUASH

Cover with water and cook until
   soft . . . .   4 medium **YELLOW SQUASH**
                                 1 tsp. **SALT**

Cut squash in half lengthwise,
   scoop out inside. Mash the
   squash removed and
   add . . . .   2 slices **BACON** fried and
                                            crumbled
                                 ½ cup chopped **GREEN PEPPER**
                                 1 **TOMATO,** chopped
                                 ½ cup chopped **ONION**
                                 1 cup grated **CHEESE**
                                 1 tsp. **SALT**
                                 ½ tsp. **PEPPER**

Spoon mixture into squash
   halves and top with . . . .   1 cup dry **BREAD CRUMBS**
                                 2 Tbsp. **BUTTER**

Place on baking sheet and cook in preheated 350-degree oven. Bake for 30 minutes.

YIELD: 8 SERVINGS

SPANISH SQUASH
For those with a garden.

Dice . . . . 3 or 4 **YELLOW SQUASH**
1 **ONION,** medium
1 can **TOMATOES** (or 2 **FRESH**)
Stew with 2 Tbsp. **MARGARINE** until thick.
Season with . . . . **GARLIC SALT**
SUGAR
PEPPER
BUTTER SALT

Layer in greased casserole with grated **CHEESE** on top. Bake in 350-degree oven for approximately 15 minutes, or until cheese melts.

YIELD: 6 SERVINGS

CORN CASSEROLE
Complements many entrees.

Saute until tender . . . . 1 medium **ONION,** chopped
½ **GREEN PEPPER,** chopped
in . . . . ¼ pound **BUTTER** or **MARGARINE**
Add and mix . . . . 2 cans **CREAM STYLE CORN**
1 cup **MINUTE RICE,** uncooked
1 jar **PIMIENTOS,** chopped
2 Tbsp. **SUGAR**
Add . . . . **SALT** and **PEPPER**

Place in a greased 1½ quart casserole. Bake in a 350 degree oven for 25 minutes. Then cover with 1 cup grated **CHEESE** and bake an additional 15 minutes.

YIELD: 8 SERVINGS

ZUCCHINI CASSEROLE

Saute . . . . 1 medium **ONION,** sliced
in . . . . ¼ cup **SALAD OIL**
Add . . . . 1½ to 2 pounds sliced **ZUCCHINI**
3 to 4 chopped ripe **TOMATOES**
1 **GREEN PEPPER,** chopped
Sprinkle with . . . . ¼ tsp. **GARLIC POWDER**
SALT and **PEPPER** to taste

Cook until tender. Sprinkle with **PARMESAN CHEESE** and serve.

Cakes/Pies

THE BETTER-THAN-SEX CAKE
Tried and untrue.

Mix according to package directions	1 **YELLOW CAKE MIX**

Pour into a greased and floured 13x9x2-inch baking dish and bake in a preheated 350-degree oven for 35 to 40 minutes.

In a medium saucepan, boil 5 minutes	1 can (15 oz.) **CRUSHED PINEAPPLE** (with juice)
Pour on hot cake. Cool completely.	1 cup **SUGAR**
Prepare, according to directions on box	1 package **INSTANT VANILLA PUDDING**

Spread over pineapple mixture.

Slice over pudding mixture	3 **BANANAS**
Spread with	**WHIPPED TOPPING**
Sprinkle with.	**FROZEN COCONUT**
Cover with.	**CHOPPED NUTS**

Refrigerate

HAWAIIAN DREAM CAKE

Combine	1 **YELLOW CAKE MIX**, dry
	4 **EGGS**
	¾ cup **OIL**
	½ can (No. 2) **CRUSHED PINEAPPLE** with **JUICE**

Beat 4 minutes.

Pour into a greased and floured 13x9x2-inch baking dish. Bake in a preheated 350 degree oven for 30 minutes or until done. Remove from oven, cool and frost with **COCONUT-PINEAPPLE ICING.**

COCONUT-PINEAPPLE ICING

Heat together	½ can (No. 2) **CRUSHED PINEAPPLE** with **JUICE**
	1 stick **BUTTER** or **MARGARINE**
Boil 3 minutes.	
Remove from heat and add	1 box **POWDERED SUGAR**
	1 can **COCONUT**

Punch holes in cake with sharp-bladed knife. Pour hot icing over cake.

7-UP CAKE

Cream together . . . . 1½ cups **BUTTER**
2¾ cups **SUGAR**
Beat until light and fluffy.
Add, one at a time . . . . 5 **EGGS**
Beat well. Add . . . . 3 cups sifted **FLOUR**
Stir in . . . . 2 tsp. **LEMON FLAVORING**
¾ cup **7-UP**

Beat 2 minutes. Pour into a greased and floured tube pan. Bake in a preheated 325 degree oven for 1 hour 15 minutes. When done, cool in pan 15 minutes. Turn out on rack and finish cooling. (May drizzle with **JUICE** of 1 **LEMON** and enough **POWDERED SUGAR** to thicken.)

COCA-COLA CAKE

Sift together and set aside . . . . . 2 cups **FLOUR**
2 cups **SUGAR**
1½ cups **MINIATURE MARSHMALLOWS**
In a saucepan, combine . . . . ½ cup **SHORTENING**
½ cup **BUTTER** or **MARGARINE**
3 Tbsp. **COCOA**
1 cup **COLA**
Heat only until melted. Remove from heat and pour over the flour mixture.
Stir in . . . . ½ cup **BUTTERMILK**
1 tsp. **SODA**
2 **EGGS,** well beaten

Grease and flour a 13x9x2-inch baking pan. Pour in batter and bake in a preheated 350 degree oven for 45 minutes or until done. When done, remove from oven, cool and frost with **COLA FROSTING.**

COLA FROSTING

Put in saucepan and bring
to boil . . . . ½ cup **MARGARINE**
3 Tbsp. **COCOA**
6 Tbsp. **COLA**
When melted, remove from heat
and add . . . . 1 box **POWDERED SUGAR**
1 cup **PECANS,** chopped

Spread on cake.

DR. PEPPER CAKE
Allie Acker's after-school treat.

In a medium saucepan, bring to
  a boil . . . . 1½ cups **DR. PEPPER**
Pour over . . . . 1 cup **QUICK OATS**
Let cool.
Cream together . . . . ½ cup **SHORTENING** or
                                MARGARINE
                       1 cup **SUGAR**
Add and beat until mixture
  is fluffy . . . . 2 **EGGS,** well beaten
Sift together and add to cream
  mixture . . . . 1 cup **BROWN SUGAR,** packed
                      1½ cups **FLOUR**
                      ½ tsp. **SALT**
                      1 tsp. **SODA**
                      ½ tsp. **CINNAMON**
Stir in . . . . Dr. Pepper-oats mixture
                      1 tsp. **VANILLA**

Pour into a greased and floured 13x9x2-inch pan. Bake in a preheated oven at 350 degrees for 40 to 45 minutes, or until done. When cake is done, remove from oven and spread **TOPPING** over cake.

YIELD: 12 TO 18 SERVINGS

TOPPING

In a small saucepan, heat until
  melted . . . . 9 Tbsp. **BROWN SUGAR**
                      5 Tbsp. **BUTTER**
                    1½ Tbsp. **CREAM**
                    1 cup **COCONUT**

Spread over cake. Put under broiler until brown and bubbly.

SWEETENED CONDENSED MILK: Blend ¼ cup hot tap water with ¾ cup sugar for 1 minute. Slowly add 1¼ cups dry non-fat milk. Mix until smooth. Refrigerate.

PINEAPPLE UPSIDE-DOWN CAKE
One of Vera's specialties.

Melt in the bottom of a large
  (12-inch) iron skillet . . . .   1 cup **BROWN SUGAR**
                                   1 stick **BUTTER**
                                   1 tsp. **VANILLA**
Drain, reserve juice and
  add . . . .   1 can (16 oz.) **CRUSHED**
                                            PINEAPPLE
Boil about 5 minutes.
In a mixing bowl cream
  together . . . . 1½ cups **SUGAR**
                                   1 stick **BUTTER**
Add . . . .   2 **EGGS**
                                   1 cup **PINEAPPLE JUICE** (add
                                       WATER to make full cup)
                                   1 tsp. **VANILLA**
                               2¼ cups **FLOUR**
                                 ½ tsp. **SALT**
                                 ½ tsp. **SODA**
                                 1 tsp. **BAKING POWDER**

Mix well and spread over the pineapple mixture. Bake in preheated 350 degree oven for 1 hour. When done, let set about 10 minutes before inverting onto serving plate.

BLACKBERRY WINE CAKE

In a large mixing bowl combine .   1 **WHITE CAKE MIX**
                                   1 pkg. (3 oz.) **BLACKBERRY JELLO**
Add . . . .   5 **EGGS**
                                   ½ cup **OIL**
                                   1 cup **BLACKBERRY WINE**

Mix well. Grease and flour a bundt pan. Sprinkle ½ cup chopped nuts in pan before adding batter. Pour in cake batter and bake in a preheated 325 degree oven for 50 to 55 minutes. Cool and drizzle with glaze.

BLACKBERRY WINE GLAZE

Dissolve and bring to a boil . . . . 1 cup **POWDERED SUGAR**
                                   ½ cup **BLACKBERRY WINE**

Drizzle half of mixture on hot cake in pan. Cool cake. Invert onto cake plate. Drizzle rest of glaze on top.

STRAWBERRY CAKE
Makes a pretty birthday cake for a little girl.

In a mixing bowl combine . . . . . .
- 1 box **WHITE CAKE MIX**
- 3 Tbsp. **FLOUR,** rounded
- 1 box **STRAWBERRY JELLO,**
    added to ½ cup **WATER**
- 1 cup plus 2 Tbsp. **OIL**
- 4 **EGGS**
- 5 ounces **FROZEN STRAWBERRIES,** thawed

Beat well. Bake in well-greased and floured 13x9x2-inch baking dish, or 3 greased and floured 9-inch cake pans. Bake in a preheated 350 degree oven 35 to 40 minutes for oblong pan, or 30 to 35 minutes for cake pans. When done, cool in pans 10 minutes. Turn out on rack to cool completely. Frost with **STRAWBERRY FROSTING.**

STRAWBERRY FROSTING

Beat on high speed of mixer . . . .
- 1 stick **MARGARINE** or **BUTTER**
- 1 box **POWDERED SUGAR**
- 5 ounces frozen **STRAWBERRIES,** thawed with juice

Spread on cold cake layers.

$25,000.00 CAKE

Mix well . . . .
- 1 box **GERMAN CHOCOLATE CAKE MIX,** dry
- 2 **EGGS,** well beaten
- 1 tsp. **ALMOND FLAVORING**

Batter will be very thick. Grease and flour a 13x9x2-inch oblong baking dish. Spread mixture evenly in bottom of pan. Carefully spoon over batter, 1 can **CHERRY PIE FILLING.** Bake in a preheated 350 degree oven for 25 minutes. Remove from oven and spread **FROSTING** on while cake is hot.

CAKE COATING: For a quick, delicious icing, spread warmed honey over cake and sprinkle with chopped nuts or grated coconut.

25,000.00 CAKE FROSTING

Combine in a small saucepan . . .   ⅓ cup **MILK**
                                             1 cup **SUGAR**
                                             5 Tbsp. **BUTTER** or **MARGARINE**
Bring to a boil. Cook 1 minute.
Remove from heat and add . . . . .   6 ounces **MILK CHOCOLATE CHIPS**

Stir and frost cake in pan.

TURTLE CAKE
Cake version of Turtle Candy.

Combine and mix well . . . . 1 **GERMAN CHOCOLATE CAKE MIX**
                                       1 stick **MARGARINE**, softened
                                       1½ cups **WATER**
                                       ½ cup **OIL**
                                       ½ can **EAGLE BRAND MILK**
Pour one-half of the batter into a greased and floured 13x9x2-inch baking dish. Bake in a preheated 350 degree oven for 20 to 25 minutes.
Melt and mix together . . . . 1 pound bag **CARAMELS**
                                         ½ can **EAGLE BRAND MILK**

Spread over the baked layer. Sprinkle generously with chopped **PECANS**. Cover with remaining cake batter. Bake 25 to 35 minutes longer. Frost with **TURTLE CAKE FROSTING**.

TURTLE CAKE FROSTING

Melt in a small saucepan . . . . . .   1 stick **MARGARINE**
                                         3 Tbsp. **COCOA**
                                         6 Tbsp. **EVAPORATED MILK**
Remove from heat and add . . . . .   1 box **POWDERED SUGAR**
                                         1 tsp. **VANILLA**

Spread over cool cake.

MAYONNAISE CHOCOLATE CAKE
Don's favorite...not a pretty cake just good!

Mix . . . .   2 cups **FLOUR**
                                   1 cup **SUGAR**
                                   4 Tbsp. **COCOA**
                                   3 tsp. **BAKING POWDER**
                            1⅓ tsp. **SODA**
Add . . . .   1 cup **COLD WATER**
                                   1 cup **MAYONNAISE**
                                   1 tsp. **VANILLA**

Mix all together and pour into 2 well-greased and floured round cake pans.
Bake in preheated 350 degree oven for 25 to 30 minutes. Let cool 10 minutes
before removing from pans. Completely cool and glaze .

GLAZE

Mix in a saucepan . . . .   ¼ cup **COCOA**
                                 1 cup **SUGAR**
                               ¼ cup **MILK**

Boil 1 minute and glaze cake immediately.

"4 L RANCH" GERMAN FRUIT CAKE

A favorite in the Birdwell residence at Christmas time.

Mix in order given . . . . ¾ cup **MARGARINE**
2 cups **SUGAR**
4 **EGGS,** well beaten
½ tsp. each **ALLSPICE, NUTMEG**
     and **CINNAMON**
¾ tsp. **SODA** *dissolved in*
1 cup **BUTTERMILK**
2 cups **FLOUR**
⅔ cup **CHERRY PRESERVES**
⅔ cup **APRICOT PRESERVES**
⅔ cup **PINEAPPLE PRESERVES**
1 cup **PECANS,** chopped
1 tsp. **VANILLA**

Pour batter into a 10-inch tube pan that has been greased and floured. Bake in a preheated oven at 325 degrees until a straw inserted in the middle of the cake comes out clean, about 1½ hours. Wrap in foil and store in a cool place. This is better if baked several weeks before Christmas.

MAN'S POUND CAKE

All our family's favorite cake.

Beat until stiff and set aside . . . . 6 **EGG WHITES**
Cream . . . . 1 cup **SHORTENING**
3 cups **SUGAR**
Add . . . . 6 **EGG YOLKS**
Sift together . . . . 3 cups **FLOUR**
½ tsp. **SALT**
¼ tsp. **SODA**
Add, alternately with . . . . 1 cup **BUTTERMILK**
2 tsp. **VANILLA**

Fold in egg whites. Bake in a greased and floured tube pan or 2 loaf pans. Cook in a preheated 350-degree oven for 1 hour and 10 minutes. When done, remove from oven and cool 10 minutes in the pan. Remove to rack and let cool. (Optional: Drizzle with ½ cup **ORANGE JUICE**, 1 tsp. grated **ORANGE RIND,** and ⅔ cup **SUGAR** boiled together for 3 minutes.)

SPICY FRESH APPLE CAKE
Very moist.

Cream together...............	¾ cup	**SHORTENING**
	2 cups	**SUGAR**
Add	3	**EGGS**
Beat until fluffy. Add..........	3 cups	**FLOUR**
	½ tsp.	**SALT**
	½ tsp.	**CLOVES**
	2½ tsp.	**SODA**
	1 tsp.	**CINNAMON**
Add by hand.................	2½ cups	**APPLES,** peeled and cubed
	1 cup	**RAISINS**
	1 cup	**PECANS,** chopped
	1 tsp.	**LEMON FLAVORING**
	½ tsp.	**MAPLE FLAVORING**
	½ tsp.	**ALMOND FLAVORING**
	2 tsp.	**VANILLA**

Pour batter into a well-greased and floured tube pan. Bake in a preheated oven at 325 degrees for 1 hour and 20 minutes. Cool in pan 15 minutes before removing. (Optional: Drizzle over cake a mixture of 1½ cups **POWDERED SUGAR,** 3 Tbsp. **WATER** and 2 tsp. **VANILLA.**)

TEXAS WESTERNER

Cream together until fluffy	3 sticks	**BUTTER** or **MARGARINE,** softened
	1 box (1-lb.)	**LIGHT BROWN SUGAR**
Add, one at a time	6	**EGGS**
Beat well after each addition.		
Sift 3 times and gradually add to batter	1 box-full	**FLOUR** (Use box sugar was in.)
Add	1 tsp.	**LEMON JUICE**
	1 Tbsp.	**VANILLA**

Bake in a greased and floured tube pan in a preheated 325 degree oven for 1½ hours. When done, cool 5 minutes, then remove from pan and place on rack. Wonderful served with **WHIPPED TOPPING, FRESH FRUIT,** or **ICE CREAM.**

APPLESAUCE CAKE

Cream together . . . . ½ cup **SHORTENING**
½ cup **BROWN SUGAR**
½ cup **WHITE SUGAR**
When light and fluffy add . . . . . . 2 **EGGS**
Sift together and add to above
   mixture . . . . 2 cups **FLOUR**
1 tsp. **SALT**
1 tsp. **SODA**
1 tsp. **BAKING POWDER**
1 tsp. **CINNAMON**
½ tsp. **NUTMEG**
¼ tsp. **CLOVES**
Alternate with . . . . ½ cup **APPLESAUCE**
Stir in . . . . ½ cup chopped **WALNUTS**
   (optional)
½ cup chopped **RAISINS** (optional)

Mix well and spread batter in a greased 13x9x2-inch pan. Bake in
350-degree oven for 35 to 40 minutes.

TOPSY-TURVY CAKE

The mixture sprinkled on top makes pudding on the bottom.

Cream . . . . ¾ cup **SUGAR**
2 Tbsp. **MARGARINE**
Add . . . . ½ cup **MILK**
1 tsp. **VANILLA**
Sift together and add . . . . 1 cup **FLOUR**
¼ tsp. **SALT**
1 Tbsp. **COCOA**
2 tsp. **BAKING POWDER**
½ cup **PECANS**, chopped
Spread in a buttered 9-inch square pan.
In a small bowl, mix . . . . ½ cup **FLOUR**
½ cup **BROWN SUGAR**, packed
1 Tbsp. **COCOA**
Sprinkle over batter.

Pour over entire cake 1½ cups **BOILING WATER.** Bake in a preheated 350
degree oven for 35 to 40 minutes. Top each individual serving with **WHIP-
PED TOPPING.**

YIELD: 6 TO 9 SERVINGS

PUMPKIN CAKE
This was always a favorite to take to the lake.

Cream together . . . . 2 cups **SUGAR**
                                     4 **EGGS**
Add . . . . 2 cups **FLOUR**
                                     1 tsp. **SALT**
                                 1½ cups **WESSON OIL**
                                 1 cup **PUMPKIN**
                                 2 tsp. **SODA**
                                 3 tsp. **CINNAMON**

Bake in a greased and floured tube pan in a preheated 325 degree oven for 1 hour. When cool, frost with **FROSTING.**

YIELD: 14 TO 16 SERVINGS

FROSTING

Mix together . . . . 1 stick **BUTTER,** room temperature
                                 1 box **POWDERED SUGAR**
                                 1 package (3 oz.) **CREAM CHEESE**
                                 1 Tbsp. **VANILLA**
                                 1 cup **PECANS,** chopped

Spread mixture on cooled **CAKE.**

RUM CAKE

Combine in mixing bowl and beat 4
   minutes 1   **YELLOW CAKE MIX,** dry
                                    4   **EGGS**
                                   ½ cup **WATER**
                                   ½ cup **OIL**
                                   ½ cup **RUM**
                                   1   small package **INSTANT VANILLA PUDDING**

Grease and flour a bundt pan. Sprinkle with ½ cup chopped **PECANS.** Pour batter over pecans in pan. Bake in a preheated 325-degree oven for one hour to 1 hour, 10 minutes. Let cool 20 minutes. Pour **GLAZE** over cake while still in the pan. Do not remove cake from pan until completely cool.

YIELD: 12 SERVINGS

RUM GLAZE

Boil for 3 minutes in a medium
    saucepan . . . .'. . . .   ¼   cup **WATER**
                               ½   cup **RUM**
                               1   cup **SUGAR**
                               1   stick **BUTTER**

Pour over cake.

SHEATH CAKE
Gets better each day.

Mix in saucepan   1   stick **MARGARINE**
                               3½   Tbsp. **COCOA** or **CHOCOLATE
                                      SYRUP**
                               1   cup **WATER**
                               ½   cup **SHORTENING**
Bring to a boil. Remove from
    heat and add   2   cups **FLOUR**
                               2   cups **SUGAR**
                               1   tsp. **SODA**
Mix well and add . . . .   ⅓   cup **BUTTERMILK**
                               2   **EGGS,** well beaten
                               1   tsp. **VANILLA**

Pour into a greased and floured 13x9x2-inch baking dish. Bake in a
preheated 400 degree oven for 30 minutes. Pour on **ICING** while cake is
still hot. Serve warm or cold.

SHEATH CAKE ICING

In a medium saucepan bring to a
    boil   1   stick **MARGARINE**
                               3½   Tbsp. **COCOA** or **CHOCOLATE
                                      SYRUP**
                               ⅓   cup **MILK**

Boil 1 minute. Remove from heat and add 1 box **POWDERED SUGAR,** 1 tsp.
VANILLA, and 1 cup chopped **PECANS.** Pour over hot cake.

ITALIAN DREAM CAKE
An "asked for" favorite of Olive Martin.

Separate . . . .   5 **EGGS**
Beat whites stiff and set aside.
Cream . . . .   2 cups **SUGAR**
   1 stick **MARGARINE,** softened
   ½ cup **SHORTENING**
Add, one at a time . . . .   egg yolks
   2 cups plus 2 Tbsp. sifted **CAKE FLOUR**
Alternate with . . . .   1 cup **BUTTERMILK,** with
   1 tsp. **SODA** dissolved in it
Fold in gently . . . .   egg whites
   1 cup **ANGEL FLAKE COCONUT**
   1 tsp. **VANILLA**

Pour into a greased and floured 13x9x2-inch baking dish. Bake 40 minutes at 350 degrees. Cool and frost.

FROSTING

Cream together . . . .   1 pkg. (8 oz.) **CREAM CHEESE**
   1 stick **MARGARINE,** softened
   1 box **POWDERED SUGAR**
   1 tsp. **VANILLA**
   ½ cup **NUTS,** chopped and toasted
Spread on cooled **CAKE.**

TEMPTATION
Edna Carroll's favorite pound cake.

Cream *well* . . . .   1 cup **MARGARINE,** softened
   ½ cup **BUTTER,** softened
   8 ounces **CREAM CHEESE**
   3 cups **SUGAR**
Add . . . .   Dash of **SALT**
   2 tsp. **VANILLA**
Add, one at a time, beating well
   after each . . . .   6 large **EGGS**
Add . . . .   3 cups plus 3 Tbsp. **FLOUR**

Beat well. Pour into a greased and floured 10-inch tube pan or 2 loaf pans. Place in a *cold* oven and turn heat to 275 degrees. Bake for about 1½ hours. Insert a toothpick in center of cake to test for doneness.

REMEMBER GRANNY'S CHOCOLATE LAYER CAKE?
This is Aunt Snook's version.

Cream together..............	1 cup **SHORTENING**
	2 cups **SUGAR**
Add	4 **EGGS,** well beaten
Sift together	2½ cups **FLOUR**
	1 tsp. **SODA**
	4 Tbsp. **COCOA**
	¼ tsp. **SALT**
Add to creamed mixture alternately with	1 cup **BUTTERMILK**
Stir in	1 tsp. **VANILLA**

Grease and flour 3 (9-inch) cake pans. Pour batter into pans, bake in a preheated 350-degree oven for 25 minutes. Remove from oven, cool 10 minutes, turn out on racks. When completely cool, fill with **CUSTARD** and frost with **FUDGE FROSTING.**

CUSTARD

Combine in a saucepan	½ cup **SUGAR**
	3 Tbsp. **FLOUR**
	¼ tsp. **SALT**
	1½ cups **MILK**

Mix and cook until slightly thickened. (10 minutes) Pour small amount into 2 slightly beaten **EGG YOLKS.** Add egg yolk mixture to saucepan and return to heat. Cook 2 more minutes. Cool and spread on layers, stack and frost.

FUDGE FROSTING

In a medium saucepan combine .	2 squares **UNSWEETENED CHOCOLATE,** cut in pieces
	⅔ cup **MILK**
Heat and stir until melted.	
Add	2 cups **SUGAR**
	2 tsp. **KARO,** light
	2 Tbsp. **BUTTER**
Stir until dissolved.	

Continue cooking without stirring until mixture forms a soft ball (238 degrees on candy thermometer). Remove from heat. Add 1 tsp. **VANILLA.** Cool without stirring to lukewarm. Beat until creamy. Frost cake. (Do not let frosting get too hard, or it will be hard to spread on cake.)

HUMMINGBIRD CAKE
So good, you will go "hmmmmm" when you eat it.

In a large mixing bowl, stir
   by hand .... 1½ cups **OIL**
                             2 cups **SUGAR**
                             3 **EGGS**
                           1½ tsp. **VANILLA**
Add .... 1 tsp. **SODA**
                             1 tsp. **CINNAMON**
                             3 cups **FLOUR**
                             ½ tsp. **SALT**
Mix well. Add............... 2 **BANANAS**, diced
                             1 can (8 oz.) **CRUSHED PINEAPPLE**, with juice
                             ½ cup **COCONUT**
                             1 cup **PECANS**, chopped

Pour well-mixed batter into a greased and floured bundt or tube pan and bake in a preheated 350-degree oven for 1½ hours. When cooked, cool before removing from pan. (Or, bake in 3 greased and floured 9-inch cake pans for 25 to 30 minutes. Cool and frost with **CREAM CHEESE FROSTING.)**

CREAM CHEESE FROSTING

Combine and beat until smooth.. 1 pkg. (8 oz.) **CREAM CHEESE**, softened
                             ½ cup **BUTTER**, softened
Add .... 1 pkg. (16 oz.) **POWDERED SUGAR**
                             1 sp. **VANILLA**

Beat until light and fluffy. Spread between layers and on top and sides of cake. Sprinkle ½ cup chopped **PECANS** on top.

PEEL AWAY: Use a vegetable peeler to remove the tough brown skin that adheres to fresh coconut meat.

BANANA NUT CAKE
A good traveler.

Cream together . . . . ½ cup **SHORTENING**
1½ cups **SUGAR**
2 **EGGS,** slightly beaten
Add . . . . 4 Tbsp. **BUTTERMILK**
1 tsp. **VANILLA**
1 tsp. **SODA**
2 cups **FLOUR**
Mash and add . . . . 3 ripe **BANANAS**
Dredge in a little flour and
add . . . . ½ cup **PECANS**

Mix well and bake in 2 greased and floured cake pans in preheated 350 degree oven for 25 minutes. Cool and spread with **BANANA NUT FILLING.**

BANANA NUT FILLING

Cream together . . . . ¼ pound **BUTTER**
1 pound **POWDERED SUGAR**
2 ripe **BANANAS**
1 cup **PECANS,** chopped

Mix together and spread on cooled **BANANA NUT CAKE.**

KANSAS APPLE CAKE
A specialty of Joy Cheyney.

Mix together and set aside . . . . . 4 cups peeled and chopped
APPLES
2 tsp. **BAKING SODA**
Combine in separate bowl . . . . . . 2 cups **SUGAR**
2 **EGGS**
1⅓ cups **OIL**
Mix together . . . . 3 cups **FLOUR**
½ tsp. **SALT**
2 tsp. **CINNAMON**
¼ tsp. **BAKING POWDER**
Mix dry ingredients with egg
mixture and add . . . . 2 tsp. **VANILLA**
Fold in . . . . 1 cup chopped **NUTS**

Add apples and pour into 2 greased and floured loaf pans or a greased and floured tube pan. Bake in preheated 350 degree oven for 50 to 60 minutes.

COCONUT CAKE
A Franklin Christmas tradition.

Cream together . . . .   2 cups **SUGAR**
   1 cup **SHORTENING**
Add . . . .   4 **EGG YOLKS,** well beaten
   2 tsp. **VANILLA**
Sift together . . . .   3 cups **FLOUR**
   3 tsp. **BAKING POWDER**
   ⅛ tsp. **SALT**
Add to creamed mixture,
   alternately with . . . . 1¼ cup **MILK**
Beat until stiff and fold in . . . . . .   4 **EGG WHITES**
Do not overbeat.

Grease and flour 4 (9-inch) cake pans. Pour batter evenly into all 4 pans. Cook in a preheated 350-degree oven for 20 to 25 minutes. Remove from oven and turn out on racks to cool. Frost with **MAM-MA'S ICING** or **GOLDIE'S ICING.**

MAM-MA'S ICING

In mixing bowl, beat until
   very stiff . . . .   5 or 6 **EGG WHITES**
In saucepan combine . . . .   2 cups **SUGAR**
   1 cup **BOILING WATER**
   1 Tbsp. **KARO,** light
   ½ tsp. **VINEGAR**

Bring to boil on medium heat, stirring only until sugar is dissolved. Continue cooking until mixture reaches soft-ball stage (238 degrees on candy thermometer). Pour slowly into egg whites, with mixer stirring. Add 1 tsp. **VANILLA.** Spread on layers of cake, sprinkling with fresh or thawed frozen **COCONUT.** Stack and frost the outside, covering with remaining coconut. (You may use Angel Flake Coconut, if you prefer.)

GOLDIE'S ICING FOR FRESH COCONUT CAKE
Henry's Christmas-time favorite for 54 years.

Combine . . . .   1 cup **MILK**
   2 cups **SUGAR**
   1 stick **MARGARINE**

Cook until slightly thickened. Add 1 tsp. **VANILLA.** Ice a 2-layer **WHITE CAKE** and put freshly-grated **COCONUT** that has soaked in its own milk, on top of each iced layer. Refrigerate, or can be frozen.

MOM'S PIE CRUST

Mix . . . .   3 cups **FLOUR**
                                     1 tsp. **SALT**
                                     1 Tbsp. **SUGAR**
Cut in with pastry blender or
   two knives, using scissor
   motion . . . .   1 cup **SHORTENING**
Add . . . .   ⅓ cup **WATER**
                                     1 **EGG,** well beaten
                                     1 tsp. **VINEGAR**

Mix with a fork until mixture forms a ball. Roll into 2 pie crusts. (This dough
can be put into a plastic bag, tightly sealed, refrigerated and kept for several
days. Let warm to room temperature before rolling.)

YIELD: 2 LARGE OR 3 SMALL PASTRY SHELLS

NEVER-FAIL BUTTERMILK PASTRY

Shared by a friend on the Coastal Bend of Texas.

Put into a mixing bowl . . . .   2 cups **FLOUR**
Make an indention in the middle of the flour.
Pour into a 1-cup glass
   measure . . . .   ½ cup **OIL**
Pour **BUTTERMILK** into the oil until it measures ¾ cup altogether.
Add . . . .   1 tsp. **SUGAR**
Mix very well.

Pour the oil-buttermilk mixture into the indention in the flour. Stirring with
a fork, begin working the flour gradually into the liquid. Mix until right consistency for pie crust. (May need only 1¾ cups flour.) Roll between pieces
of waxed paper. This dough is very soft, so it is easy to work with. When
recipe calls for pre-baked pastry, cook in preheated 375 degree oven for
10 minutes.

YIELD: 1 PASTRY SHELL

*PIE SHELL HINT: Paint unbaked pie shell with a little of the beaten egg.
Bake it at 450 degrees for 7 to 10 minutes. Do not brown. The egg keeps
it crisp after it's filled.*

PECAN CRUST
This is from Beth Smith and it is delicious.

Mix . . . . 1 cup chopped **PECANS**
1½ sticks **BUTTER,** softened
1½ cups **FLOUR**
2 Tbsp. **SUGAR**

Pat into a pie pan and bake at 325 degrees for 20 minutes.

YIELD: 1 PASTRY SHELL

"PRACTICALLY" FOOL-PROOF MERINGUE

Beat until soft peaks . . . . 3 **EGG WHITES**
Dash of **SALT**
Gradually add. . . . . 1 cup **MARSHMALLOW CREME**

Beat until stiff peaks form. Spread over **PIE FILLING,** sealing to edge of crust. Bake in preheated 350 degree oven for 12 to 15 minutes.

YIELD: MERINGUE FOR 1 PIE

"PRACTICALLY" NEVER-FAIL MERINGUE

Blend together in a medium
saucepan. . . . . 1 Tbsp. **CORNSTARCH**
2 Tbsp. **COLD WATER**
Add . . . . ½ cup **BOILING WATER**
Cook until clear and thickened, stirring constantly. Let stand until cold.
Beat until foamy. . . . . 3 **EGG WHITES**
Gradaully add. . . . . 6 Tbsp. **SUGAR**
Beat until stiff, but not too dry.
Turn mixer to "Low", add . . . . . 1 tsp. **VANILLA**

Gradually add cornstarch mixture. Mix on high speed for 2 minutes. Spread over **PIE FILLING,** sealing to edge of crust. Bake in preheated 350 degree oven for 10 minutes.

YIELD: MERINGUE FOR 1 PIE

ALL AMERICAN APPLE PIE
Make ahead, freeze and bake when needed.

Pare, core and slice thin	6 tart **APPLES**
Combine and mix with	
apples	1 cup **SUGAR**
	1 Tbsp. **FLOUR**
	1 tsp. **CINNAMON**
	¼ tsp. **SALT**
If apples are not tart, add	1 Tbsp. **LEMON JUICE**

Fill a 9-inch **PASTRY**-lined pie pan with apple mixture. Dot with ½ stick **BUTTER**. Cover with a top **CRUST**, cut slits to allow steam to escape. Bake at 400 degrees for 50 minutes or until done.

YIELD: 8 SERVINGS

AUNT TOOTSIE'S CHOCOLATE CREAM PIE

Combine and cook over low heat	
until thick	¼ cup **FLOUR**
	⅔ cup **SUGAR**
	⅛ tsp. **SALT**
	2 Tbsp. **COCOA**
	2 cups **MILK**
Stir ½ cup above mixture	
into	3 **EGG YOLKS,** well beaten
Pour back into saucepan and cook until very thick.	
Add	1 Tbsp. **BUTTER**
	½ tsp. **VANILLA**

Mix well and cool. Pour into baked **PASTRY SHELL** and top with **ME-RINGUE**. Brown in pre-heated 375 degree oven for 10 to 12 minutes.

YIELD: 8 SERVINGS

1-2-3 LEMONADE PIE

Blend well	1 small can frozen **LEMONADE**
	1 can **EAGLE BRAND MILK**
Fold into	1 carton (8 oz.) **COOL WHIP**

Pour into a cooked **PASTRY SHELL** or **GRAHAM CRACKER CRUST**. Chill.

BEST EVER LEMON PIE

Mix in a double boiler . . . . 1¼ cups **SUGAR**
6 Tbsp. **CORNSTARCH**
Add . . . . 2 cups **WATER**
Combine . . . . 3 **EGG YOLKS**
⅓ cup **LEMON JUICE**
Beat well and add to mixture. Cook until thick (about 25 minutes).
Add . . . . 1½ tsp. **LEMON FLAVORING**
3 Tbsp. **BUTTER,** melted
2 tsp. **VINEGAR**

Stir well and pour into a 9-inch baked **PASTRY SHELL.** Let cool. Cover with **MERINGUE** and brown.

YIELD: 8 SERVINGS

LEMON ANGEL PIE

Macky Turner shared this "heavenly" dessert with us.

Beat until fairly stiff . . . . 4 **EGG WHITES**
Add . . . . ¼ tsp. **CREAM OF TARTAR**
Continue beating. Gradually
add . . . . ¾ cup **SUGAR**

Beat until meringue mixture is stiff. Spread in a baked **PASTRY SHELL,** making an indention in the middle. Bake in a preheated 300 degree oven for 1 hour. Do not open oven door during cooking. Cool. Fill with **LEMON FILLING.**

YIELD: 8 SERVINGS

LEMON FILLING

Mix in top of double-boiler . . . . . 8 **EGG YOLKS,** slightly beaten
¾ cup **SUGAR**
½ tsp. **SALT**
Add . . . . 3 Tbsp. **ORANGE JUICE**
3 Tbsp. **LEMON JUICE**
1 tsp. each grated **LEMON** and
ORANGE RIND
Cook until thick. Stir occasionally.

Cool and spread over baked **MERINGUE.** Cover with 2 cups **WHIPPED CREAM.** Garnish with toasted **ALMONDS.**

JANET HARRIS' WONDER RECIPE
Wonder what we would do without it?

Use for pudding or pie filling. Use a large bowl or it will boil over in microwave.

Microwave on "high" (100%
    power) until warm . . . . 1½ cups **MILK**
Mix together and add to
    milk . . . . 1½ cups **SUGAR**
                          4 Tbsp. **FLOUR**
Microwave 5 minutes.
Blend together . . . . 2 **EGG YOLKS,** well beaten
                          ½ cup **MILK**
Mix well and pour into milk mixture.
Cook for 1 minute intervals until
    custard is thick, stirring
    between each minute of
    cooking. Stir in . . . . 1 tsp. **VANILLA**

Cook and pour into **PASTRY SHELL**. Top with **MERINGUE**.

YIELD: 8 SERVINGS

VARIATIONS:
CHOCOLATE: Add 3 Tbsp. **COCOA** to sugar-flour mixture.
BANANA: Pour over sliced **BANANAS** in pastry shell. For BANANA PUD-
    DING, layer custard with **BANANAS** and **VANILLA WAFERS**.
COCONUT: Stir 1 can **ANGEL FLAKE COCONUT** into the custard mixture.
PINEAPPLE: Stir *well-drained* **PINEAPPLE** into custard mixture.

PEANUT BUTTER PIE
One of Mary Taylor's culinary delights.

Combine until texture of coarse
    cornmeal . . . . 1 cup **POWDERED SUGAR**
                          ½ cup **CREAMY PEANUT BUTTER**
Put ¾ of mixture in a baked 9-inch **PASTRY SHELL**
Combine in a saucepan and cook
    over medium heat until thick,
    stirring constantly . . . . 4 Tbsp. **CORNSTARCH**
                          3 **EGG YOLKS**
                          ⅔ cup **SUGAR**
                          2 cups **MILK**

Pour custard over peanut butter mixture. Top with **MERINGUE**. Sprinkle remainder of peanut butter mixture over meringue. Bake in 325 degree oven for 20 minutes or until brown.

YIELD: 8 SERVINGS

QUICK CRUSTLESS RITZ PIE
Make the Lemon Angel Pie, use the leftover
egg whites and make this one.

Beat at high speed on mixer
   until very stiff . . . .   3 or 4 **EGG WHITES**
                                ½ cup **SUGAR**
Add . . . .   1 tsp. **VANILLA**
Set aside. Crush with rolling
   pin . . . .   20 **RITZ CRACKERS**
Mix with . . . .   ½ cup **SUGAR**
                                ½ cup **NUTS**

Fold mixtures together and spoon into a greased and floured 9-inch pie pan. Cook in a preheated 350-degree oven for 25 minutes. (Do not open oven during cooking.) Pie will fall, so fill cavity with **WHIPPED TOPPING** after pie has completely cooled.

YIELD: 6 TO 8 SERVINGS

HARVEST PIE
Perfect for Thanksgiving dinner.

Mix together . . . .   2 **EGGS**
                                1½ cups **PUMPKIN**
                                ½ tsp. **SALT**
                                ½ tsp. **ALLSPICE**
                              1 tsp. **CINNAMON**
                              ½ tsp. **NUTMEG**
                              ¾ cup **SUGAR**
                              1½ cups **MILK**

Pour into unbaked **PASTRY SHELL.** Bake in preheated 425 degree oven for 15 minutes. Reduce heat to 350 degrees and bake for 45 more minutes.

YIELD: 8 SERVINGS

HALF PRICE MILK: Keep nonfat dry milk mixed and in refrigerator to cook with.

OLE' TIME OSGOOD PIE
H.G.'s mom's recipe.

Beat until stiff   2   **EGG YOLKS**
Add   1   cup **SUGAR**
                              1½ tsp. **VINEGAR**
                              ¼ tsp. **CINNAMON**
                              ¼ tsp. **CLOVES**
                              1 Tbsp. **BUTTER,** melted
Beat until fluffy.
Fold in ....   ½   cup **PECANS,** chopped
                              ½   cup **RAISINS**
                              2   beaten **EGG WHITES**

Pour into a 9-inch unbaked **PASTRY SHELL.** Bake in a preheated oven at 300 degrees for 40 to 50 minutes.

YIELD: 8 SERVINGS

PANHANDLE RAISIN PIE

In a medium saucepan combine   ¾ cup **SUGAR**
                              1 Tbsp. **CORNSTARCH**
                              ¼ tsp. **SALT**
                              1 tsp. **CINNAMON**
                              ½ tsp. **NUTMEG**
                              ¼ tsp. **CLOVES**
Stir in ....   1 cup **SOUR CREAM**
                              1 Tbsp. **LEMON JUICE**
Add   1   cup **RAISINS**
Bring to a boil, stirring constantly. Cook until thick.
Remove from heat and stir a
    small amount of hot mixture
    into ....   2 **EGG YOLKS,** well beaten
Pour back into hot mixture and cook 1 minute. Cool.
Add ....   ½ cup **WALNUTS**

Pour into an 8-inch baked **PASTRY SHELL.**

YIELD: 8 SERVINGS

FRUIT IN CAKE: Keep raisins, dried fruits or nuts from sinking to bottom of cake by using small amount of flour from recipe to coat.

COCONUT LOVER'S CHESS PIE

Beat in an electric mixer at
medium speed . . . . 3 **EGGS**
1½ cups **SUGAR**
2 Tbsp. **FLOUR**
Cut in with knife . . . . ½ stick **MARGARINE**
Stir in . . . . 1 cup **MILK**
1 tsp. **VANILLA**

Sprinkle bottom of an unbaked **PASTRY SHELL** with 1 can **COCONUT**. Pour mixture over top of coconut. Bake in a preheated 325 degree oven until golden brown, about 50 minutes.

YIELD: 6 TO 8 SERVINGS

CHOCOLATE FUDGE PIE

Mix together . . . . 1 cup **SUGAR**
2 **EGGS**
4 Tbsp. **COCOA**
2 Tbsp. **FLOUR**
½ cup **MILK**
3 Tbsp. **BUTTER**, melted
Dash of **SALT**
1 Tbsp. **VANILLA**

Pour into an unbaked **PASTRY SHELL**. Bake in preheated oven at 350 degrees for 30 minutes.

YIELD: 8 SERVINGS

PINEAPPLE CHESS PIE

Beat well . . . . 3 **EGGS**
Add . . . . 2 cups **SUGAR**
2 Tbsp. **CORNMEAL**
2 Tbsp. **FLOUR**
1 small can **CRUSHED PINEAPPLE**
with juice

Pour into an unbaked **PASTRY SHELL.** Chip over the top, 1 stick **MARGARINE.** Bake in a preheated 325 degree oven until toothpick comes out clean, about 1 hour.

YIELD: 8 SERVINGS

FAWN PIE

Cream together	1 stick **MARGARINE,** melted
	2 cups **SUGAR**
Add, one at a time	4 **EGGS**
Beat well and stir in	1 Tbsp. **FLOUR**
	1 Tbsp. **CORNMEAL**
	1 tsp. **VANILLA**
Fold in	1 small can **CRUSHED PINEAPPLE** with juice
	1 can **COCONUT**

Place in prepared unbaked **PASTRY SHELL.** Bake in preheated 375 degree oven for 10 minutes. Reduce oven temperature to 325 degrees and bake for additional 50 minutes, or until set.

YIELD; 6 SERVINGS

BUTTER PIE

Barbara's Grandmother, Mrs. Rich Miller, brought this recipe to Borden County in 1900.

Combine	1 cup **SUGAR**
	6 Tbsp. **FLOUR**
Add	1 cup **MILK**
	1 tsp. **VANILLA**

Pour into an 8-inch unbaked **PASTRY SHELL.** Slice ½ cup **BUTTER** over top of mixture. Sprinkle with **NUTMEG.** Bake at 350 degrees for 10 minutes. Lower temperature to 300 degrees and cook until set.

BUTTERMILK PIE

Cream together	½ cup **BUTTER**
	2 cups **SUGAR**
Add	3 rounded Tbsp. **FLOUR**
	3 **EGGS,** slightly beaten
Stir in	1 cup **BUTTERMILK**
	1 tsp. **VANILLA**
	Dash **NUTMEG**

Beat until smooth.

Place in uncooked pastry shell. Bake at 350 degrees for 45 to 50 minutes.

GRANNY'S LEMON CHESS
Easy make-ahead pie for holidays.

Mix together	2 cups **SUGAR**
	1 Tbsp. **CORNMEAL**
	1 Tbsp. **FLOUR**
Cut in with pastry blender	4 Tbsp. **MARGARINE**
Add, one at a time	4 **EGGS**
Stir and add	¼ cup **MILK**
	¼ cup **LEMON JUICE**
	1½ Tbsp. grated **LEMON RIND**

Pour into an unbaked **PASTRY SHELL** and bake in a preheated oven at 375 degrees for 45 minutes. (Can be frozen after cooking.)

VARIATION: Add 1 cup **PECANS** to mixture.

YIELD: 6 TO 8 SERVINGS

CATHY'S CHERRY PIE DELIGHT

Refrigerate in an airtight container	1 can **CHERRY PIE FILLING**
In a medium bowl, beat until light and fluffy	1 pkg. (8 oz.) **CREAM CHEESE**
Add and blend well	1 can **EAGLE BRAND MILK**
Stir in	⅓ cup **LEMON JUICE**
	1 tsp. **VANILLA**

Pour cream cheese mixture into prepared **GRAHAM CRACKER CRUST**. Chill at least 3 hours. To serve, top pie slices with cherry pie filling. This recipe refrigerates well. (Use any of your favorite pie fillings.)

MRS. OGLETREE'S PECAN PIE

Mix all ingredients	1 cup **SUGAR**
	1 cup **WHITE KARO**
	⅛ tsp. **VANILLA**
	2 Tbsp. **MARGARINE**
	3 **EGGS,** slightly beaten
Add last	1 cup **PECANS,** chopped (not fine)

Bake at 400 degrees for 15 minutes. Reduce heat to 325 degrees and bake 30 to 35 minutes longer. When done, edges should be set and center slightly soft. Cool and it is ready to eat or wrap in foil and freeze for later use.

GRANDMOTHER'S PECAN PIES
75 year old recipe.

Combine in order . . . . 4 **EGGS,** well beaten
1¼ cups **WHITE KARO**
3 Tbsp. **CREAM**
3 Tbsp. **SUGAR**
½ Tbsp. **CORNSTARCH**
1 tsp. **VANILLA**
1 cup **PECANS**

Mix well. Pour into unbaked **PASTRY SHELL.** Sprinkle with **NUTMEG.** Bake in a preheated 350-degree oven for 10 minutes. Reduce oven temperature to 300 degrees and continue baking for 1 hour, or until set.

YIELD: 6 SERVINGS

NONA'S PECAN PIE
The secret is in the stirring.

Slightly stir together with a fork   3 **EGGS**
3 Tbsp. **FLOUR**
1 cup **WHITE KARO**
1 cup **SUGAR**
Dash of **SALT**
1 tsp. **VANILLA**
Melt and add . . . . 3 Tbsp. **BUTTER**

Put a layer of **PECANS** (either halves or chopped, whichever you prefer) into an unbaked **PASTRY SHELL.** Pour mixture over, covering all the pecans. Bake in a preheated 300 degree oven until mixture is set in the middle, between 1 hour and 1 hour, 10 minutes.

VARIATION:
Brown **COCONUT** in a small amount of **BUTTER** in the oven, stirring occasionally. Substitute for pecans.

YIELD: 8 SERVINGS

DID YOU KNOW? Keep your shelled nuts in plastic bags in the freezer to prevent their becoming rancid.

CARAMEL-NUT PIE
Calories: One Zillion

Mix in a medium saucepan and
   cook over medium heat . . . . . .   1 can **EAGLE BRAND MILK**
                               ½ cup **BROWN SUGAR,** packed
                               Dash of **SALT**
Cook until thick. Stir in . . . .   ¼ cup **PECANS,** chopped
Cool mixture and put into baked **PASTRY SHELL.**
Sprinkle over mixture . . . .   ¼ cup **PECANS,** chopped
Whip until stiff . . . .   1 cup **HEAVY CREAM**
Fold in . . . .   ¼ cup **POWDERED SUGAR**

Spread on top of filling. Garnish with **TOASTED COCONUT.** Refrigerate.

YIELD: 8 SERVINGS

"HIGH AS THE SKY" STRAWBERRY PIE

In a small mixing bowl, whip . . .   ½ cup **WHIPPING CREAM**
Set aside. Chill a medium mixing bowl and beaters.
Combine and beat for 15 minutes
   at high speed . . . .   1 pkg. (10 oz.) frozen
                                    STRAWBERRIES
                               2 **EGG WHITES**
                               ¼ tsp. **SALT**
                               ¾ cup **SUGAR**
                               1 Tbsp. **LEMON JUICE**
Add . . . .   1 tsp. **VANILLA**

Fold the two mixtures together gently. Pour into a pre-baked **PASTRY SHELL.** Swirl the top. Place uncovered in the freezer. Serve frozen. Garnish with **WHOLE STRAWBERRIES.**

YIELD: 8 SERVINGS

SYRUP PIE

*Really more of a caramel pie. Recipe has been in the Franklin family
for 150 years.*

Mix all ingredients in a medium
   skillet.....................   2 **EGGS**
                               2 Tbsp. **FLOUR**
                               1 cup **WHITE KARO**
                               ½ cup **SHORTENING**
                               1 cup **SUGAR**

Cook over medium heat, stirring constantly, until mixture reaches a rolling
boil. (It will probably stick, but this does not affect the results of the pie.)
Continue cooking for 2 or 3 more minutes. Add 1 tsp. **VANILLA.** Pour into
a baked **PASTRY SHELL.** Bake in a preheated 350 degree oven for 15
minutes. Texture resembles caramel. Serve warm or cold.

YIELD: 6 TO 8 SERVINGS

JAYME J'S CALYPSO PIE

Melt.......................   ¼ cup **BUTTER**
Add ....   18 crushed **OREO COOKIES**
Press into a 9-inch pie pan.
In a medium saucepan,
   melt.....................   3 squares **UNSWEETENED
                                        CHOCOLATE**
                               ¼ cup **BUTTER**
Remove from heat and
   stir in ....   ⅔ cup **SUGAR**
                               ⅛ tsp. **SALT**
Blend well. Gradually add,
   mixing well ....   1 can (13 oz.) **EVAPORATED MILK**

Cook over low heat, stirring constantly, for about 4 minutes or until thick.
Remove from heat and stir in 1 tsp. **VANILLA.** Chill in refrigerator.

Soften 1 quart **MOCHA ICE CREAM** (or any other flavor). Put ice cream
into crust. Pack down and put into freezer. Cover with cooled Chocolate
Fudge Sauce. Top with **WHIPPED TOPPING** that has 3 Tbsp. **POWDERED
SUGAR** added to it. Garnish with slivered **ALMONDS.** Return to freezer
until ready to serve.

YIELDD: 8 SERVINGS

KIWI AND STRAWBERRY TART

Prepare a rich **PASTRY SHELL.** Line with aluminum foil, fill with dried beans. Bake at 425 until brown (about 12 minutes). Remove beans and foil. Cool.

Combine .... 1½ cups **WHIPPING CREAM**
½ cup **SUGAR**
2 **EGG YOLKS**
1 tsp. **VANILLA** or 2 Tbsp. **COINTREAU**

Pour into cooled pastry shell. Bake at 325 degrees until firm (about 35 minutes). Cool completely. Arrange a row of **STRAWBERRIES** around outside edge of tart (1½ to 2 cups fresh strawberries). Fill the inside with a single layer of sliced **KIWI.** Heat ¼ cup **APRICOT JAM** just until melted and brush over fruit with pastry brush.

YIELD: 10 TO 12 SERVINGS

SWINNEY STRAWBERRY PIE

Cream together .... ½ cup **HEAVY CREAM**
½ cup **POWDERED SUGAR**
3 oz. **CREAM CHEESE**
½ tsp. **VANILLA**
¼ tsp. **ALMOND FLAVORING**
In small saucepan, crush....... ½ cup **STRAWBERRIES**
Add .... ½ cup **WATER**
¼ cup **SUGAR**
1 Tbsp. **CORNSTARCH**
Cook until thick on low heat, stirring constantly. Cool completely.

Wash and drain on paper towels, 1 cup **STRAWBERRIES.** Remove stems and place over cream cheese mixture in prepared **PASTRY SHELL** (Vanilla wafer, graham or regular). Pour glaze over strawberries and refrigerate. To serve, garnish with **WHIPPED TOPPING.**

YIELD: 8 SERVINGS

SARAH'S FRENCH SILK PIE

Cream until fluffy. . . . .   1 stick **BUTTER**
Gradually add. . . . .   ¾ cup **SUGAR**
Beat thoroughly.
Add . . . .   1 square **UNSWEETENED**
                                    CHOCOLATE, melted
                              1 tsp. **VANILLA**

Add, one at a time, beating 3
  minutes after each
  addition . . . .   2 **EGGS**

Pour mixture into a baked 9-inch **PASTRY SHELL**. Top with 1 cup **HEAVY CREAM**, whipped. Garnish with chopped **BLACK WALNUTS** or toasted **ALMOND SLIVERS**. Freeze for several hours. Remove from freezer 10 to 15 minutes before serving.

YIELD: 8 SERVINGS

PUNKIN'S MUD PIE

Mix together . . . . 1½ cups crushed **CHOCOLATE**
                                  WAFERS (about 30 wafers)
                             6 Tbsp. **BUTTER,** melted
                             1 tsp. **CINNAMON**
Pat into a 9-inch pie plate and bake for 15 minutes at 300 degrees. Let cool
  completely.
While crust is cooling,
  soften . . . .   ½ gallon **BUTTER ALMOND ICE**
                                  CREAM (may prefer **MOCHA**)
Mound in cooled crust. Cover and freeze.
When frozen solid, top with . . . .   1 jar (about 12 oz.) **FUDGE** or
                                  CHOCOLATE TOPPING
                             1 cup **TOASTED ALMONDS,**
                                  slivered

Cover again and re-freeze. To serve, spread with **WHIPPED TOPPING**.

YIELD: 8 SERVINGS

MILLIONAIRE PIE

Makes 4 pies. Eat one and freeze three, or share with friends.

Cream together..............	1 pkg. (8 oz.) **CREAM CHEESE,** softened
	2 sticks **MARGARINE**
	1 cup **EGG YOLKS**
Add	¼ tsp. **SALT**
	1½ pounds **POWDERED SUGAR**

Spread in bottom of 4 baked **PASTRY SHELLS.** Cool.

Whip until stiff..............	2 cups **HEAVY CREAM**
Fold in	4 Tbsp. **POWDERED SUGAR**
	2 cups **PINEAPPLE,** *well*-drained
	1 cup **PECANS,** chopped

Spread over cream cheese mixture. Chill.

YIELD: 4 PIES

CUT-OUT CRUST: When making a two-crust pie, roll out dough as usual. Cut out various appropriate shapes with cookie cutters and place them on top of filling before baking. Gives pies a festive touch on special special occasions.

Desserts

EASY DESSERT - ELEGANT ENTERTAINING
Crepes.

Make crepes ahead of time and freeze. Fill with your favorite mixture. Serve.

BATTER:

Gradually blend	2 cups **FLOUR**	
into	4 **LARGE EGGS,** well beaten	
Beat in by spoonsful	1 cup **MILK**	
	1 cup **COLD WATER**	
Add	¼ cup **BUTTER,** melted	
	½ tsp. **SALT**	

Cover and refrigerate 2 hours. (This allows the flour particles to swell and soften so the crepes will be light in texture.) Put scant ¼ cup batter in a moderately hot, lightly greased 6-inch skillet. (Crepe-maker is best.) Tilt pan to spread. Brown and turn. Cook about 1 minute on each side. Place on a clean towel to cool. Stack between layers of waxed paper to prevent sticking together.

TO SERVE: Place 3 Tbsp. **FILLING** into center of each crepe, roll up, and place seam-side-down on a serving plate. Garnish.
TO FREEZE: Stack with waxed paper between each crepe. Wrap tightly in foil. Thaw to room temperature before filling.

YIELD: 12 CREPES. SERVE 2 CREPES PER PERSON.

CREPES SUZETTE:

In center of each **CREPE,** place	1 Tbsp. **ORANGE MARMALADE** (from 8 oz. jar)	
Fold into quarters. Melt in a large skillet	4 Tbsp. **BUTTER**	
Add remaining marmalade and	¼ cup **FRESH ORANGE JUICE**	
Simmer until blended.		
Place crepes in sauce, overlapping in a circle around the skillet.		
Just before serving, pour in	1 ounce **BRANDY,** warmed	

Light with match. When flame has gone out, place crepes on serving plate. Spoon sauce over crepes and sprinkle tops with **SUGAR.** Garnish.

YIELD: 12 CREPES

GRAND MARNIER CREPES:

In a skillet, melt	2 sticks **MARGARINE**
Add	1 cup **POWDERED SUGAR**
	½ cup **FRESH ORANGE JUICE**
Cook over low heat, stirring until thickened. Add	⅛ tsp. **CINNAMON**
Add	2 ounces **GRAND MARNIER,** warmed

Flame, stirring until flame goes out. Place crepes in skillet, one at a time, folding into quarters. Serve with remaining sauce. Garnish with **WHIPPED TOPPING** and **SLIVERED ALMONDS.**

YIELD: 12 CREPES

ORANGE CREPES:

Beat until light and fluffy	1 pkg. (3 oz.) **CREAM CHEESE,** softened
Add	8 oz. **SOUR CREAM**
	¼ cup **ORANGE MARMALADE** (from small jar)
	2 tsp. grated **ORANGE RIND**
	¼ Tbsp. grated **LEMON RIND**

Spread mixture evenly over each **CREPE.** Roll up, and place seam down in a lightly buttered 13x9x2-inch baking dish. Spread remaining marmalade over crepes. Sprinkle with toasted slivered **ALMONDS.** Broil until marmalade begins to bubble.

YIELD: 12 CREPES

RUM-CHOCOLATE CREPES:

Combine and beat at low speed on mixer for 2 minutes	1 small pkg. **INSTANT CHOCOLATE PUDDING MIX**
	1½ cups **COLD MILK**
Fold in	¼ cup **RUM**
	1¼ cups **WHIPPED TOPPING**
	¼ cup chopped **TOASTED ALMONDS**

Chill. When ready to serve, spoon pudding into center of each **CREPE,** roll up, and place seam down on a serving plate. Garnish.

YIELD: 12 CREPES

HURRY-UP FILLINGS:

BANANAS
Roll **BANANAS** in a mixture of 1 small package **INSTANT PUDDING MIX** and **SOUR CREAM,** according to taste. Roll in **COCONUT.** Try different variations.

FRUIT
Fill **CREPES** with favorite **FRUIT** and top with **WHIPPED TOPPING** or sprinkle with **POWDERED SUGAR.**

ICE CREAM
Fill **CREPES** with **ICE CREAM** and top with favorite **FRUIT** that has been partially thawed and sweetened.

CREAM PUFFS

In a saucepan, boil............	1 cup **WATER**
Add	1 stick **MARGARINE**
	¼ tsp. **SALT**
When melted, *quickly* stir in....	1 cup **FLOUR**

Mix well. The dough will form a ball. Remove from heat. Cool for 5 minutes. Add, *one at a time,* 4 **EGGS.** Dough will be smooth and shiny. Mound puffs with a spoon onto a lightly-greased cookie sheet. Place about 2 inches apart. They will triple in size. Bake in a preheated 450 degree oven for 15 minutes. Reduce oven temperature to 325 degrees and bake for 20 minutes more. Remove when done. Turn off oven. Slit puffs about halfway through horizontally. Put back into open oven to dry out 2 or 3 minutes. Place on rack to cool. Store in an air-tight container until ready to serve.

YIELD: 12 LARGE OR 25 TO 28 MINIATURE

VARIATIONS:
CUSTARD FILLING: Fill cooled puffs with your favorite **CUSTARD.** Top with FUDGE SAUCE.
IN A HURRY: Place puff in bowl. Pour **CUSTARD** or **SAUCE** on top.
PARTY PUFFS: Make miniature puffs. Fill with **CHICKEN SALAD, TUNA SALAD,** or any of your favorite **MEAT FILLINGS.**

FRIED PIES

Our beloved baby-sitter, Gannaway, spoiled the children with these.

Combine and chill for
2 hours . . . .

4 cups **FLOUR**
1 tsp. **SALT**
1 tsp. **SUGAR**
2 tsp. **BAKING POWDER**
1 can (13 oz.) **EVAPORATED MILK**
1 **EGG,** well beaten
⅔ cup **SHORTENING,** melted (do not use oil)

Remove about ⅓ of the dough from the refrigerator at a time. Keep the rest of the dough chilled. Pinch off enough dough to roll into a circle about the size of a saucer, when rolled thin. (Make tiny ones for parties.) Place your favorite **FRUIT FILLING** or **PRESERVES** in center of the circle. Prick one side with a fork and fold over. Seal the edges well. Fry in hot, but not smoking, **SHORTENING.** Cook until golden brown, turning only once, to prevent sogginess. Drain well on paper towels. (May also be baked, to save on the calories.)

To glaze: Combine ½ cup **POWDERED SUGAR,** 1 Tbsp. melted **BUTTER,** 1 Tbsp. **MILK.** Spread on hot pies.

Gannaway's Specialty: Extra-thick **VANILLA CUSTARD** filling.

YIELD: 5 DOZEN LARGE OR 8 TO 9 DOZEN SMALL PIES

QUICK APPLE DUMPLINGS

Just Heavenly.

In a medium saucepan, make a
syrup of . . . .

2 cups **SUGAR**
2 cups **HOT WATER**
¼ tsp. **CINNAMON**
¼ tsp. **NUTMEG**
½ stick **MARGARINE**

Bring to a boil. Pour over 8 frozen **APPLE DUMPLINGS.** Bake at 400 degrees for 35 minutes. Turn dumplings over once during cooking.

YIELD: 8 SERVINGS

CALORIES A-PLENTY

Melt in a 13x9x2-inch
    oblong pan .... 1 stick **BUTTER**
Add and pat into a crust .... 1½ cups **FLOUR**
    ¼ cup **BROWN SUGAR**
    ¼ cup **PECANS**
Bake for 15 minutes at 375 degrees.
Mix and pour over crust .... 2 packages (8 oz. each) **CREAM CHEESE**
    1 cup **SUGAR**
    2 tsp. **VANILLA**
    4 **EGGS**
Bake for 15 to 20 minutes at 350 degrees, until firm. Let cool.
Cook until thick .... 3 Tbsp. **CORNSTARCH**
    JUICE from 2 large bags frozen **STRAWBERRIES**
Add strawberries. Pour over last mixture. Cool.
Whip until stiff .... 2 cartons **WHIPPING CREAM**
Add .... ½ cup **POWDERED SUGAR**

Spread on mixture. Garnish with a few of the strawberries or pecans. Very good!

CHEESECAKE
This is a really special dessert!!!

Preheat oven to 375 degrees.
Mix together and press into a
    spring pan .... 1⅓ cup **VANILLA WAFERS,** crushed into crumbs
    ¼ cup **MARGARINE**
Bake 15 minutes. Crust can be frozen.
Beat until smooth .... 4 **EGGS**
    1 cup **SUGAR**
    3 pkgs. (8 oz. each) **CREAM CHEESE**
    1 tsp. **VANILLA**
Pour into crust and bake for 35 minutes.
Cool for 10 minutes.
Reheat oven to 475 degrees.
    Beat until smooth .... 1 cup **SOUR CREAM**
    ½ cup **SUGAR**
    1 tsp. **VANILLA**

Pour over cheesecake and bake for 5 minutes. Cool for 45 minutes. Then refrigerate for 2 or 3 hours before serving. Can be frozen indefinitely.

DOOLIE'S PIZZARIA

Something almost sinful.

Slice very thin .... 1 pkg. **REFRIGERATOR SUGAR COOKIE DOUGH**

Place on a pizza pan close enough so they will run together when baked. Bake at 350 degrees until golden brown. Cool.

Cream together.............. 8 ounces **CREAM CHEESE**
⅓ cup **SUGAR**
1 Tbsp. **FRUIT JUICE**

Spread evenly over crust.
Arrange in a circle on the
outside edge of crust .... 2 cups **MANDARIN ORANGES,** well-drained

Arrange a circle just inside the
oranges of................. 1 can (8 oz.) **CHUNK PINEAPPLE,** well-drained

Inner circle .... **STRAWBERRIES** or **SLICED BANANAS**

Heat and spoon over top .... **APRICOT PRESERVES** or **ORANGE MARMALADE**

Combine and sprinkle over all .. ½ cup **PECANS,** chopped
½ cup **COCONUT**

Top with **WHIPPED TOPPING** and refrigerate. Slice and serve.

YIELD: 8 SERVINGS

FORGOTTEN DESSERT

Preheat oven to 450 degrees.
Beat until foamy.............. 6 **EGG WHITES**
¼ tsp. **SALT**
Add .... ½ tsp. **CREAM OF TARTAR**
Then add, 1 Tbsp. at a time .... 1½ cups **SUGAR**
Add .... 1 tsp. **VANILLA**

Spread in a greased 13x9x2-inch pan. Put in oven, turn off heat, go to bed! *Do not peek!* Next morning, remove from oven. Spread with 1 pint **WHIPPED CREAM** to which 1 Tbsp. **POWDERED SUGAR** has been added. Refrigerate until serving time. Cut into squares and top each with frozen or fresh **STRAWBERRIES** or **RASPBERRIES**.

YIELD: 6 TO 8 SERVINGS

PEACH ROLL

Melt in a 13x9x2-inch
   casserole .... 1 stick **MARGARINE** or **BUTTER**
In a small saucepan boil
   3 minutes .... 2½ cups **SUGAR**
                         2 cups **WATER**
Make a pastry of .... 1 cup **FLOUR**
                         1 tsp. **BAKING POWDER**
                        ⅓ cup **SHORTENING**
                         SALT

Add enough **MILK** to moisten.

Pour pastry dough onto a floured board or waxed paper. Knead a few times and roll into a rectangle. Spread with 4 cups **PEACHES,** thinly-sliced. (If using canned peaches, be sure to *drain well*.) Roll up as a jelly roll. Slice and lay flat in the casserole with butter. Cover with the syrup. Bake in a preheated 350 degree oven until brown, about 45 to 50 minutes.

YIELD: 8 SERVINGS

PUMPKIN ROLL

Beat 5 minutes at
   high speed .... 3 **EGGS**
Slowly add .... 1 cup **SUGAR**
Then add.................... ⅔ cup **PUMPKIN**
                         1 tsp. **LEMON JUICE**
Mix separately .... ¾ cup **FLOUR**
                         1 tsp. **BAKING POWDER**
                         2 tsp. **CINNAMON**
                         1 tsp. **GINGER**
                         ½ tsp. **SALT**
                         ½ tsp. **NUTMEG**
Fold mixtures together.

Grease and flour jelly roll pan (15x10-inches). Spread cake mixture evenly in pan. Sprinkle 1 cup **PECANS,** finely chopped, on cake and bake at 375 degrees for 15 minutes. Turn out on towel covered with **POWDERED SUGAR.** Roll up and allow to cool completely. Unroll and frost with **FROSTING.** Reroll and chill.

YIELD: 8 SERVINGS

PUMPKIN ROLL FROSTING

Mix thoroughly . . . .   6 ounces **CREAM CHEESE**
                                          4 Tbsp. **BUTTER**
                                          ½ tsp. **VANILLA**
                                          1 cup **POWDERED SUGAR**

After frosting and rerolling, roll cake in waxed paper and keep in the refrigerator until all is eaten.

RED TART CHERRY DELIGHT CAKE

Crumble into a 13x9x2-inch
 pan . . . .   1 **ANGEL FOOD CAKE**
Whip according to package
 directions . . . .   2 packages **DREAM WHIP**
Add . . . .   1 cup **POWDERED SUGAR**
                                          1 pkg. (8 oz.) **CREAM CHEESE,**
                                            softened

Pour mixture over cake. Top with **GLAZE:**

In a medium size saucepan
 combine. . . . .   1 pound **FROZEN CHERRIES,**
                                            thawed
                                          ¼ cup **WATER**

Cook over medium heat until
 cherries begin to simmer.
 Add . . . .   ½ cup **SUGAR**
Mix together and put into cherry
 mixture . . . .   3 Tbsp. **CORNSTARCH**
                                          Small amount of **WATER** to
                                            moisten

Simmer until mixture thickens, about 3 or 4 minutes, stirring constantly while cooking to prevent sticking. Cool. Pour over cake mixture. Refrigerate. Cut into squares to serve. Garnish with teaspoon of **COOL WHIP.**

YIELD: 12 SERVINGS

RACHEL'S PRETZEL TORTE

Cream . . . .   ½ cup **SUGAR**
                                              1 stick **MARGARINE,** softened
Crush . . . .   **PRETZELS** to make 1½ cups
Mix with butter-sugar mixture and press into the bottom of a 13x9x2-inch pan. Refrigerate.
Prepare . . . .   1 package **LEMON PUDDING.**
Cool, but not long enough to get very thick.
Prepare . . . .   2 packages **WHIPPED TOPPING MIX**
Refrigerate.
Mix together . . . .   1 package (8 oz.) **CREAM CHEESE,** softened
                                              1 cup **POWDERED SUGAR**

Spread cream cheese mixture in crust. Top with pudding, then whipped topping. Refrigerate overnight.

YIELD: 10 TO 15 SERVINGS

ROXANNE'S RAPTURE

Mix together . . . .   1 cup **FLOUR**
                                              1 cup **BUTTER** or **MARGARINE,** room temperature
                                              1 cup **NUTS,** chopped
Spread into a 13x9x2-inch baking dish. Bake 25 minutes at 350 degrees. Cool.
Mix together . . . .   1 cup **CONFECTIONERS SUGAR**
                                              8 ounces **CREAM CHEESE,** softened
                                              1 cup **WHIPPED TOPPING**
Spread over nut crust.
Mix together . . . .   1 pkg. **VANILLA INSTANT PUDDING**
                                              1 pkg. **CHOCOLATE INSTANT PUDDING**
                                              3 cups **MILK**
Spread over cream cheese filling.
Top with **WHIPPED TOPPING** and **NUTS.**

The puddings can be mixed together or mixed and spread on one at a time. (Use 1½ cups milk for each pudding.) A pretty effect for a party: marbelize, by dropping spoonsful and swirling around.

YIELD: 12 SERVINGS

BROWN CARAMEL CUSTARD

In a medium skillet stir until
  melted and brown . . . . 1½ cups **SUGAR**
Set aside.
In a medium saucepan, mix and
  cook until thick . . . . 2½ cups **MILK**
                                    5 **EGG YOLKS**
                                    3 Tbsp. **FLOUR**
Add browned sugar and mix well.
Beat until stiff . . . .   5 **EGG WHITES**
Gradually add . . . . 10 Tbsp. **SUGAR**

Pour custard mixture into individual **BAKED CRUSTS**. Cover with beaten
egg whites. Bake in preheated 325 degree oven for 15 minutes.

YIELD: 6 SERVINGS

BITSIE'S LEMON FROMAGE
Use fresh lemon juice and rind.

Beat well . . . .   3 **EGGS**
Add slowly and continue to beat
  until mixture is thick and
  creamy . . . . ½ cup **SUGAR**
Add . . . . 1 Tbsp. grated **LEMON RIND**
Combine and stir until
  dissolved . . . . 1 package **GELATIN,** plain
                                    ¼ cup **LEMON JUICE**
Add to egg mixture. Fold in . . . .   2 cups **WHIPPING CREAM**, stiffly
                                        beaten

Pour mixture into a one-quart mold. Chill until firm (4 to 6 hours). Serve
with sliced, sweetened **STRAWBERRIES.**

YIELD: 4 SERVINGS

PEELED BANANA: Toss with pineapple juice to prevent turning dark.

STUFF

Recipe from the Worleys' kitchen.

Mix in a medium-size
    mixing bowl . . . .   ¼ cup **MARGARINE**, softened
                                   2 Tbsp. **BROWN SUGAR**
                                   1 cup **PECANS**, chopped
                                   1 cup crushed **VANILLA WAFERS**
Press half the mixture into a 13x9x2-inch baking dish. Bake at 425 degrees
    for 6 or 7 minutes. Cool.
Put one-half . . . .   1 jar (18 oz.) **APRICOT**
                                        PRESERVES
and one-half . . . .   ½ gallon **VANILLA ICE CREAM**
over pastry mixture.

Repeat with the rest of the preserves and ice cream. Sprinkle remainder
of first mixture over entire Stuff. Chill.

YIELD: 20 SERVINGS

IRRESISTIBLE PUDDING

Chocolate chips, coconut, brickle chips, and calories.

Combine in medium saucepan . . .   3 cups cooked **RICE**
                                    3 cups **MILK**
                                   ½ cup **BROWN SUGAR**, packed
                                   3 Tbsp. **BUTTER**
                                   Dash of **SALT**
Cook over medium heat until thick and creamy (20 to 25 minutes). Stir
    occasionally.
Remove from heat, add . . . .   1 tsp. **VANILLA**
Cool.
Combine in small mixing
    bowl . . . .   ¼ cup **COCONUT**, toasted
                                      ¼ cup **ALMOND BRICKLE CHIPS**
                                      ¼ cup **SEMI-SWEET CHOCOLATE**
                                      CHIPS

Fill 8 dessert dishes one-half full with pudding mixture. Sprinkle 1 Tablespoon coconut mixture on top. Repeat layers. Garnish with **WHIPPED TOP-
PING** and **MARASCHINO CHERRIES**.

YIELD: 8 SERVINGS

"THE ULTIMATE" DESSERT
A cross between Fudge and Pudding.

In a medium saucepan melt	1 cup **BUTTER**
Add and stir until dissolved	3 Tbsp. **COCOA**
	2 cups **SUGAR**
Remove from heat and add	4 **EGGS**
	1 Tbsp. **VANILLA**
	1 cup **FLOUR**
	1 to 2 cups **PECANS,** chopped

Stir as little as possible.

Pour into an 8x8x2-inch buttered dish. Place this dish into a larger pan that has 1 cup of hot **WATER** in it. Place in a preheated 300 degree oven and bake for 1 hour and 10 minutes. Serve warm or cold, it's delicious either way. (The secret is in the mixing. Stir only to mix.)

YIELD: 6 SERVINGS

BAKED CUSTARD BY TERRI LONG

Heat in double boiler until hot, but not scalding	1 pint **WHIPPING CREAM**
	1 pint **HALF AND HALF**
Add and stir until dissolved	2 Tbsp. **SUGAR**
Beat until light	8 **EGG YOLKS**
Add to cream. Stir in	2 tsp. **VANILLA**

Mix well, *strain,* and pour into custard cups. Place in hot **WATER** in a pan and bake at 350 degrees for 30 to 40 minutes. Cool and place in the refrigerator for several hours.

Cover each custard with ¼-inch **LIGHT BROWN SUGAR** that is soft and has no lumps. Place under a red hot broiler. When glazed, remove, and cool. Serve cold.

YIELD: 8 SERVINGS

HEAVENLY CHERRY PUDDING
Sooooo good.

Mix together in saucepan ...... 1½ cups **SUGAR**
2 heaping tsp. **FLOUR** or
CORNSTARCH
Gradually add and stir
together .... 1½ cups **WATER**
Add .... 1 can pitted **SOUR CHERRIES** with
juice
½ to 1 cup **PECANS**, chopped

Cook until thick like custard. While hot, layer in a bowl (like banana pudding) with crushed **VANILLA WAFERS**. Let set overnight in refrigerator. Before serving, top with **WHIPPED CREAM** or **COOL WHIP**.

YIELD: 6 TO 8 SERVINGS

MOTHER'S DESSERT

Remove label from .... 1 can **EAGLE BRAND MILK**
Place *unopened* can in a saucepan and cover with **WATER**. Boil gently for 4 hours, making sure that the water never boils away. Check frequently and add water as necessary. Remove from heat and cool completely before opening can. The milk will have completely caramelized and turned brown in color. To serve as an elegant, rich dessert, for each serving
Spread caramelized milk on .... **GRAHAM CRACKER**
Place on serving dish and
top with .... 1 slice canned **PINEAPPLE**
WHIPPED CREAM or **TOPPING**
MARASCHINO CHERRY

Store caramelized milk in refrigerator. Will keep indefinitely, unless there are kids around.

QUICK BANANA PUDDING
Have the recipe handy to give when you serve this.

Mix according to package
directions .... 1 box (3⅝ oz.) **INSTANT VANILLA**
PUDDING
Fold in .... 1 can **EAGLE BRAND MILK**
1 cup **COOL WHIP**

Layer with **VANILLA WAFERS** and sliced **BANANAS**. Cover with 1 cup **COOL WHIP**. Chill and serve.

RUTHIE'S "LEMON FLUFF"

Dissolve . . . .   1 pkg. (3 oz.) **LEMON JELLO**
in . . . . 1¾ cups **HOT WATER**
Add . . . .   1 cup **SUGAR**
                                    ¼ cup **LEMON JUICE**
Mix and place in refrigerator until partially set. Whip until fluffy.
Have well chilled . . . .   1 cup **EVAPORATED MILK**
Whip and fold into Jello mixture.

Line the bottom of a 13x9x2-inch pyrex pan with ¾ cup **VANILLA WAFER CRUMBS.** Carefully spread Jello mixture over crumbs. Sprinkle with an additional ¾ cup **VANILLA WAFER CRUMBS.** Chill until firm. Cut into squares and top each with a **MARASCHINO CHERRY.**

YIELD: 12 SERVINGS

VELTA'S "VELVET" CUSTARD

Beat well with a mixer . . . .   6 **EGGS**
Add . . . .   1 cup **SUGAR**
                                    ¼ tsp. **SALT**
Scald and add, slowly . . . .   4 cups **MILK**
Add . . . .   1 tsp. **VANILLA**

Butter 8 oven-proof custard cups. Pour mixture into cups. Place into a pan that has 2 cups hot **WATER** in it. Bake in a preheated 425 degree oven for 10 minutes. Reduce heat and bake at 325 degrees for 30 to 40 more minutes. Insert blade of knife in middle of custard. When knife comes out clean, custard is done. (Optional: Sprinkle with **NUTMEG** before baking.) Serve either warm or cold.

YIELD: 8 SERVINGS

FOR JUST A SQUIRT: Poke a hole in one end of lemon for juice.

GRATED RIND: Wash fruit and grate before juicing.

CAREER GAL COBBLER
Recipe from Southern Wells Bush.

Make a crust of . . . . 1½ sticks **BUTTER** or **MARGARINE,**
softened
2 Tbsp. **POWDERED SUGAR**
1½ cups **FLOUR**
¾ cup **PECANS**

Bake in a 13x9x2-inch casserole at 350 degrees for 20 minutes.

Blend . . . . 2 cups **WHIPPED TOPPING**
8 ounces **CREAM CHEESE,**
softened
2 cups **POWDERED SUGAR**

Pour over completely cooled crust and top with favorite **PIE FILLING.** Refrigerate.

YIELD 10 TO 12 SERVINGS

WASH-DAY COBBLER

In a medium saucepan heat until
boiling . . . . 1 can **FRUIT,** your choice
Set aside.
In a medium mixing bowl
combine . . . . 1 cup **FLOUR**
1 cup **SUGAR**
1 cup **MILK**
2 tsp. **BAKING POWDER**
Dash of **SALT**

Melt 1 stick **MARGARINE** in a quart casserole. Pour in batter. Add hot fruit. Sprinkle ¾ cup **SUGAR** over entire casserole. Bake in preheated 400-degree oven for 20 to 30 minutes. Serve warm with **ICE CREAM.**

YIELD: 4 TO 6 SERVINGS

SNOW ICE CREAM

Beat well . . . . 1 **EGG**
Add and beat 3 minutes . . . . ¾ cup **SUGAR**
Stir in . . . . 1 cup **MILK**
1½ Tbsp. **VANILLA**

Beat well. Add **SNOW** until thick and creamy.

YIELD: 1 SERVING

"AUNTIE L's" HOMEMADE ICE CREAM
Definitely worth the trouble.

Separate into two bowls . . . . 6 **EGGS**
Add to egg whites and beat until
   very fluffy . . . . 1 cup **SUGAR**
Set aside.

Add to egg yolks and beat until
   fluffy . . . . 1 cup **SUGAR**
Set aside.

Beat until stiff . . . . 2 cups **HEAVY CREAM**
Blend all mixtures together and
   add . . . . 2 tsp. **VANILLA**

Pour into prechilled freezer can. Finish filling with **MILK** or **HALF AND HALF CREAM.** Freeze according to manufacturer's manual. Try this once! You will never make ice cream any other way.

YIELD: 1 GALLON

CORKY BOZEMAN'S FAVORITE ICE CREAM
With Margie's SECRET ingredient for vanilla ice cream.

Beat on high speed of mixer
   until light and fluffy . . . . 5 **EGGS**
                            2 cups **SUGAR**
Add . . . . 1 pint **WHIPPING CREAM**
                            1 large can **EVAPORATED MILK**
                            1 Tbsp. **VANILLA**
Add Margie's secret
   ingredient . . . . 3 Tbsp. **LEMON JUICE CONCENTRATE**

Add enough **MILK** to fill freezer within 2 inches of top of bucket. Freeze according to manufacturer's instructions.

VARIATIONS:

STRAWBERRY: Add a few drops of **RED FOOD COLORING.** When almost frozen, add 2 cups **STRAWBERRIES.**
PEACH: Add few drops **YELLOW FOOD COLORING.** When almost frozen, add 2 cups **FRESH PEACHES.**
BANANA: Add a few drops **YELLOW FOOD COLORING,** 5 ripe **BANANAS** to vanilla mixture. When almost frozen, add 1 cup **TOASTED PECANS,** chopped.
PINEAPPLE: Thicken 1 large can **CRUSHED PINEAPPLE** with 2 Tbsp. **CORNSTARCH.** Cool. Add to vanilla mixture. When almost frozen, add 1 cup **TOASTED PECANS.**

11 FLAVORS OF ICE CREAM THE JAN-SU WAY
Forget the diet, "Pig Out!"

Beat well	6 **EGGS**
Gradually add	2 cups **SUGAR,** scant
Beat at least 5 minutes.	
Add and beat well	1 can **EAGLE BRAND MILK**
	1 cup **HEAVY CREAM**
	1 small can **EVAPORATED MILK**
	2 tsp. **VANILLA**

Pour into prechilled freezer can. Finish filling with **MILK** or **HALF AND HALF CREAM.** Freeze according to manufacturer's manual.

YIELD: 1 GALLON

VARIATIONS:

ALMOND TOFFEE: Add 1 Tbsp. **INSTANT COFFEE,** 3 Tbsp. **COCOA,** and ¾ cup slivered **TOASTED ALMONDS.**

BANANA: Add 3 mashed **BANANAS** to mixture. May add 1 cup chopped **NUTS.**

BUTTER PECAN: Reduce sugar to 1½ cups. Add 1 small package **INSTANT VANILLA PUDDING,** 2 tsp. **BUTTER FLAVORING,** ¼ tsp. **MAPLE FLAVORING,** and 1 cup chopped **TOASTED PECANS.**

CHERRY NUT: Add 1 jar (6 oz.) **MARASCHINO CHERRIES,** chopped, with the juice. Add 1 cup chopped **NUTS** and 1 tsp. **RED CAKE COLORING.**

COKE: Pour mixture into freezer can. Add 16 oz. **COCA-COLA** as part of the liquid.

HEATH BAR: Freeze **HEATH** candy bars. Remove from the freezer and crush immediately. Add to mixture just before putting into freezer can.

KAHLUA: Add ¾ cup **KAHLUA** to mixture. Omit ½ cup of the sugar.

MILKY WAY: Chop 1 pound **MILKY WAY** candy bars into the evaporated milk, and melt over low heat (or use microwave). When thoroughly melted, add to the rest of the mixture.

RUM RAISIN: Reduce sugar to 1½ cups. Add ⅔ cup **RAISINS** that have soaked in 1 cup of **RUM** for 30 minutes. (Add rum to ice cream with the raisins.)

STRAWBERRY: Reduce sugar to 1½ cups. Add 1 cup **STRAWBERRY PRESERVES.** (Or 1 package frozen **STRAWBERRIES,** thawed. Include juice).

GERMAN ICE CREAM
For chocolate lovers.

Beat until fluffy	6	**EGGS**
Blend together and add		
to eggs	1½ cups	**SUGAR**
	½ cup	**COCOA,** heaping
	½ cup	**FLOUR**
Beat about 5 minutes. Add	1 can	**EAGLE BRAND MILK**
	½ tsp.	**RED CAKE COLORING**
	2 tsp.	**VANILLA**

Blend well and pour into ice cream can. Finish filling with **MILK**. Freeze according to manufacturer's manual.

YIELD: 1 GALLON

BETTER THAN DOLLY'S

Melt in a 13x9x2-inch baking		
dish	½ stick	**MARGARINE**
Layer in order given	1 cup	**GRAHAM CRACKER CRUMBS**
	1 cup	**COCONUT**
	6 ounces	**SEMI-SWEET CHOCOLATE CHIPS**
	6 ounces	**BUTTERSCOTCH CHIPS**
Drizzle over all	1 can	**EAGLE BRAND MILK**
Sprinkle with	1 cup	**PECANS,** chopped

Bake in a preheated 325 degree oven for 30 minutes. Cool and cut into squares.

YIELD: 24 SQUARES

FORGOTTEN COOKIES

Beat with an electric mixer until		
stiff	2	**EGG WHITES**
Add gradually...............	½ cup	**SUGAR**
Fold in	1 cup	**CHOCOLATE CHIPS**
	½ cup	**PECANS**

Place sheet of foil on cookie sheet. Drop batter by teaspoonsful onto foil. Preheat oven to 350 degrees. *Turn off oven.* Place cookies in oven and leave 4 hours or longer. *Do not open oven door* until 4 hours have passed.

YIELD: 3 DOZEN

"OREO" COOKIE DESSERT

In a medium-size saucepan, soak
    for 1 hour ....   1 envelope **KNOX GELATINE**
                              1 cup **MILK**

Combine and add to
    mixture ....   1 cup **SUGAR**
                              2 **EGG YOLKS**

Cook 5 minutes. Remove from heat and *cool.*
Beat until very stiff ....   2 **EGG WHITES**
Fold into cooled mixture.
Fold in ....   1 carton **WHIPPED TOPPING**

Crush 1 package **OREOS**. Place half in the bottom of a serving dish. Add
mixture. Use rest of the Oreos for topping. Chill.

YIELD: 4 TO 6 SERVINGS

THANGS
Quick and easy.

Boil for 2 minutes ....   1 cup **BROWN SUGAR**
                              2 sticks **MARGARINE**
Stir in ....   1 cup **NUTS,** chopped
Place in a large flat pan ....   3 dozen **GRAHAM CRACKERS,**
                                     whole

Pour syrup mixture over crackers. Bake in preheated 350-degree oven for
10 minutes. Cool. Break apart.

YIELD: 3 DOZEN

CHIP AHOY CHOCOLATE COOKIES
Feeds lots of hungry little boys.

Cream in a large mixing
    bowl . . . .   ⅔ cup **SHORTENING**
                                 ⅔ cup **BUTTER** or **MARGARINE,**
                                      softened
                                   1 cup **SUGAR**
                                   1 cup **BROWN SUGAR,** packed
Add . . . .   2 **EGGS,** slightly beaten
                                   2 tsp. **VANILLA**
Stir in . . . .   3 cups all-purpose **FLOUR**
                                   1 tsp. **SODA** (omit if using self-
                                      rising flour)
                                   1 tsp. **SALT** (omit if using self-
                                      rising flour)
                                   1 cup **PECANS,** chopped
                                   2 pkgs. (6 oz. each) **SEMI-SWEET**
                                         CHOCOLATE CHIPS

Drop by rounded teaspoonsful 2 inches apart onto an ungreased baking sheet. Bake in a preheated 375-degree oven until light brown, for 8 to 10 minutes. Cool slightly before removing from baking sheet. (For a softer, rounder cookie, add ½ cup **FLOUR** more.)

YIELD: ABOUT 7 DOZEN COOKIES

PLEASURE WITHOUT LIMITATION
Caramel chocolate bars.

Combine and melt over
    low heat . . . .   1 bag (14 oz.) **CARAMELS**
                                   ⅓ cup **EVAPORATED MILK**
Keep warm after all is melted.
Combine . . . .   1 **YELLOW CAKE MIX**
                                   ¾ cup **BUTTER,** melted
                                   ⅓ cup **EVAPORATED MILK**
Beat at medium speed on mixer for 2 minutes. Spread half the batter in a greased 13x9x2-inch baking dish. Bake at 350 degrees for 6 minutes. Cool 5 minutes. Spread the caramel mix carefully over the baked layer.
Sprinkle with . . . .   1 pkg. (6 oz.) **CHOCOLATE CHIPS**

Drop the rest of the batter by spoonfuls over all very carefully. Sprinkle with **NUTS.** Bake at 350 degrees for 18 minutes.

YIELD: 24 BARS

BOSTON DROP COOKIES

Cream together . . . .   1 cup **SHORTENING**
                                              1⅓ cups **SUGAR**
Beat in, one at a time . . . .   4 **EGGS**
Stir in . . . .   3 cups **FLOUR**
                                              1 tsp. **BAKING POWDER**
                                              1 tsp. **SALT**
                                              2 tsp. **VANILLA**

Mix well. Drop by teaspoonsful onto a lightly greased cookie sheet. Bake in a preheated 375 degree oven for 10 minutes. Remove from oven and place on rack to cool.

YIELD: 4 DOZEN

CHERRY TOPS
Party cookies.

Cream in a medium bowl . . . . . .   1 cup **SHORTENING**
                                       1 package (3 oz.) **CREAM CHEESE**
Gradually add . . . .   1 cup **SUGAR**
Beat until fluffy. Add . . . .   1 **EGG**
                                       1 tsp. **ALMOND FLAVORING**
Beat well. Combine and add . . . . 2½ cups **FLOUR**
                                       ¼ tsp. **BAKING SODA**
                                       ½ tsp. **SALT**

Beat well and chill 1 hour. Shape dough into 1-inch balls. Roll in 1¼ cup finely chopped **PECANS**. Place on ungreased cookie sheet. With thumb, press indention in the center of each cookie. Press a **CHERRY** half into each indention. Bake in a preheated 350 degree oven for 15 to 18 minutes.

YIELD: 4 DOZEN COOKIES

COOKIES: Remove just moments after they are baked to prevent sticking to the pan.

FRESH ORANGE COOKIES

Cream together . . . .   1 cup **SHORTENING**
                                             1½ cups **BROWN SUGAR**
Add . . . .   2 **EGGS,** slightly beaten
                                             1 tsp. **VANILLA**
Add . . . .   1 cup **BUTTERMILK**
                                             1 tsp. grated **ORANGE RIND**
Sift together and add . . . .   3 cups **FLOUR**
                                             1 tsp. **SODA**
                                             ½ tsp. **SALT**
                                             2 tsp. **BAKING POWDER**

Drop from a teaspoon onto a greased cookie sheet. Bake in preheated oven at 375 degrees for 8 to 10 minutes. When cool, ice with **ORANGE ICING.**

ORANGE ICING

Mix together to a smooth
  consistency . . . .   2 cups **POWDERED SUGAR**
                                             1 tsp. grated **ORANGE RIND**
                                             1 tsp. **LEMON JUICE**
                                             3 tsp. **ORANGE JUICE**
                                             2 tsp. soft **MARGARINE**

NANCY DRYBREAD'S COOKIES
You guessed it, the Drybreads once ran a bakery.

Cream . . . .   1 cup **SHORTENING**
                                             1 cup **SUGAR**
                                             1 cup **BROWN SUGAR,** packed
Add and beat . . . .   2 **EGGS,** well beaten
Stir in . . . .   2 cups **FLOUR**
                                             1 tsp. **SODA**
                                             1 tsp. **VANILLA**
                                             2 cups crushed **POTATO CHIPS**
                                             1 small package **BUTTERSCOTCH BITS**

Drop by teaspoonsful onto a cookie sheet. Bake in a preheated oven at 325 degrees for 10 to 12 minutes.

YIELD: 8 DOZEN

TEXAS RANGER COOKIES
These go fast.

Cream	1 cup **SHORTENING**
	1 cup **SUGAR**
	1 cup **BROWN SUGAR**
Add	2 **EGGS**
Stir in	2 cups **FLOUR**
	1 tsp. **BAKING SODA**
	½ tsp. **BAKING POWDER**
	¼ tsp. **SALT**
	2 cups **OATMEAL,** uncooked
	2 cups **RICE KRISPIES**
	1 cup **COCONUT**
	1 tsp. **VANILLA**

Mix well. Mold with hands into balls the size of walnuts. Press flat with a fork. Bake in a preheated 350 degree oven for 12 to 14 minutes. (May substitute 2½ cups **CORN FLAKES** for 2 cups Rice Krispies.)

YIELD: 4 TO 5 DOZEN

SUGAR COOKIES
Mam-ma Cook always sent these to the lake for the kids.

Cream together in large mixing bowl	1 cup **SUGAR**
	1 stick **MARGARINE** or **BUTTER**
Add, one at a time	2 **EGGS**
Add	2 Tbsp. **MILK**
	3 tsp. **BAKING POWDER**
	2 tsp. **VANILLA**
Stir in	2 cups **FLOUR** (may need more)

Chill 10 minutes so dough will handle better. Turn out onto a lightly floured board or waxed paper. Roll to about ¼-inch thick. Cut into desired shapes. Place on cookie sheet. Bake in a preheated 325-degree oven for 15 minutes, or until only slightly brown.

YIELD: 7 OR 8 DOZEN.

PREPARED MIXES: There are so many good mixes on the market now, don't be afraid to try them and add your own variations.

RUM DUMS

Mix well, using hands
    if necessary ....   3 cups very finely crushed
                              VANILLA WAFERS
                            1 cup **POWDERED SUGAR**
                          1½ cups **NUTS,** chopped very fine
                          1½ Tbsps. **COCOA**
                          2 Tbsps. **WHITE KARO**
                          ½ cup **RUM** (May use ¼ cup Rum
                                and ¼ cup **ORANGE JUICE**)

Form into small balls about the size of a pecan. Place **POWDERED SUGAR** in a small bowl and roll balls until coated well. Wrap in waxed paper. These freeze well.

WHISKEY BISCUITS
Always found at Mussy's house at Christmas.

Cream together in a large mixing
    bowl ....   1 stick **BUTTER,** softened
                            1 cup **BROWN SUGAR,** packed
Add ....   4 **EGGS,** slightly beaten
Mix until dissolved and add to
    sugar mixture.............   3 tsp. **SODA**
                            3 Tbsp. **BUTTERMILK**
Stir in ....   ½ cup **WHISKEY** (may use
                             ORANGE JUICE)
In a large bowl, put ....   3 cups **FLOUR**
Stir into flour ....   1 tsp. **CLOVES**
                            1 tsp. **CINNAMON**
                            1 tsp. **ALLSPICE**
                          ½ box **WHITE RAISINS** (may use
                             cut up **DATES**)
                          1 pound **CANDIED CHERRIES**
                          1 pound **CANDIED PINEAPPLE**
                          2 pounds **PECANS**

Combine flour with creamed mixture. Drop by teaspoonsful on cookie sheet, 2 inches apart. Bake in a preheated 375-degree oven for 8 to 10 minutes. *Do not get too brown.* Cookies should be slightly soft. Store in an air-tight container. Will freeze well.

YIELD: 12 DOZEN

C.T.'S CARAMEL CANDY

In a heavy saucepan melt . . . . . .   1 cup **BUTTER**
Add and cook over medium
   heat. . . . .   1 box (1 pound) **BROWN SUGAR**
                         dash of **SALT**
Stir well. Blend in . . . .   1 cup **LIGHT KARO**
                         1 can **EAGLE BRAND MILK**

Cook and stir until candy reaches the firm ball stage (245 to 248 degrees on candy thermometer). Remove from heat. Add 1 tsp. **VANILLA** and 2 cups **PECANS.** Pour into a buttered 9x9x2-inch baking dish and cool. Cut into 1-inch squares and wrap in pieces of Saran Wrap.

DIVINITY

Avoid making on a humid day.

In a medium saucepan over
   medium-high heat,
     bring to a boil . . . .   3 cups **SUGAR**
                         ½ cup **LIGHT CORN SYRUP**
                         ½ cup **WATER**
Stir until sugar is dissolved. Set candy thermometer in place and cook, without stirring, until temperature reaches 248 degrees.
Meanwhile, in a medium mixing
   bowl, beat at high speed . . . . .   2 **EGG WHITES,** room temperature
When egg whites form stiff peaks, slowly pour half of the syrup into the whites. Continue beating at medium speed while heating the other half of the syrup to 272 degrees.

While turning bowl and continuing beating, slowly pour hot syrup into mixture. (Mixture will be stiff.) Add 1 tsp. **VANILLA** (and **COLORING,** if desired) and beat until mixture holds stiff, glossy peaks. Drop by teaspoonsful onto waxed paper. Cool, store in covered container.

YIELD: 1½ POUNDS CANDY

MARSHMALLOWS: Avoid stickiness when cutting by freezing first.

EASY PRALINES

Combine in a heavy saucepan
and bring to a boil . . . . 2½ cups **SUGAR**
2 Tbsp. **KARO**
2 Tbsp. **BUTTER**
⅔ cup **EVAPORATED MILK**

Cook on high to 238 degrees on candy thermometer (soft ball). Remove from heat and beat until creamy. Add 1½ to 2 cups **PECANS**. Drop by teaspoons onto waxed paper.

EDDIE'S "LAZY MAN'S" WHITE FUDGE

Combine and cook on
medium high . . . . 2 cups **SUGAR**
1 carton **SOUR CREAM**
dash of **SALT**
Stir only occasionally. Cook to 238 degrees on candy thermometer (soft ball.)
Add . . . . 1 Tbsp. **VANILLA**
2 Tbsp. **BUTTER**
½ to 1 cup **PECANS,** chopped

Beat until mixture thickens. Pour into a buttered dish. Cut into squares when almost cool.

G-O-O-D POPCORN BALLS

Colleen Tucker always doubles this recipe,
because there are never enough.

Combine in a heavy saucepan . . . 1 cup **WHITE KARO**
1 cup **WHITE SUGAR**
¼ cup **WATER**
¼ tsp. **SALT**

Bring to a rapid boil, stirring constantly. Lower heat to a slow boil. When syrup forms a hard ball in cold water, remove from heat (260 degrees on candy thermometer). Add 3 Tbsp. **BUTTER** and 1 tsp. **VANILLA**. Stir well and pour evenly over 4 quarts popped **POPCORN**. Mix well. Put **BUTTER** on hands, and form into balls as soon as you can handle the hot popcorn.

HERSHEY'S COCOA BOX FUDGE
Chocaholic's downfall.

Mix in a medium saucepan and
    cook over medium heat . . . . . .   2 cups **SUGAR**
                   2 Tbsp. **COCOA**
                   ⅓ cup **WHITE KARO**
                   ⅔ cup **MILK**
Bring to a slow boil. Cook to soft ball stage on candy thermometer (234 degrees).
Remove from heat and add . . . . .   1 tsp. **VANILLA**
                   2 Tbsp. **BUTTER**
                   1 cup **PECANS,** chopped (optional)

Beat until mixture begins to harden. Pour into a buttered dish. Cool and cut into squares.

JIM BOB'S PEANUT BRITTLE
The best darn COOK in TEXAS.

Combine in bottom of a pressure
    pan . . . .   2 cups **RAW PEANUTS**
                   2 cups **SUGAR**
                   1 cup **WHITE KARO**
                   ⅓ cup **WATER**
Cook until light brown on medium heat.
Turn off heat and add . . . .   dash of **SALT**
                   2 Tbsp. **BUTTER**
                   1 tsp. **VANILLA**
Mix well. Quickly stir in . . . .   1 tsp. **SODA**

Put on 3 greased cookie sheets in circles. about plate sized. When candy starts to set up, lift with forks and go underneath candy. Begin to spread very thin. Keep pulling and spreading the candy until almost transparent. Work very fast.

NEVER FAIL CHOCOLATE SAUCE: Mix 1 can sweetened condensed milk with 1 cup chocolate chips. Heat in double boiler, or microwave 1 minute on HIGH and stir for 30 seconds. Delicious topping for ice cream, cake, etc.

MICROWAVE CANDY
So good, one batch won't do.

On "Roast" setting, microwave
in a glass bowl for about 3
minutes . . . . 1 pkg. (12 oz.) **PEANUT BUTTER CHIPS**
1 pkg. (12 oz.) white **ALMOND BARK**

Remove and stir in . . . . 1 can **SALTED SPANISH PEANUTS**
1 tsp. **VANILLA**

Drop by teaspoonsful on waxed paper. If it begins to get too hard, return
to microwave for a few seconds.

VARIATION:
PEANUT-PECAN: Substitute . . . . 1 pkg. (12 oz.) **DARK ALMOND BARK**
1 pkg. (12 oz.) **PEANUT BUTTER CHIPS**
1½ cups **PECANS**

CHOCOLATE CHIP: Substitute . . 1 pkg. (12 oz.) **DARK ALMOND BARK**
1 pkg. (12 oz.) **CHOCOLATE CHIPS**
1½ cups **PEANUTS** or **ALMONDS**

PEANUT BRITTLE

Use a cast-iron skillet or a heavy
saucepan. Bring to a fast boil
on high heat . . . . 2 cups **SUGAR**
¾ cup **LIGHT KARO**
½ cup **WATER**

Stir as little as possible.
Using a wooden spoon, dip into
syrup. Hold over pan and
allow to drizzle off spoon.
When it spins a thread 4 to 6
inches,
add . . . . 1 pkg. (12 oz.) **RAW PEANUTS**
Reduce heat to medium and cook
until a golden brown (not
dark). Remove from heat and
add . . . . dash of **SALT**
1 tsp. **VANILLA**
1 Tbsp. **BUTTER**
Mix well. Add . . . . 2 tsp. **BAKING SODA**

Mix quickly only until mixture looks milky. Pour immediately onto ungreased cookie sheets. Cool and break into pieces.

MICRO PRALINES
Reba suggests not trying to double this recipe.

Combine in a 3-quart casserole . 1½ cups **LIGHT BROWN SUGAR,**
                                     firmly packed
                          ⅔ cup **HALF-AND-HALF CREAM**
                          ⅛ tsp. **SALT**
Mix well. Stir in . . . . 2 Tbsp. **BUTTER**

Microwave on High (100% power) for 7 to 9 minutes, to soft ball stage. Stir once while cooking. Add 1½ cups **PECAN HALVES.** Cook 1 more minute. Beat until creamy, about 3 minutes. Drop by teaspoonfuls on waxed paper.

P. P. C.
Peanut pattie candy.

Combine in a very heavy
    saucepan . . . . 3 cups **RAW PEANUTS**
                            1 cup **MILK**
                       2½ cups **SUGAR**
                       ⅔ cup **WHITE KARO**
Cook 1 hour and 10 minutes over
    low heat. Then add . . . . 1 Tbsp. **BUTTER**
                          1 tsp. **VANILLA**
                         RED CAKE COLORING

Hand beat until cool. Pour out on waxed paper. Cool and break into pieces. (Or drop into patties with tablespoon.)

TAFFY
Treat the children to a real old-fashioned Taffy Pull. Real fun!

Combine in saucepan . . . . 2 cups **SUGAR**
                              1 cup **WATER**
                           ½ cup **VINEGAR**

Cook to 265 degrees on candy thermometer (hard ball stage). Pour onto buttered pans. Let cool enough to handle. Pull and stretch (with buttered hands) until almost white. Let taffy get completely hard. Break or cut into bite-size pieces.

POPCORN BALLS
Pruddie's popcorn.

Boil together . . . .   1 cup **WHITE KARO**
½ cup **SUGAR**

When sugar is melted, remove
from heat and add . . . .   1 pkg. (3 oz.) **JELLO,** any flavor
Mix well and pour over . . . .   2 to 5 quarts **POPPED POPCORN**

Stir in with wooden spoon. Grease hands with **BUTTER** and form into balls.
Be very careful not to burn hands.

POPCORN DELIGHT
Shorty Mc's favorite.

Bring to a boil in a heavy
saucepan, stirring
constantly . . . .   ½ cup **WHITE KARO**
1⅓ cups **SUGAR**
1 cup **BUTTER** or **MARGARINE**
dash of **BUTTER SALT**
Lower heat to medium low and cook to 280 degrees on candy thermometer
(light crack stage). Stir occasionally.
Remove from heat and add . . . . .   2 tsp. **VANILLA**
½ tsp. **BUTTER FLAVORING**

Pour over 4 quarts popped **POPCORN**. Spread on a buttered pan. Let cool.
Break apart and serve in baskets. (Add toasted **PECANS, ALMONDS,** or
roasted **PEANUTS** to popcorn before adding syrup. So good!)

PEANUT BUTTER FUDGE

Mix in a heavy saucepan . . . . . .   2 cups **SUGAR**
1 Tbsp. **LIGHT KARO**
⅔ cup **MILK**
2 Tbsp. **BUTTER**
Cook to soft ball stage (234-238 degrees on candy thermometer).
Remove from heat and add . . . . .   1 cup **PEANUT BUTTER**
1 tsp. **VANILLA**
dash of **SALT**

Blend. Pour quickly into a buttered dish. Cool 10 minutes and cut into
squares.

MILLIONAIRE DATE LOAF
This is the recipe for those who have trouble with regular Date Loaf.

Mix in a heavy saucepan ...... 4½ cups **SUGAR**
                                    1 can (13 oz.) **EVAPORATED MILK**
Boil 5 minutes. Add .... 1 small package **DATES**, chopped
Cook 4 more minutes, stirring constantly. (Mixture may stick slightly, but
    it doesn't affect the results.)
Remove from heat and add ..... 1 pint **MARSHMALLOW CREME**
                                    2 cups **PECANS**
                                    1 tsp. **VANILLA**

Beat until cool. Pour into a buttered dish. Cool and cut into squares.

TEXAS MILLIONAIRES

In a heavy saucepan mix ...... 1 cup **BROWN SUGAR,** packed
                                    1 cup **DARK KARO**
                                1½ cups **EVAPORATED MILK**
                                    1 cup **WHITE SUGAR**
                                    2 sticks **BUTTER**

Bring to a boil, stirring constantly. Add 1 more cup **MILK** slowly. Do not
allow to stop boiling. Cook to a soft ball stage (234 to 238 degrees on candy
thermometer). Add 1 pound **PECANS.** Drop by teaspoonsful on foil. Chill
overnight.
Melt .... 1 package **MILK CHOCOLATE**
                                        CHIPS
                                 ⅛ pound **PARRAFIN**
Dip candy pieces in chocolate mixture.

VELVEETA CHEESE FUDGE
Delicious and nutritious.

Heat until melted in
    microwave .... 1 pound **VELVEETA CHEESE**
                                    1 pound **MARGARINE**
                                    1 Tbsp. **VANILLA**
Meanwhile, combine .... 4 pounds **CONFECTIONER'S**
                                        SUGAR
                                    1 cup **COCOA**
                                    6 cups **PECANS**

Combine the two mixtures, using hands. When completely mixed, spread
in two 13x9x2-inch buttered dishes. Chill for 1 hour and slice. Freezes well.

DOUBLE T CHINESE CHEWS

Mix . . . .   ¾ cup **FLOUR**
   1 tsp. **BAKING POWDER**
   ¼ tsp. **SALT**
   1 cup **SUGAR**
Add . . . .   1 cup chopped **NUTS**
   1 cup chopped **DATES**
   ½ cup shredded **COCONUT**
   2 **EGGS,** well beaten
   1 tsp. **VANILLA EXTRACT**

Mix all together and spread about ½-inch thick in a buttered pan. Bake in preheated 350-degree oven for 10 to 15 minutes. When done, cut immediately into small squares and roll in granulated **SUGAR.**

YIELD: 1½ DOZEN

LOTTIE'S LEMON BARS
A favorite of our Bridge Club.

Melt in a 13x9x2-inch pan . . . . .   1 cup **BUTTER,** do not substitute
Add . . . .   2 cups **FLOUR**
   ¼ tsp. **SALT**
   ½ cup **POWDERED SUGAR**
Mix and press in bottom and up sides of pan. Bake 20 to 25 minutes at 350 degrees.
Mix . . . .   4 **EGGS,** slightly beaten
   2 cups **SUGAR**
   5 Tbsps. **LEMON JUICE**
   RIND of 1 **LEMON,** grated

Mix and pour over baked crust. Bake in preheated 325 degree oven for 25 minutes. Let cool and cut into bars.

YIELD: 24 BARS

CLEAN AS A WHISTLE: When pressing a crumb crust into the bottom of the pan, place hand in a plastic bag. The crumbs will form a perfect crust and will not stick to your hands.

MELTING MOMENTS
Praline brownie bars.

Melt in medium saucepan	¼ cup **BUTTER** or **MARGARINE**
Add and cook until	
dissolved	1 cup **BROWN SUGAR,** packed
Cool. Add	½ cup **FLOUR**
	1 **EGG**
	1 tsp. **BAKING POWDER**
	¼ tsp. **SALT**
	1 cup **PECANS,** chopped
	1 tsp. **VANILLA**

Pour into a greased and floured 8-inch square baking dish. Bake in a preheated oven at 350 degrees for 30 minutes.

MERN LEWIS'S BROWNIES
I've tried them all, the these are still the BEST.

Melt in a medium saucepan	1 stick **MARGARINE**
	3 heaping Tbsps. **COCOA**
Add	1 cup **SUGAR**
	1 cup **FLOUR**
	2 **EGGS**
	¼ tsp. **SALT**
	1 tsp. **VANILLA**
	PECANS

Mix by hand, only enough to moisten. Bake in a well greased and floured oblong pan at 375 degrees for 20 to 30 minutes. Do not overbake. When done, pour on **CHOCOLATE ICING** while brownies are still hot. Let cool. Cut into squares.

CHOCOLATE ICING

Bring to boil	¼ cup **MARGARINE**
	2 level Tbsp. **COCOA**
	3 Tbsp. **MILK**
Boil 1 minute. Remove from heat	
and add	½ box **POWDERED SUGAR**
	1 tsp. **VANILLA**

Pour over hot **BROWNIES.**

VARIATION: **PEANUT BUTTER BROWNIES:** Add 1 small pkg. **PEANUT BUTTER CHIPS** to brownie mixture.

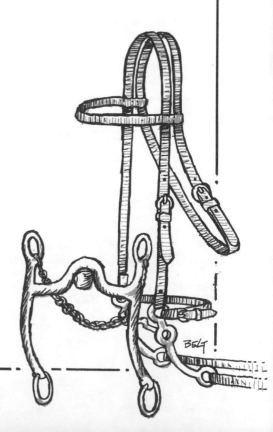

HOT CHOCOLATE MIX
Great for little gifts.

Blend well . . . .   6 cups **POWDERED MILK**
1½ cups **SUGAR**
1 cup **COCOA**
¼ tsp. **SALT**
Store in an air-tight container in a dry place.

For each serving, place 4 Tablespoons of mix in each cup. Fill with boiling **WATER.** (Top with **WHIPPED CREAM** and a dash of ground **CINNAMON.**)

"SUGAR FREE" SPICED COCOA MIX
30 calories per cup.

Mix . . . . 2¼ cups **DRY MILK POWDER**
⅓ cup **COCOA**
¼ cup **SUGAR SUBSTITUTE**
½ tsp. **CINNAMON**
¼ tsp. **NUTMEG**

Place in a container with lid and store in a dry place. Place 3 to 5 Tablespoons of mix in each cup. Fill with boiling **WATER.**

HOT MOCHA MIX
Spiced.

Mix in container with lid . . . . . . 2¼ cups **SUGAR** or **SUGAR SUBSTITUTE**
2 cups **DRY MILK**
2 cups **NONDAIRY CREAMER**
1 cup **COCOA**
½ cup **INSTANT COFFEE**
1½ Tbsp. **CINNAMON**
½ Tbsp. **CLOVES**
1 Tbsp. dry **ORANGE PEEL** (optional)

Store in dry place. To mix, add 2 heaping Tablespoons to 1 cup boiling **WATER.**

TEA AND TANG MIX
Good on a cold day with tea cakes.

Mix . . . .
    1 cup **INSTANT TEA**
    1 cup **TANG**
    1½ cup **SUGAR**
    ½ tsp. **CINNAMON**
    ½ tsp. **CLOVES**

Store in an air-tight container in a dry place. To serve, place 2 heaping teaspoonsful in a cup. Fill with hot **WATER**. (Optional: Add **RED HOT CIN-NAMON CANDY.**)

"SUGAR FREE" SPICED TEA MIX
4 calories per cup.

Mix . . . .
    1 cup **INSTANT TEA**
    1 package (24 oz.) **UNSWEETENED LEMONADE MIX**
    ¾ tsp. **CINNAMON**
    ¼ tsp. **CLOVES**
    ⅓ cup **SUGAR SUBSTITUTE**

Store in an air-tight container in a dry place. To serve, place 2 teaspoonsful in each cup. Fill with boiling **WATER**.

CHOCOLATE SAUCE
Very smooth.

Stir over low heat for
  2 minutes . . . .
    1 cup **SUGAR**
    2 Tbsp. **COCOA**
Then add . . . .
    ⅞ cup **EVAPORATED MILK**
    2 Tbsp. **BUTTER**

Stir constantly. Bring to a rapid boil. Boil for 1 minute. Serve warm or cold. Excellent on **ICE CREAM, POUND CAKE,** etc.

PERFUME HOUSE: *Combine 12 pieces ginger, 9 pieces stick cinnamon, 48 whole cloves, 3 teaspoons allspice, 6 teaspoons pickling spices. Place in jar. Simmer 3 Tablespoons in 1 quart water as needed.*

LEMON CURD
Spread on English muffins or toast.

Melt in double boiler over simmering water	1	stick **BUTTER**
Add and blend well	1½	cups **SUGAR**
	1¼	cups fresh **LEMON JUICE,** strained
	4	**EGGS,** slightly beaten
	2	Tbsp. grated **LEMON RIND**

Continue cooking, stirring frequently, until thick and smooth, about 25 to 30 minutes. Spoon into sterilized jars and seal.

YIELD: 4 HALF-PINT JARS

LEMON SAUCE
Good spread on banana cake.

Cook over medium heat	6	Tbsp. **CORNSTARCH**
	1	cup **WATER**
	1	cup **SUGAR**
	4	Tbsp. **LEMON JUICE**
	1	tsp. **LEMON RIND,** grated
Cook until thickened. Put 2 Tablespoons cornstarch mixture in	2	**EGG YOLKS,** well beaten
Pour back into mixture and cook 1 more minute.		
Remove from heat and add	2	Tbsp. **BUTTER**
	1	**BANANA,** mashed

Cool completely, Spread between any kind of cake layers.

NELL'S "CHRISTMAS RUSH" CRANBERRY SAUCE

Spread in 13x9x2-inch baking dish	1	pkg. (12 oz.) **CRANBERRIES**
Sprinkle over berries	2	cups **SUGAR**
Cover tightly with foil. Bake 45 to 50 minutes at 350 degrees.		
Cool and add	1	Tbsp. to ¼ cup **BRANDY**

Stir well and store in container in refrigerator until time to serve.

JUICE JELLY
The easy way.

Wash, rinse and scald 6 medium jelly jars.
Measure and set aside .... 3¾ cups **SUGAR**
Combine in large saucepan ..... 1 can (6 oz.) **FROZEN JUICE**
                    WATER to make 2 cups plus 6
                    ounces
Add .... 1 box **SURE-JELL**

Cook over high heat, stirring constantly until bubbles form around edge of pan. Add sugar all at once and cook, stirring constantly until bubbles again form around the edge. Remove from heat and skim off foam with metal spoon. Pour quickly into glasses and seal. Any flavor frozen juice will work.

NANNIE BELL HARRIS'S FIG PRESERVES
Her Aunt Nannie Swope still made this recipe when she was 97 years old.

Cut in half and use .... 1 pound of **FIGS**
To .... ¾ pound **SUGAR**

Wash figs in hot water and leave in water for 5 minutes. Rinse in cool water. Cook like peach preserves. Use as little water as you can to melt sugar. There will be a lot of juice when it starts to cook. You may have to take figs out of juice and boil juice down, then put figs back into syrup. Cook slowly. May add **LEMON JUICE** if desired. Place in jars and seal while hot.

WINE JELLY
For Christmas gifts, pour into small Brandy snifter
and tie with red ribbon.

Wash, rinse, and scald 6 medium jelly jars.
Combine in a large
   saucepan .... 1 box **"SURE-JELL"**
                       PREPARATION
                2 cups **RED WINE**
                6 ounces **WATER**
Cook over high heat, stirring constantly until bubbles form around edge of
   pan.
Add, all at once .... 3¾ cups **SUGAR**

Stir constantly until bubbles again form around edge. Remove from heat and skim off foam with metal spoon. Pour quickly into glasses and seal.

PEACH JELLY

To make **JUICE**, cook **PEELINGS, SEEDS** and some **PEACHES** in **WATER**.
Strain to make . . . . 3½ cups Peach Juice
Pour into a large saucepan and
   add . . . . 1 box **SURE JELL**
Bring to a hard boil and
   pour in . . . . 4½ cups **SUGAR**

Boil about 2 minutes, or until two drops slide together to make a big drop.
Pour into sterilized jars and seal.

PICKLED PEACHES
Looks good enough to enter in the county fair.

In a large pan mix . . . . 8 cups **SUGAR**
                              1½ cups **VINEGAR**
                              3 cups **WATER**
Add enough to make spicy . . . . . **CINNAMON STICKS**
                              WHOLE CLOVES
                              WHOLE ALLSPICE

Bring to a boil and add peeled cling **PEACHES**. Boil about 15 minutes, or
until peaches look clear. Pack hot peaches in sterilized jars; cover with syrup
and seal. They look pretty if you put some of the spice in the jars. If you
have more peaches than syrup, just add more syrup to the pan as needed.

SPICY PINEAPPLE PICKLES
Excellent served with ham.

Drain and set aside . . . . 2 large cans **PINEAPPLE CHUNKS**
Combine and bring to a boil . . . . **PINEAPPLE JUICE**
                              ⅔ cup **SUGAR**
                              ¼ tsp. **SALT**
                              ½ cup **VINEGAR**
                              5 or 6 **WHOLE CLOVES**
                              3 to 4 **WHOLE ALLSPICE**
                              ½ bag **RED HOTS CANDY**

Simmer about 10 minutes, or until all red hots are melted. Pour over pineapple chunks and let cool before refrigerating. Best if prepared several days
in advance. These will keep indefinitely.

AUNT EFFIE'S PEAR PRESERVES

Purchase **CANNING PEARS**. Peel and cut into small pieces. Place in container. For each 2 cups of pears, add 1 cup of **SUGAR**. Let set overnight, or long enough to make its own juice.
Cook on low heat for 2 to 3 hours. (Will turn honey-colored.) While still hot, place in sterilized jars and seal.

SWEET DILL PICKLES
Put in small jars and give for gifts.

Drain   1   quart plus 1 pint **HAMBURGER DILL SLICES**

Mix together and pour over
   pickles   3   Tbsp. **PICKLING SPICES**
                                             3   cups **SUGAR**
                                           ½   cup **WHITE VINEGAR**
                                           ½ to ⅓ Tbsp. crushed **RED PEPPER**
                                       3⅛ tsp. **GARLIC CHIPS**

Stir well. (It will be very thick.) Do not heat. Cover and refrigerate at least 2 days before eating.

FUSS-FREE PICKLES
As good as homemade.

Alternate layers in a glass or
   crock bowl   6   cups very thinly sliced **CUCUMBERS**
                                           2   cups very thinly sliced **ONIONS**

Combine in a medium saucepan
   and bring to a boil . . . . 1½ cups **SUGAR**
                                           1½ cups **VINEGAR**
                                         ½ tsp. **SALT**
                                         ½ tsp. **MUSTARD SEED**
                                         ½ tsp. **CELERY SEED**
                                         ½ tsp. **TUMERIC**

Stir until sugar is dissolved. Pour over top of cucumber and onion mixture. Cool slightly. Cover tightly and refrigerate at least 24 hours before serving. Store up to 1 month in the refrigerator.

YIELD: 7 CUPS

LAZY WIFE PICKLES
Hot garlic dill pickles.

Boil together until salt
    dissolves   1   quart **VINEGAR**
                                  ½   cup **ICE CREAM SALT**
                                  1   pint **WATER**
Wash and pack **CUCUMBERS** in sterilized jars. Quarter the large ones
    lengthways.
To each pint jar add   2   buttons **GARLIC**
                                  1   **HOT PEPPER**
                                  ½   tsp. **DILL SEED**

Pour hot vinegar over cucumbers and seal. Let set several weeks before
opening.

SEASONED SALT
Try this and you will never buy seasoning salt again.

Combine   26   ounces **SALT**
                                  1½   ounces **PEPPER**
                                  2   ounces **CAYENNE** (red pepper)
                                  1   ounce **GARLIC POWDER**
                                  1   ounce **CHILI POWDER**
                                  1   ounce **ACCENT**

This makes 32 ounces. Use on **ROASTS, STEAK, RIBS,** etc., also in **SOUPS**
and **STEWS.** *Just about everything.*

*Put into aluminum shakers, tie with Christmas ribbon and share with your
neighbors. Don't forget the recipe, they will be asking for it. Easy to double.*

HUSH PUPPY MIX
Great for a fish fry.

Mix in a large bowl   8   cups **FLOUR**
                                    8   cups **CORNMEAL**
                                    5   Tbsp. **BAKING POWDER**
                                  2½   Tbsp. **SUGAR**
                                    2   Tbsp. **SALT**

Keep in an air-tight container. Store in refrigerator. To mix, take out amount
needed, add **MILK** to make a thick batter. (Add chopped **ONIONS,** if desired.)
Drop by teaspoonsful into hot **OIL** (1 to 1½-inches deep). When brown,
remove and drain on paper towels. Serve warm.

YIELD: COMPLETE RECIPE WILL SERVE ABOUT 50 PEOPLE. 1½ CUPS
OF MIX, ABOUT 4 PEOPLE.

INDEX

Calf Fries to Caviar

Jan-Su Publications
1012 North 9th
Lamesa, Texas 79331
Phone 806-998-5010 • 872-8667

Please send me _____copies of *Calf Fries to Caviar* @ $11.95
Postage and Handling (per book)   2.00
Texas residents add 5¼% sales tax (per book)   .63
Gift Wrap (per book)   2.25

                 Total Enclosed $_____

Name: _____

Address: _____

City: _____ State: _____ Zip: _____

Make checks payable to: Jan-Su Publications

Calf Fries to Caviar

Jan-Su Publications
1012 North 9th
Lamesa, Texas 79331
Phone 806-998-5010 • 872-8667

Please send me _____copies of *Calf Fries to Caviar* @ $11.95
Postage and Handling (per book)   2.00
Texas residents add 5¼% sales tax (per book)   .63
Gift Wrap (per book)   2.25

                 Total Enclosed $_____

Name: _____

Address: _____

City: _____ State: _____ Zip: _____

Make checks payable to: Jan-Su Publications

If you would like to see *Calf Fries to Caviar* in your area, please send the names and addresses of your local gift or book stores.

If you would like to see *Calf Fries to Caviar* in your area, please send the names and addresses of your local gift or book stores.